Lodging

Management

Program

Second Edition

American
Hotel & Lodging
Educational Institute

Disclaimer

This publication is designed to provide accurate and authoritative information in regard to the subject matter covered. It is sold with the understanding that the publisher is not engaged in rendering legal, accounting, or other professional service. If legal advice or other expert assistance is required, the services of a competent professional person should be sought.

> —From the Declaration of Principles jointly adopted by the American Bar Association and a Committee of Publishers and Associations

Nothing contained in this publication shall constitute a standard, an endorsement, or a recommendation of the Educational Institute (Institute) or American Hotel & Lodging Association (AH&LA). The Institute and AH&LA disclaim any liability with respect to the use of any information, procedure, or product, or reliance thereon by any member of the hospitality industry.

The authors are solely responsible for the contents of this publication. All views expressed herein are solely those of the authors and do not necessarily reflect the views of the Institute or the AH&LA. The contents of this book were adapted taken from the following Institute publications:

Angelo, R.M. & Vladimir, A.N., *Hospitality today: An introduction, fifth edition* (2004)

Jefferies, J.P., *Understanding hospitality law, third edition* (1995)

Kappa, M.M., Nitschke, A., & Schappert, P.B., *Managing housekeeping operations, second edition* (1997)

Kasavana, M.L. & Brooks, R.M., *Managing front office operations, seventh edition* (2005)

Kasavana, M.L. & Cahill J.J., *Managing technology in the hospitality industry, fourth edition* (2003)

Lattin, G.W., *The lodging and food service industry, fourth edition* (1998)

© 2005
By the EDUCATIONAL INSTITUTE of the
AMERICAN HOTEL & LODGING ASSOCIATION
2113 N. High Street
Lansing, Michigan 48906

The Educational Institute of the American
Hotel & Lodging Association is a nonprofit educational foundation.

Printed in the United States of America
    3 4 5 6 7 8 9 10 09 08 07

ISBN 978-0-86612-276-4

Project Editor: Bridgette Redman

Acknowledgements

We would like to thank the following organizations and people for their contributions to helping this program achieve excellence:

American Hotel & Lodging Association
Joseph McInerney, President and Chief Executive Officer

American Hotel & Lodging Educational Foundation
Michelle Poinelli, Vice President

National Restaurant Association
Herman Cain, former President and Chief Executive Officer

Educational Foundation of the National Restaurant Association
Stephen J. Caldeira, former President and Chief Operating Officer
Reed Hayes, former President and Chief Operating Officer
Jennifer Hulting, Product Development Leader
Bettina Tahsin, Group Product Manager, Professional Development

Instructors, Contributors, and Reviewers

Patricia G. Breeding, Coordinator, Orange County Public Schools

Nancy F. Dillon, Director, Arizona Education Foundation

Leta Durrett, Hospitality Services Coordinator, Skyline Career Center

Milton Ericksen, Director of Public Relations and Education, Arizona Hotel & Motel Association

Jeralyn Forcier, Georgia Hospitality and Travel Association

Mary Kreps, former Director of Educational Programs, Texas Hotel & Motel Association

Carol Parker, Education Director, Florida Hotel & Motel Association

Connie Porter, CHI, DECA Advisor

Christopher Rott, Sunburst Hospitality Corporation

Jill Staples, CHA, Coordinator, Hotel/Motel Program, Virginia Beach, VA

Heath Trehame, Hospitality Instructor, Wood County Technical Center

Camille L. M. Wright, Academy of Hospitality & Tourism, Hungerford Prep High School, Eatonville, FL

Welcome!

You are about to embark on the adventure that is hospitality. The Lodging Management Program introduces you to the wealth of careers available in one of the world's major industries.

What opportunities are available in lodging? There are literally hundreds of careers in lodging and the number is constantly growing. With the right education and training, you can be a general manager, a controller, a sales and marketing executive, a gourmet chef, an interior designer, an engineer, a landscaper. Possibilities abound!

You might end up working in a resort hotel in an exotic location, a medical spa, a cruise ship, an elegant private club, a quaint bed-and-breakfast, or a busy downtown hotel. There are lodging operations in every corner of the globe and they are always looking for talented and hard-working individuals.

Even if you decide not to pursue a career in hospitality, the skills you learn in this course will aid you in whatever you do. You'll see certain symbols throughout this text that identify skills that are transferable or other points of interest:

Communication Skills: No matter what career you pursue, you'll need basic communication skills. This symbol identifies core skills of writing, communicating, and listening.

Math Skills: You'll be putting your math skills to practical use throughout this course. This symbol alerts you to when math applications are being used.

Symbol of Hospitality: The pineapple has long been a symbol of hospitality. Look for the pineapple to read fun, interesting facts about lodging past and present.

Under the Gavel: The shaded boxes with these symbols address some of the legal issues that are inherent in lodging management. They are based on actual court rulings and cases.

Whatever your interests and whatever your goals, the lodging industry has a destination and a career that can fit your plans. The skills you'll learn today will help you navigate throughout your life.

Now, let your journey begin!

Contents

Chapter 13—Guestroom Cleaning

Chapter 14—On-Premises Laundry Management

Unit

Overview of Lodging Management

Profile

Joseph McInerney
President and Chief Executive Officer,
American Hotel & Lodging Association

Joseph McInerney gets tagged as Man of the Year for good reason. The president and chief executive officer of the American Hotel & Lodging Association—the largest trade association representing the U.S. lodging industry—knows hospitality and is eager to make it a better industry for everyone.

A former president of Pacific Asia Travel Association, Forte Hotels, Hawthorn Suites, and ITT's Sheraton franchise division, McInerney has seen the industry from many sides. As the AH&LA president, he's worked hard to make lodging an attractive career option. An avid supporter of school-to-career programs, McInerney helped consolidate the association's affiliates to produce the only educational dollar-dispensing, not-for-profit premier organization for scholarships, professional certification, and instructional material.

Under his leadership, the association has sponsored a three-day event that allows outstanding high school students to demonstrate their knowledge and various skill sets needed for advancing within the lodging industry.

"This competition brings together the best and brightest high school students in the hospitality industry from across the nation to showcase their skills and abilities. This venue also allows AH&LEF to continue its mission of making noteworthy financial contributions to the educational endeavors of future hoteliers," said McInerney. "Additionally, these students' participation will help set standards for others who may have an interest in pursuing a hospitality industry career."

McInerney is an honor graduate of Boston College. He also is a Certified Hotel Administrator via the Educational Institute (EI), an affiliate of AH&LA.

His labors have not gone unnoticed by the industry. The Pacific Area Travel Writers Association called him the "Tourism Man of the Year. *Hospitality Magazine* in 1999 gave him the Stephen Brener, Silver Plate Lifetime Achievement Award. In 1994, AH&LA named their future president the Economy Lodging's "Person of the Year."

No matter who is singing his praises, one thing is certain, McInerney will continue to labor at making careers in the lodging industry a more exciting, opportunity-filled path to pursue.

Organization and Structure

Sections

1.1 Types of Hotels

AFTER STUDYING SECTION 1.1, YOU SHOULD KNOW HOW TO:

♦ Describe commercial hotels

♦ Describe airport hotels

♦ Describe suite hotels

♦ Describe extended stay hotels

♦ Describe residential hotels

♦ Describe resort hotels

♦ Describe bed and breakfast hotels

♦ Describe vacation ownership and condominium hotels

♦ Describe casino hotels

♦ Describe conference centers

♦ Describe convention hotels

♦ Identify alternative lodging properties

The profession of hotel management is one of the most challenging and least understood in the American economy. Although most communities have one or more lodging properties, and although the average citizen has had some contact with them, few people realize the diversified knowledge, variety of skills, and creativity demanded of the successful hotel manager.

Hotels are in every country and city of the world. Classifying hotels is not always easy. Many hotels do not fit into one, or only one, well-defined category. Nonetheless, there are several useful general classifications according to the markets the hotels attempt to attract and serve.

Commercial Hotels

The first hotels and inns were usually in the towns and villages they served. It was not until railroads that the hotel business began to expand in the United States. Railroads

Pineapple Power

When early European explorers traveled to the West Indies, they discovered the pineapple. Enchanted by its appearance, taste, and texture, they brought pineapples home. By the seventeenth century, pineapples had become a popular symbol of society and royalty. Later, sea captains would announce their homecoming by placing pineapples at their doors. The pineapples broadcast: "I'm back! Stop in and we'll celebrate!"

Today, the pineapple remains a symbol of hospitality and welcome, and you can find it carved into the entrances of many hotels and restaurants.

connected the country. Travelers getting off trains usually needed a place to stay. As more people traveled, the demand for hotels grew. In turn, more hotels were built, many conveniently located near railroad stations. In time, hotels in the city center catered to travelers and became the social centers of the community.

Like their historic counterparts, today's commercial hotels are usually in dowtown or business districts. These hotels are the largest group of hotel types and cater to business travelers. Although commercial hotels primarily serve business travelers, many tour groups, individual tourists, and small conference groups find these hotels attractive.

Airport Hotels

Air travel encouraged a distinct type of hotel growth in the 1950s through the 1970s. Demand skyrocketed for lodging facilities located near airports—especially international airports.

Airport hotels, which vary widely in size and level of services, are popular because they are close to major travel centers. Typical target markets include business clientele, airline passengers with overnight travel layovers or canceled flights, and airline personnel.

Hotel-owned limousines or courtesy vans often transport guests between the hotel and the airport. Signs announcing direct telephone service to nearby hotels for reservations and pick-up service are a common sight in most airports.

Many airport hotels feature conference rooms to attract a particular market: those who travel to a meeting by air and wish to minimize ground travel. Guests who stay at airport hotels often enjoy significant cost savings and convenience from such arrangements.

Suite Hotels

Suite hotels feature guestrooms with a living room or parlor area and a separate bedroom. Some guest suites include a compact kitchenette with a refrigerator and in-room beverage service. In exchange for more complete living quarters, suite hotels generally have fewer and more limited public areas and guest services than other hotels. This helps keep suite hotels' guestroom prices competitive in the marketplace.

Suite hotels appeal to several different market segments. People who are relocating transform suites into temporary living quarters; frequent travelers enjoy the comforts of a "home-away-from-home"; and vacationing families discover the privacy and convenience of non-standard hotel accommodations designed with a family in mind. Professionals such as accountants, lawyers, and executives find suite hotels particularly attractive since they can work or entertain in an area besides the bedroom.

Extended Stay Hotels

Extended stay hotels are similar to suite hotels, but usually offer kitchen amenities in the room. They are designed for travelers who intend to stay five days or longer and require reduced hotel services. Extended stay hotels usually do not provide uniformed services, and often do not provide food, beverage, or guest laundry service (though they do provide guest laundromats). They attempt to foster a homelike feeling. In addition, room rates are often determined by the length of stay.

Residential Hotels

Residential hotels provide long-term or permanent accommodations for people in urban or suburban areas. Located primarily in the United States, these properties house residents who want and can afford daily, limited hotel services. Residential hotels are not nearly as popular as they once were. They have been replaced in part by condominium and suite hotel properties.

Residents may choose to contract for some or all of the services provided to guests in a commercial hotel. A residential hotel may provide daily housekeeping, telephone, front desk, and uniformed services. There may also be a restaurant and lounge on the premises.

Resort Hotels

Guests often choose resort hotels as their planned destination or vacation spots. A resort may be in the mountains, on an island, or in some other exotic location away from crowded residential areas. They feature recreational facilities and scenery.

Most resort hotels provide extensive food and beverage, valet, and room services for vacationers. Many resorts also provide special activities for guests such as dancing, golf, tennis, horseback riding, nature hikes, sailing, skiing, and swimming. Most resort hotels try to be a "destination within a destination" by providing a wide range of facilities and activities, giving the guest many choices and fewer reasons to leave the property.

Bed and Breakfast Hotels

Bed and breakfast hotels, sometimes called B&Bs, range from houses with a few rooms converted to overnight facilities, to small commercial buildings with 20 to 30 guestrooms. The owner of a B&B—the host or

hostess—usually lives on the premises and serves breakfast to guests. Breakfast may range from a continental breakfast to a full-course meal. B&Bs derive popularity from intimate, personal service for leisure travelers. Most B&Bs offer only lodging and limited food service or—as the name implies—breakfast only.

Vacation Ownership and Condominium Hotels

Another expanding segment of the hospitality industry is the *vacation ownership hotel.* Vacation ownership properties typically involve individuals who purchase the ownership of accommodations for a specific period of time—usually one or two weeks a year. These owners then occupy the unit—usually a condominium—during that time. Owners may also have the unit rented out by the management company that operates the hotel.

These hotels are becoming especially popular in resort areas. One popular feature of vacation ownership hotels is the ability to trade ownership time with another owner in another location. For example, an owner of a beach-front vacation ownership unit may want to trade time in the unit for time in a winter ski unit.

Condominium hotels are similar to vacation ownership hotels. The difference between the two lies in the type of ownership. Units in condominium hotels have only one owner. In a condominium hotel, an owner informs the management company of when he or she wants to occupy the unit. The management company is then free to rent the unit for the remainder of the year. When the management company rents the unit, the revenue goes to the owner.

Casino Hotels

Hotels with gambling facilities may be categorized as a distinct group: casino hotels. Although the guestrooms and food and beverage operations in casino hotels may be quite luxurious, their function is secondary to casino operations. Casino hotels tend to cater to leisure, vacation travelers.

Casino hotels attract guests by promoting gaming and headliner entertainment. A recent trend in casino hotels is to provide a broad range of entertainment opportunities, including golf courses, tennis courts, spas, and theme recreational activities. Casino hotels frequently provide specialty restaurants and extravagant floor shows, and may offer charter flights for guests planning to use the casino facilities.

Gambling activities at some casino hotels operate 24 hours a day, 365 days a year; this may significantly affect the operation of the rooms and food and beverage divisions. Some casino hotels are very large, housing as many as 4,000 guestrooms.

Conference Centers

While many hotels provide meeting space, conference centers are specifically designed to handle group meetings. Most full-service conference centers offer overnight accommodations for meeting attendees. Because meetings are their focal point, conference centers typically place great emphasis on providing all the services and equipment necessary to ensure a meeting's success—for example, technical production assistance, high-quality audiovisual equipment, business service centers, flexible seating arrangements, flip charts and display screens, and so forth.

Conference centers typically charge meeting planners a single price, which includes attendee guestrooms, meals, meeting rooms, audiovisual equipment, and other related services. Guest amenities may not be as plentiful since these centers concentrate more on fulfilling the needs of meeting planners and organizers than on meeting the needs of program attendees.

Convention Hotels

The demand for the convention market has nearly doubled in the past 20 years. While most commercial hotels have fewer than 600 rooms, convention hotels—designed to accommodate large conventions—offer as many as 2,000 rooms or more.

Convention hotels have enough guestrooms to house all the attendees of most conventions. Convention hotels often have 50,000 square feet or more of exhibit hall space—plus ballrooms and meeting rooms. A full line of business services is generally available, including teleconferencing, secretarial assistance, language translation, and facsimile (fax) machines.

Convention hotels usually attract the convention market for state, regional, national, and international associations. They also attract regional, national, or international corporate meetings.

Alternative Lodging Properties

There are several other types of lodging establishments which compete for travelers. Recreational vehicle parks, campgrounds, and mobile home parks involve the rental of space for overnight accommodations. But although similarities exist, these alternatives stand apart from other facilities, sometimes vigorously competing for overnight accommodation revenues. In some resort areas, parks and campgrounds appeal to a broad range of travelers.

Still another form of alternative lodging is the corporate lodging business. Corporate lodging is designed for guests wishing to stay longer periods of time, often up to six months or longer. Guests often include business executives moving from one city to another, consultants on temporary assignments, corporate training programs, and special projects connected with movie or sporting events. Corporate lodging usually provides fully furnished apartments for guests. Corporate lodging is usually cost-competitive with hotels, since apartments can be rented and furnished by the owner or service provider for a lower daily cost than that incurred by hotels.

Another example of alternative lodging is the cruise ship industry. Cruise ships have become major competition for resorts, especially in the Caribbean region, and are primary competitors of resort hotels. They offer many amenities similar to those offered at island resorts, while having the unique advantage of moving from island to island as part of the experience.

Apply Your Learning 1.1

Please write all answers on a separate sheet of paper.

For questions 1–8, in which type of hotel would the guest be most likely to make a reservation?

1. Airplane attendant with a 12-hour layover

2. Honeymooners planning to gamble

3. Family that plans to return to the same vacation spot for two weeks each year

4. Business traveler attending a downtown sales meeting

5. Executive who will be visiting a city for two weeks

6. Vacationer wanting a week on the beach

7. Retired couple taking a nostalgic trip to a small, quiet town

8. Meeting planner for a regional conference

1.2 Service Levels

AFTER STUDYING SECTION 1.2, YOU SHOULD KNOW HOW TO:

♦ List the services found in world-class service properties

♦ Describe the hotels that offer mid-range service

♦ Identify the services offered by economy/limited service hotels

Another way to classify lodging properties is by level of guest service. The level of guest service offered in a hotel varies without regard to hotel size or type, and some hotels offer more than one level of service. The level of service is usually reflected in the room rate.

World-Class Service

Hotels offering **world-class service**—sometimes called luxury service—target top business executives, entertainment celebrities, high-ranking political figures, and wealthy clientele as their primary markets. World-class hotels provide upscale restaurants and lounges, exquisite decor, concierge service, and opulent meeting and private dining facilities. Guests may be treated to oversized guestrooms, heated and plush bath towels, large soap bars, shampoo, shower caps, clock radios, refreshment centers, and more

expensive furnishings, decor, and artwork. Housekeeping services are typically provided twice daily including a nightly bedroom turn-down service.

The public areas of a world-class hotel may be large and elaborately decorated and furnished. Several food and beverage outlets are frequently available to cater to the tastes of the hotel's guests and visitors. There may also be a variety of retail outlets, such as gift shops, clothing and jewelry stores, specialty retail shops, and international newsstands.

Above all, world-class hotels stress personalized guest services and maintain a relatively high ratio of staff members to guests. This ratio lets the hotel offer extensive amenities and unique services and respond quickly to guest requests. Some of

From Hollywood to Holiday

The first Holiday Inn was built in Tennessee in 1952. The name was reportedly supplied by the architect based on the classic Bing Crosby movie. In eight years, there were 100 Holiday Inn Hotels affiliated hotels operating in the United States, and by 1968, there were 1,000.

the finest hotels in Asia boast a ratio of two or more employees per guest. Many of the world-class hotels in North America have more than one employee per guest.

Executive Floors. In some hotels, certain floors are designated to provide some of the hotel's guests with world-class attention. Properties offering *executive floors* (sometimes known as *tower, concierge,* or *club floors*) provide upgraded guestroom furnishings and additional guest services in these areas of the hotel. Executive floors usually are designed with larger, deluxe guestrooms that may contain a number of unique amenities. Recent trends for these floors include in-room fax machines, DVD players, large televisions, and computers. Executive-level guestrooms or suites might also feature an in-room refreshment center and may be stocked with signature bathrobes, fresh fruit, and fresh-cut flowers.

Usually, the luxury services offered on executive floors are not confined to the guestroom. A concierge, or personal butler, may be stationed on each executive floor. Access to these floors may be restricted by the use of special elevator keys that allow only authorized guests to enter. In many cases, the executive or tower floors contain a private lounge. Special complimentary food and beverage services may be offered in the evening, and a continental breakfast may be served in the morning. Secretarial services may also be available.

Mid-Range Service

Hotels offering **mid-range service** appeal to the largest segment of the traveling public. Mid-range service is often modest but sufficient. Although the staffing level is adequate, the mid-range property does not try to provide elaborate services. A mid-range property may offer uniformed guest services, airport limousine service, and food and beverage room service. Like world-class hotels, mid-range properties range in size from small to large. The typical hotel offering mid-range service is of medium size—roughly 150 to 300 rooms.

The property may offer a specialty restaurant, coffee shop, and lounge that cater to visitors as well as hotel guests. Guests likely to stay at a mid-range hotel include businesspeople, individual travelers, and families. Rates are lower than world-class hotels since the properties offer fewer services, smaller rooms, and a smaller range of facilities and recreational activities. Such factors often make mid-range hotel properties appealing to those travelers desiring some hotel services, but not the full range of luxuries. Meeting rooms are usually available at mid-range hotels.

Economy/Limited Service

Economy/limited service hotels provide clean, comfortable, inexpensive rooms and meet the basic needs of guests. Economy hotels appeal primarily to budget-minded travelers who want rooms with the minimal amenities required for a comfortable stay, without unnecessary, often costly, extra services. Since a large proportion of the population travels on limited funds, economy lodging properties have a potentially large market from which to attract clientele. The clientele of economy properties may include families with children, bus tour groups, traveling businesspeople, vacationers, retirees, and groups of conventioneers.

In the early 1970s, the only amenities offered by many economy properties were an in-room telephone, a bar of soap, and a television set with local channels. Most economy properties now offer cable or satellite television, swimming pools, limited food and beverage service, playgrounds, small meeting rooms, and other special features. What most economy properties *do not* usually offer is room service, uniformed guest services, large group meeting rooms, laundry or dry-cleaning services, banquet rooms, health clubs, or any of the more elaborate amenities.

An economy property generally does not provide full food and beverage service, which means guests may need to eat at a nearby restaurant. Many economy hotels do, however, provide a free continental breakfast in the lobby area.

Apply Your Learning 1.2

Please write all answers on a separate sheet of paper.

1. What amenities are offered by world-class properties?

2. What amenities are offered by mid-range service properties?

3. What amenities are offered by economy/limited-service properties?

What service level would each of the following guests be most likely to select?

4. Family traveling to visit relatives

5. Corporate salesperson for a Fortune 500 company

6. Chief Executive Officer of a multi-national corporation

7. Bus tour group on a mystery weekend

8. Lead singer for a rock group on tour

1.3 Ownership and Affiliation

AFTER STUDYING SECTION 1.3, YOU SHOULD KNOW HOW TO:

♦ Identify the advantages and disadvantages of independent hotel ownership

♦ Identify the advantages and disadvantages of chain ownership

♦ Describe how management contracts are implemented

♦ Explain how franchises and referral groups work

Ownership and affiliation provide another means by which to classify hotel properties. Two basic structures exist: independent hotels and chain hotels. An **independent hotel** has no affiliation with other properties. **Chain hotel** ownership may take a number of forms, depending on the association that the chain organization has with each property. There are several distinct forms of chain ownership, including management contracts, franchises, and referral groups. Many chain hotel companies tend to be a mixture of several types of ownership.

Independent Hotels

Independent hotels have no relationship to other hotels regarding policies, procedures, marketing, or financial obligations. A typical example of an independent property is a family-owned-and-operated hotel.

The unique advantage of an independent hotel is its autonomy. Since there is no need to adhere to a particular image, an independent operator can offer a level of service geared toward attracting a specific target market. Moreover, the flexibility inherent in a smaller organization often allows the independent hotel to quickly adapt to changing market conditions. An independent hotel, however, may not enjoy the broad advertising exposure or management insight of an affiliated property, and is unable to take advantage of the volume purchasing power of a chain hotel.

Chain Hotels

Chain ownership usually imposes certain minimum standards, rules, policies, and procedures to restrict affiliate activities. In general, the more centralized the organization, the stronger the control over the individual property. Chains with less dominant central organizations typically allow individual hotel managers to exercise more creativity and individual decision-making.

Several different structures exist for chain hotels. Some chains own affiliated properties, but many do not. Some chains have strong control over the architecture, management, and standards of affiliate properties. Other chains only concentrate

Hotel Management Contracts

UNDER THE GAVEL

Many major franchise companies use management contracts for hotel properties to supplement their franchise arrangements. At least 10 major chains now operate more than 700 properties under management contracts.

Chain companies furnish management for hotel and motel properties that are owned by other parties throughout the nation. The use of the management contract has proven very successful to major chains as a way of rapidly expanding their operations with far less investment per property than direct ownership requires. Under the management contract, the owner often retains all or most of the financial and legal responsibilities. There are usually extensive provisions in the contract, which depend on the bargaining power of the management company and the owner.

---

on advertising, marketing, and purchasing. Some chains may have only a small corporate structure and minimum membership standards and therefore would not be equipped to provide a high level of assistance to local ownership.

A chain is usually classified as operating under a management contract or as a franchise or referral group.

Management Contracts. Management companies are organizations that operate properties owned by other entities. These entities range from individual businesspeople and partnerships to large insurance companies. Here's an example of how a management company might be hired to run a hotel. A group of businesspeople may decide that a hotel would enhance local business conditions. If the group's preliminary business feasibility study was favorable, the group might try to get a loan to build the hotel. Many lending institutions, however, would require professional hotel management, and possibly chain affiliation, before they would approve a loan. At this point, the group could contract with a professional hotel management company to operate the proposed property, probably on a long-term basis. The developers and the management company would sign a **management contract.**

The owner or developer usually retains the financial and legal responsibility for the property. The management company usually operates the hotel, pays its expenses and, in turn, receives an agreed-upon fee. After operating expenses and management fees have been paid, any remaining cash usually goes to the owners, who must pay debts, insurance, taxes, and so forth.

Management contracts have proven successful for many major hotel chains. Some management contract companies do not have a brand name. These companies usually operate franchises or independents for property owners. The franchising company provides the purchasing power, advertising, and central reservation system, while the management company provides the management expertise.

Franchise and Referral Groups. Some of the best-known U.S. hotels belong to franchise and referral groups. Travelers often prefer to stay with brands they recognize and owners trust in brand names to attract business. There is an organizational distinction between these two types of chain hotels.

Franchising is a method of distribution whereby one entity that has developed a particular pattern or format for doing business—the *franchisor*—grants to other entities—*franchisees*—the right to conduct such a business provided the franchisee follows the established pattern. In the lodging industry, most organizations offering franchises have first established the quality of their product and expertise in operations by developing parent-company (franchisor-owned) hotels. Franchise organizations typically have established standards for design, decor, equipment, and operating procedures to which all franchised properties must adhere. This standardization is what enables franchise chains to expand while maintaining a consistent, established product and level of service.

The franchisor usually provides the franchisee with other reasons for purchasing a franchise aside from a strong brand

Franchising

UNDER THE GAVEL

The franchise relationship is based upon the franchise contract. Therefore, before entering into any franchise contract, the owner assesses the franchisor's business history and reputation, as well as actual operations and the franchise system. Also, the owner seeks the advice and review of an attorney and business consultant.

The Federal Trade Commission rules require franchisors and franchise brokers to furnish prospective franchisees with information about the franchisor, the franchisor's business, and the terms of the franchise agreement through a "Basic Disclosure Document."

name. These include national or international central reservation networking, national advertising campaigns, management training programs, advanced technology, and central purchasing services. Some franchisors also provide architectural, construction, and interior design consulting services. In some cases, a company may provide management contract services as well as sell franchises.

Some operations are so distinct that belonging to a franchise system and conforming to a set of standards may be perceived as harmful. For these operations, a referral group might be more appropriate. **Referral groups** consist of independent hotels that have banded together for some common purpose. While each property in a referral system is not an exact replica of the others, there is sufficient consistency in the quality of service to consistently satisfy guest expectations. Hotels within the group refer their guests to other affiliated properties. Through this approach, an independent hotel may gain a much broader level of exposure.

As with franchise organizations, referral groups provide central purchasing services. These services reduce expenses to the individual hotels since items are purchased in larger quantities. Owners can purchase interior furnishings, bath amenities, linen and towels, and restaurant items at quantity prices. Referral groups do require members to maintain certain operating standards.

Apply Your Learning 1.3

Please write all answers on a separate sheet of paper.

1. A(n) _____ _____ has no affiliations with other properties.

2. Management contracts, franchises, and referral groups are distinct forms of _____ _____.

3. A _____ _____ is an organization that operates properties owned by other entities.

4. _____ is a method of distribution whereby one entity grants another entity the right to do business in the way that the first entity has established.

5. _____ _____ consist of independent hotels that have banded together for a particular purpose.

1.4 Property Organization

AFTER STUDYING SECTION 1.4, YOU SHOULD KNOW HOW TO:

♦ Create an organization chart

♦ Classify functional areas by revenue or support centers

♦ Classify functional areas by front-of-the-house and back-of-the-house

An organization requires a formal structure to carry out its mission and goals. It may divide its structure into functional areas by either revenue and support or front-of-the-house and back-of-the-house (also known as heart-of-the-house).

Organization Chart

A common way to represent an organization's structure is the **organization chart.** An organization chart is a picture of the relationships between positions within an organization. It shows where each position fits in the overall organization, as well as where divisions of responsibility and lines of authority lie. Solid lines on the chart indicate direct-line accountability. Dotted lines indicate relationships that involve a high degree of cooperation and communication, but not a direct reporting relationship.

An organization chart should be flexible. It should be reviewed and revised yearly, or more often if business conditions significantly change. Employee responsibilities may change as individuals assume more duties, depending on their qualifications and strengths. Some organizations list each employee's name on the chart along with his or her title.

Since no two hotels are exactly alike, organizational structures are tailored to fit the needs of each individual property. The charts in this section illustrate two organizational possibilities: a full-service property and a rooms-only hotel.

A full-service property that offers both lodging and food and beverage service will probably have an extensive organizational structure. Exhibit 1 shows an organization chart outlining the management-level positions in a large full-service property. All but two of the lines on the chart are solid,

Resorts Got Drafted

Nearly all of the 333 resort hotels in Miami, Florida, were used by the army during World War II for lodging or hospitals. In many cases, the Army took possession with little notice to the hotel owners.

Exhibit 1
Organization Chart: Management Positions in a Full-Service Hotel

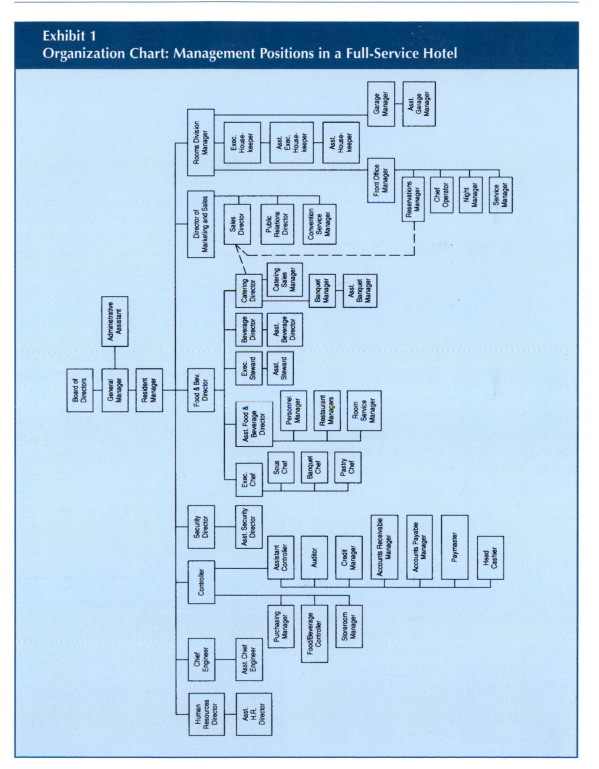

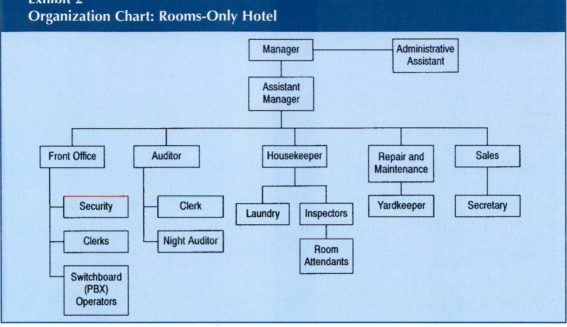

**Exhibit 2
Organization Chart: Rooms-Only Hotel**

indicating reporting relationships. The dotted lines connecting the sales director to the catering director and the reservations manager represent the close working relationship needed among these positions.

Exhibit 2 presents a possible organizational structure for a hotel without a restaurant. These organization charts illustrate some of the many organizational variations that are possible among lodging properties.

Classifying Functional Areas

A hotel's divisions and departments (its *functional areas*) can be classified in almost as many ways as the hotel itself. One method involves classifying an operating division or department as either a **revenue center** or **support center.** A revenue center sells goods or services to guests, thereby

generating revenue for the hotel. Typical revenue centers include the front office, food and beverage outlets, room service, retail stores, full-service spas, and telephone.

Support centers, also referred to as cost centers, include the housekeeping, accounting, engineering and maintenance, and human resources divisions. These divisions do not generate direct revenue, but provide important support for the hotel's revenue centers. Designers of accounting and information systems often find it useful to segment a hotel by revenue and support centers.

The terms **front of the house** and **back of the house** may also be used to classify hotel departments, divisions, and personnel. Front-of-the-house areas are areas where guests interact with employees. Such areas include the front office, restaurants, and lounges. In back-of-the-house areas, interaction between guests and employees is less common. Such areas include house-keeping, engineering and maintenance, accounting, and human resources. House-keeping staff do occasionally interact with guests, but it is not part of their primary duties as it is for front desk and bell staff. Although back-of-the-house employees may not interact with the guest, the employee does serve the guest by cleaning the guestroom, repairing a leaky faucet, or correcting an error in a guest account. That is why they are often called the "heart-of-the-house."

Apply Your Learning 1.4

Please write all answers on a separate sheet of paper.

1. What does a dotted line on an organization chart stand for?

2. What does a solid line on an organization chart stand for?

3. Which of the following departments would be considered a support center?

   a. Reservations
   b. Front desk
   c. Auditor
   d. Hotel lounge

4. Which of the following departments would be considered front-of-the-house?

   a. Laundry
   b. Switchboard operators
   c. Security
   d. Housekeeping

1.5 Hotel Divisions and Departments

AFTER STUDYING SECTION 1.5, YOU SHOULD KNOW HOW TO:

♦ List the departments found within the rooms division

♦ Describe the functions of the food and beverage division

♦ Explain the functions of the engineering and maintenance division

♦ List the activities of the marketing and sales division

♦ Describe the duties of the accounting division

♦ Identify the function of the human resources division

♦ Explain the structure and duties of the security division

Within each property, the functional areas are often divided into major divisions that contain one or more departments. While the functional areas vary among properties, depending upon market segment, service level, and ownership and affiliation, some of the common major divisions are:

• Rooms

• Food and beverage

• Engineering and maintenance

• Marketing and sales

• Accounting

• Human resources

• Security

Rooms

The rooms division provides hotel services directly to guests. It includes the front office, housekeeping, uniformed service, reservations, and telecommunications departments. (The reservations and telecommunications functions are sometimes part of the front office.) Hotels with garages or other parking facilities often place responsibility for this function with the rooms division. This division, a revenue center, usually earns the most money for the hotel.

> ### "Gimme a double decaf skim cap to go!"
>
> The first coffeehouse in Boston was established in 1670. As far as we know, it was *not* operated by anyone named "Starbuck."

Front Office. The most visible area in a property, with the greatest amount of guest contact, is the front office. The front desk itself is the focal point of activity in the front office because it is where the guest is registered, assigned to a room, and checked out.

The mail and information section of the front office department was once a very prominent section of most properties. In recent years, however, the responsibility for providing guests with information and messages has been divided among the desk agents, PBX (private branch exchange—the term used for the switchboard equipment) operators, and cashiers, so a single full-time person is usually not required for these duties.

Cashiers receive payments and post charges to guest accounts. Point-of-sale terminals (electronic cash registers) help reduce the manual posting of charges. The busiest time for the cashier occurs when guests check out of the property.

Concierge services are also part of the front office function. These are special services to hotel guests, such as making theater reservations and obtaining tickets; organizing special functions, such as VIP cocktail parties; and arranging for secretarial and typing services for guests. In a sense, the concierge section is simply an extension of the front office that specializes in guest service.

Communications. The telecommunications section of the rooms division has a complex communications network. Staff may be responsible for receiving calls, placing calls (local and/or long-distance) for guests, tracking and relaying charges, answering questions about the hotel, making wake-up calls, monitoring automated systems, and coordinating emergency communication systems.

In hotels using advanced equipment, routing the charges for long-distance calls to guest accounts and making wake-up calls may be done automatically.

Reservations. The reservations section of the rooms division is responsible for receiving, accepting, and making reservations for guests of the hotel. In addition, this department must keep exact records regarding the status of guestrooms and make sure that future dates are not overbooked. Reservations staff members work closely with sales and marketing personnel.

Uniformed Service. Parking attendants, door attendants, porters, limousine drivers, and bell staff make up the uniformed service staff. They meet, greet, and help guests to the front desk and to their rooms. At the end of the stay, they escort guests to the cashier, out the front door, and to their transportation.

Housekeeping. This department's staff cleans vacant rooms to make them ready for occupancy, cleans occupied rooms, and helps the front office keep the status of every room current. An executive housekeeper heads the department and may be assisted by inspectors, room attendants, a laundry manager, housepersons, and, if the department is large enough, an assistant housekeeper. Some large properties may employ people to monitor the housekeeping inventory and people to do sewing repairs.

Some hotels have their own laundries. In larger properties, the laundry equipment can be quite complicated. It may include folding and ironing machinery in addition to commercial washers and dryers.

Food and Beverage

The food and beverage division is another important revenue center of the hotel. This division is often second only to the rooms division in the amount of revenue it earns.

In properties operating their own food and beverage facilities, a food and beverage director manages the activities of the division. Other positions depend upon the nature of the property's food and beverage operations.

There are many varieties of hotel food and beverage operations—for example, gourmet and specialty restaurants, coffee shops (which may offer 24-hour service), lounges or dining rooms in which live music or shows are performed, room service, and combined banquet and meeting room facilities. Food service in hospitality suites or employee food service may be additional operations.

The sale and service of alcoholic beverages is usually a distinct operation, purposely separated from food sales and service. The beverage section has separate storerooms, servers, sales areas, and preparation people (bartenders); its hours of operation may extend well past the hours of the food service operations.

Banquets and catered meals are sometimes handled by food and beverage staff or specially designated personnel. While revenue from banquets are included in the total food and beverage sales, the banquets themselves usually take place in special function rooms or areas of the property. Both banquet and catering services may contribute a significant portion of the revenue earned by the food and beverage division.

Engineering and Maintenance

The engineering and maintenance division maintains the appearance of the property and keeps all equipment operational. It is sometimes called an operations department when combined with housekeeping. A chief engineer or director of property operations directs the division in larger properties.

This division's work can be divided into four main activities—regular maintenance, emergency work, preventive maintenance, and special project assignments.

The staff members of this division are often skilled in carpentry, plumbing, and electrical work. The maintenance staff performs such tasks as painting, minor carpet repairs, furniture refinishing, and preventive equipment maintenance. However, major problems or projects may require outside specialists. For example, full-scale refurbishing of public areas and guestrooms is usually contracted to specialists in interior decorating.

Outside, this division handles swimming pool cleaning and sanitation. It also does landscaping, which entails cutting the grass, planting flowers, caring for shrubs and trees, watering plants, and keeping the property's grounds in good condition.

Guest satisfaction depends upon well-maintained rooms. As a result, the engineering and maintenance division must stay in close contact with the front office, handling guest complaints quickly and notifying front office staff when rooms cannot be rented because repairs are necessary.

Marketing and Sales

Although some hotels do not have formal marketing divisions, every hospitality enterprise conducts marketing activities. The primary activities of marketing and sales operations are sales, convention services, advertising, and public relations.

The size of the marketing and sales division in a hotel can vary from just one person, usually the manager spending only part of his or her time handling this function, up to a staff of 15 or 20 full-time people. Coordination with and knowledge of all other departments and divisions in the hotel is essential for smooth functioning in the marketing and sales division.

Accounting

The accounting division, headed by a controller, handles the financial activities of the operation. A hotel's accounting division must work very closely with the front office's cashiering and guest accounting functions. The number of people on the accounting staff varies, depending partly upon whether most of the accounting is done off the property or on-site.

If the accounting is done off-site, the local property's accounting staff simply collects and sends out the data, without computing results. For example, time sheets are forwarded to corporate offices where payroll checks are drawn and mailed back to the properties. Operating figures may be sent out daily, weekly, or at some other regular interval. Income statements are then computed and transmitted from the corporate office to the local property.

If all accounting functions are performed within the hotel, the accounting staff has many more responsibilities and is therefore larger. These responsibilities include paying all bills (accounts payable), sending out statements and receiving payments (accounts receivable), computing payroll information and printing payroll checks, accumulating operating data (income and expenses), and compiling the monthly income statement. In addition, the accounting staff makes bank deposits, secures cash, and performs any other control and monitoring functions required by the hotel's ownership or management.

Human Resources

The human resources division (sometimes called the personnel division) assists other divisions in recruiting and selecting the most qualified job applicants. It also administers insurance and other benefit programs, handles personnel-related complaints, ensures compliance with labor laws, is involved with labor union matters, and administers the property's wage and salary compensation program.

In properties that are not large enough to justify a separate office or position, the general manager may handle the human resources functions.

Security

Security procedures are generally developed on an individual property basis, because every property has different security needs. The security division usually reports directly to the general manager. The staff might be made up of in-house personnel, contract security officers, or personnel with police experience. Some local police departments allow their officers to hold off-duty jobs, and their trained personnel may be hired to work in security at a hotel.

However a hotel's security program is structured, the safety and security of guests, visitors, and employees requires the participation of all staff. For example, front desk staff should issue room keys only to registered guests and make sure all keys are returned at check-out. Housekeeping staff should note any damage to locks, doors, or windows, and the engineering and maintenance division should repair these promptly. All employees should report suspicious activities anywhere on the property to the appropriate security personnel.

The security staff is responsible for helping guests and employees stay safe and secure at the hotel. Specific duties may include patrolling the property or monitoring any television surveillance cameras. The division may also develop and implement procedures for emergencies such as fires, bomb threats, and natural disasters.

The security division should maintain a good working relationship with local police and fire departments, since their cooperation and assistance is critical to the security division's effectiveness.

Other Divisions

Many hotels staff a variety of other divisions. Hotels are highly diverse in the ways they serve the needs of their guests.

Retail outlets. Lodging properties often have gift shops, newsstands, or other retail outlets. These outlets might be owned by the hotel or pay the hotel a fixed space rental fee or share a percentage of sales with the hotel.

Recreation. Some hotels, primarily resorts, staff a division dedicated to providing recreational activities for guests. Some recreation divisions landscape the grounds and maintain the pool. Golf, tennis, bowling, snorkeling, sailing, walking tours, bicycle trips, horseback riding, hikes, and other activities may be arranged by recreation division staff. The division may also plan and direct activities such as arts and crafts shows or children's programs.

Casino. Casino hotels will have a casino division that operates games of chance for guests and protects the property's gambling interests. The casino division may offer various forms of entertainment and other attractions to draw customers into the property and its gambling facilities.

Spas. Many hotels, especially resorts, offer some sort of spa services. These might range from a salon to a full-blown modern health resort with body treatments, stone therapy, and hydrotherapy. Modern spas cater to people who want to lose weight, get in shape, relax, or be pampered. A spa within a resort or hotel typically provides professional spa services, fitness and wellness activities, and spa cuisine menu choices.

Apply Your Learning 1.5

Please write all answers on separate sheet of paper.

1. List the departments that make up the rooms division.
2. List the activities that food and beverage divisions engage in.
3. What are the responsibilities of the engineering and maintenance division?
4. What are some of the duties performed by the security department?

Quick Hits

SECTION 1.1—TYPES OF HOTELS

- Commercial hotels are usually in a downtown area and are used primarily by business travelers.

- Airport hotels are near major travel centers and typically cater to business travelers, airline passengers with overnight travel layovers or canceled flights, and airline personnel.

- Suite hotels feature guestrooms with a large living room or parlor area and separate bedrooms. Some include a compact kitchenette.

- Extended-stay hotels offer kitchen amenities and reduced hotel services. They are for travelers who plan to stay five days or longer.

- Residential hotels house residents who want long-term or permanent accommodations with daily, limited hotel services.

- Resort hotels are in vacation spots and have recreational facilities and scenery.

- Bed and breakfast hotels are houses with a few rooms converted to overnight facilities or small commercial buildings with 20 to 30 guestrooms.

- Timeshare and condominium hotels are properties where there are many owners. Each unit is owned by the a different person, sometimes for only a few weeks out of the year.

- Casino hotels are hotels that have guestrooms as a support to the casino operations.

- Conference centers are specifically designed to handle group meetings.

- Convention hotels can accommodate large conventions—they usually have 2,000 or more rooms.

- Alternative lodging properties include campgrounds, recreational vehicle parks, mobile home parks, corporate lodging, and cruise ships.

SECTION 1.2—SERVICE LEVELS

- Hotels offering **world-class service** (or luxury service) target top business executives, entertainment celebrities, high-ranking political figures, and wealthy clientele. The entire hotel may provide luxury service or just certain floors, also known as executive floors, tower, concierge, or club floors.

- Hotels offering **mid-range service** offer modest, but sufficient service. It may include food and beverage, airport limousine service, uniformed guest services, and room service.

- **Economy/limited service** hotels provide clean, comfortable, inexpensive rooms with limited services.

SECTION 1.3—OWNERSHIP AND AFFILIATION

- **Independent hotels** have no relationship to other hotels regarding policies, procedures, marketing, or financial obligations.

- **Chain hotels** have certain minimum standards, rules, policies, and procedures that are set by the corporate owner. Chain hotel ownership may take the form of **management contracts, franchises,** or **referral groups.**

SECTION 1.4—PROPERTY ORGANIZATION

- The **organization chart** is a picture of the relationships between positions within an organization.

- Functional areas of the hotel may be divided up into **revenue centers** (departments or divisions that generate revenue for the hotel) and **support centers** (departments or divisions that do not generate direct revenue, but support the revenue centers). Another way of dividing them up are **front of the house** and **back of the house** areas. Front-of-the-house employees directly interact with guests, back-of-the-house employees do not.

SECTION 1.5—HOTEL DIVISIONS AND DEPARTMENTS

- The rooms division provides hotel services directly to the guests. Departments within the rooms division include front office, telecommunications, reservations, uniformed services, and housekeeping.

- The food and beverage division is a revenue center that includes all of the food and beverage operations. A property may have restaurants, lounges, coffee shops, dining rooms, banquet services, room service, and meeting room services. Alcoholic beverage sales are usually a separate department within the food and beverage division.

- The engineering and maintenance division takes care of the interior and exterior of the property.

- The marketing and sales division handles sales, convention services, advertising, and public relations.

- The accounting division handles the financial activities of the operation.

- The human resources division handles all issues related to employment.

- The security division helps ensure the safety and security of guests, visitors, employees, and the hotel property.

- Other divisions include retail outlets, recreation services, casinos, and spas.

Terri Haack

Vice President and Managing Director
Wild Dunes Resort

It took Terri Haack only five years to snag a top-level job. She started in the lodging industry at age 17, as a hostess in Denver's Inn at the Mart. By age 22, she was general manager there. For the next 20 years, she worked as a general manager or assistant general manager at inns, resorts, and hotels, including Hiltons, Sheratons, and independent properties. Her career has taken her from Colorado to Washington state, Delaware, and now, Virginia.

In 1998, she was named Outstanding General Manager of the Year by the American Hotel & Lodging Association, one of the first two people to earn that honor.

As a managing director of a once-struggling luxury resort, Haack must pay attention to financial details, marketing, staff development, and guest relations.

"It's been a full court press all the way," she says. "I've had to hone my marketing skills. There is much more attention necessary to the financial aspect. There is so much pressure that you need to constantly find ways to get more yield from rooms, meeting space, whatever you can sell."

Now, while the job is challenging, it's also appealing.

In 2002, she took over as managing director of the Wild Dunes Resort, leading a turnaround that cut expenses, boosted profits, and refocused their marketing efforts.

"It's exciting to be able to try to please both employees and guests while also spending a great deal of time on business strategy," says Haack.

Haack is also very involved in hotel associations and community organizations. She is a past chairman of the Virginia Hospitality and Travel Association and past president of the Williamsburg Hotel and Motel Association.

While she was general manager of Kingsmill Resort, Haack completed a master's degree in organizational management to help her become more competitive. She also sits on the board at Virginia Polytechnic Institute, where she works with the continuing education program of the hospitality school.

"I tell students this can be a viable and respectable career," says Haack.

Portions of this article are excerpted with permission from Lodging *magazine.*

Guest Service

Sections

2.1   What Is Service?

AFTER STUDYING SECTION 2.1, YOU SHOULD KNOW HOW TO:

♦ Identify the elements of good service

♦ Distinguish between marketing tangible products and intangible products

♦ Explain how the nature of products is different from the nature of service

♦ Describe the involvement of customers in service

♦ Describe the concerns of maintaining quality control

♦ Distinguish between controlling inventory and controlling demand

♦ Explain the importance of time and distribution channels to service

Hospitality consumers look for ways to tell one hospitality brand apart from another. One difference is availability. Some chains have one or more locations in just about every major city; others have just a few. Another difference is price. A steak at Denny's costs much less than one at the Outback Steakhouse. The most compelling difference, however, in the minds of many consumers, is **service.**

Defining Service

Service is generally defined as "work done for others." But this definition falls far short of the real meaning of the word. If a guest orders a sirloin steak, medium rare, and then after waiting 30 minutes receives a baked chicken breast, we can hardly characterize this as "service." Yet it fits the definition of "work done for others"!

Hotel customers have certain expectations. If reality *exceeds* expectations, they rate the service as better than average, or high. If reality *matches* expectations—guests get no more or less than they expected—service is satisfactory. But if reality is less than what is expected, then service is poor.

Price may play an important part in how service is evaluated because it influences customers' expectations. When someone buys a hamburger at a fast-food chain unit, what they expect is very different from when they buy a hamburger in the dining room of a fine hotel. They expect more because they are paying more.

It is the person who is receiving the service (the customer), not the person who is delivering it, whose expectations count.

One approach to defining good service is to look at service as a *performance* directed at satisfying the needs of customers. Good service is *meeting customer needs in the way that they want and expect them to be met.* Superior service is exceeding their expectations.

People are part of the product offered at hotels and restaurants. As a result, their service attitude plays a large part in delivering such "service products" as friendliness and positive experiences. (Courtesy of The Olive Garden Restaurants)

Intangible Products

Hotels—which deal in such **intangible products** as comfort, security, and positive experiences—have very different management and marketing problems than tangible products such as automobiles or boxes of cereal:

- The nature of the product is different.

- Customers are more involved in the production process.

- People are part of the product.

- It's harder to maintain quality control standards.

- There are no inventories.

- The time factor is more important.

- Distribution channels are different.

The Nature of the Product

Manufactured goods are tangible products. We can pick them up, carry them around, or in some other way physically handle them. A service is a performance or process. Marketing a service, like a hotel or restaurant, which of course involves the use of physical objects and goods such as beds and food, is quite a different thing from marketing the goods themselves. For example, when guests choose a hotel, they take into account such factors as the convenience of the location, amenities (spas, business

Other guests are an important part of the overall hospitality experience.

centers, etc.), and the kind of service they expect. When they call for a reservation, we reserve a certain category of room based on price, size, or location, but we seldom reserve the exact room itself. When guests arrive they use the physical facilities and eat the food, but that's not all they are buying. They are also purchasing the performance of a host of services of people who work in the hotel—room service, concierge service, valet service—all of which are intangible.

The Customer's Role in Production

Customers have no involvement in the production of manufactured goods. Production and consumption are completely separate. This is not true in a service-based business.

A restaurant or a hotel is, in a very real sense, a factory. It is a factory where service is produced for customers who come inside, see the workers who are putting together the service, and may even participate with them in producing it. A good example is the typical salad bar, where guests assemble their own salads and thus become part of the production process. Because it is part of the service (product), that interaction between employees and customers needs to be managed—a task which a manager of manufactured goods never has to face.

People Are Part of the Product

Customers not only come in contact with employees but with other customers as well. That makes the other customers a part of the product (which we define as a performance), and often defines the quality of the service. Have you ever been to a movie or play where the people behind you wouldn't keep quiet and spoiled some of your enjoyment? What about a restaurant where you went for a quiet, romantic evening and there was a party of 12 loud people at the next table celebrating someone's birthday? Business travelers who pay $200 a night for a room in an elegant city hotel can get very annoyed when their check-in is delayed by a busload of tourists who have just arrived, or when a group of conventioneers insists on being served breakfast before anyone else, so they can be finished in time for their first meeting.

All of the people whom a guest comes in contact with, both other guests and employees, are an integral part of the product. They often are the main difference in the quality of the experience one hotel provides over another.

Maintaining Quality Control

When a factory produces a product, it can be inspected for quality before it goes out the door. As long as proper quality control procedures and inspections are in place, defective products are not delivered. But services, like other live performances, take place in real time. That means that mistakes are bound to occur.

No Inventories

Manufacturers can store their inventory in warehouses until needed. But because services are live performances, they cannot be made in advance or stored for future use.

That means that there are times when the supply can't be produced on time because the demand is too great. Guests must be turned away from hotels that are completely occupied, or restaurant guests may wait an hour or more for a table. For this reason, service marketing often focuses on controlling demand.

The Importance of Time

Because most hospitality services are delivered (performed) in the "factory," customers have to be present to receive them. When customers are present, they expect the service to be performed "on time," which in their minds means "when they want it." Time, then, often plays a more important role in producing services than in producing goods (although "just in time" delivery systems are crucial in certain manufacturing operations). If customers must be kept waiting, hospitality enterprises must devise strategies to keep them from feeling that they are being ignored or are not important.

Different Distribution Channels

Companies that manufacture goods move their products from the factory by trucks, trains, or airplanes to wholesalers, distributors, or retailers, who then resell them to the ultimate consumer. This is not the case with services where customers come right into the factory or contact it directly. Service industries must train their employees to handle some marketing functions such as dealing with customers.

Apply Your Learning 2.1

Please write all answers on a separate sheet of paper.

1. Contrast poor service, good service, and superior service.

2. List the seven ways that intangible products are different from tangible products.

Complete the following sentences:

3. A hotel is a _____, where service is produced for customers who come inside.

4. To a customer, "on time" means _____ _____ _____ _____ _____.

5. Because there is no inventory of service, service marketing often focuses on _____ _____.

2.2 Superior Service

AFTER STUDYING SECTION 2.2, YOU SHOULD KNOW HOW TO:

♦ Explain the importance of strategic planning, missions, and objectives

♦ List the steps needed in a strategic planning process

♦ Define moments of truth

The most important operational competency of top-level service managers is the ability to plan for the future. While others can perform day-to-day operations, top-level managers must be thinking about next year and beyond. This is the job of top managers—to develop the strategy for survival that any business needs to succeed. It is also the key to providing superior service, which must begin at the very top of the organizational ladder.

Strategic Planning, Missions, and Objectives

Broad, long-range planning is called strategic planning. Companies must form general business objectives for themselves, otherwise there is bound to be confusion about where they are going and how they intend to get there. These general business objectives are most commonly called a company's mission and are expressed as a mission statement. Here is the complete mission statement of Chili's Restaurants:

• To be a premier and progressive growth company, with a balanced approach toward people, quality, and profitability.

• To be focused, sensitive, and responsive to our employees, customers, and our environment.

• To empower our team to exceed customers' expectations...to become customer obsessed.

• To enhance a high level of excellence, innovation, integrity, and ethics.

Blessed be the Industry

The patron saint of hoteliers is St. Amand, a French monk who lived from 584 to 679. He sought to provide travelers with a safe, clean atmosphere in his monasteries in Belgium. His motive was the joy he received from helping his fellow man traveling far from their homes. His monasteries were well known for the outstanding hospitality and sustenance he supplied to his guests. He himself was highly regarded as an efficient, organized manager.

- To attract, develop, and retain a superior team.

- To enhance long-term shareholder wealth.

Note the use of the words *quality, empower, team, customer obsessed, innovation, employees,* and *environment.*

Ritz Carlton's mission statement is short and simple:

We are ladies and gentlemen serving ladies and gentlemen.

The Strategic Planning Process

Once a mission has been clearly established and articulated, there is a series of steps a company must take to make that mission a guiding force.

Perform a SWOT Analysis. SWOT stands for *strengths, weaknesses, opportunities,* and *threats.* To do a **SWOT analysis,** a company examines the internal and external environment in which it is operating. What are the strengths and weaknesses of its operation? What opportunities exist for growth? What threats exist, either from competitors or changing trends? The ultimate goal of this analysis is to determine how well the operation is serving current markets.

Form Strategies. Strategies might include appealing to new market segments such as diet-conscious people, adding more units, or developing new products. Marriott did this when it developed three new types of Marriott hotels—Courtyard by Marriott (limited–service), Residence Inns (extended–stay), and Fairfield Inns ("road warriors").

Implement Strategies. Once strategies have been developed, they must be implemented. If one of a restaurant chain's strat-

egies is to add salads to its menu, the chain must create a salad that can be made in a uniform manner in all of its units. The chain must also identify suppliers and devise methods of preparation.

Before a company can implement strategies, some fundamental issues must be addressed:

Leadership. Managers must explain their strategies to employees. Continuing with the restaurant example, the managers must explain why they are introducing salads and persuade them that, even if it involves more work, it will produce benefits for them and the organization.

Organizational structure. Sometimes the organizational structure must be changed to implement a strategy. When Taco Bell decided to concentrate on improving customer service, it freed its unit managers from 15 hours of weekly paperwork so they would have time to coach employees and satisfy customers.

Corporate culture. To implement a strategy, you need employees who buy into the corporate culture or way of doing business. They must share the same values and work ethic. Disney spends two days of employee orientation in telling new employees the history of the company. Walt Disney's life story is retold at length. Early Mickey Mouse cartoons are shown. New hires are taught the Disney language—words and concepts unique to the Disney organization. This helps promote a family or "tribal" feeling.

Monitor and Evaluate Results. After implementing strategies, managers must monitor them to make sure they are working. Some examples: Marriott reads guest comment cards carefully; Domino's Pizza surveys customers by phone; South Seas Plantation on Captiva Island, Florida, holds customer focus groups.

Guests may experience more "moments of truth" with a door attendant than with any other employee.

Moments of Truth

Moments of truth occur whenever hospitality providers and guests interact, when the hospitality services extended by a provider are delivered to guests. It refers to that defining moment when guests actually experience hospitality services. As a result of their experiences, guests form perceptions and opinions of hospitality organizations.

A moment of truth is the point where the guest enters the encounter with expectations shaped by the reputation of the hotel and is either satisfied or disappointed. On occasions where a guest is disappointed, it is inevitable that the guest's disappoint-

ment will spill over into other aspects of a visit. To recover and win the guest back, the hotel has to work that much harder. Every moment of truth—whether good or bad—has a cumulative effect on guest perceptions, influencing the degree of satisfaction felt and thus the perceived quality of the hospitality experience.

Good businesses concentrate their efforts on making sure that moments of truth are handled correctly For hotels, an important moment of truth occurs when guests check in or out and come face-to-face with a hotel employee. Although there are certain check-in/check-out routines that must be followed, guests should be given individual attention so they feel their needs are being addressed in a personal way. One way to do this is to make certain that front desk employees are trained to look up from their computer screens to give guests a warm welcome (by name, if possible), and continue to smile and make eye contact as they perform their duties for the guests. Such seemingly small gestures go a long way toward establishing an overall atmosphere of attentive and pleasing guest service.

Apply Your Learning 2.2

Please write all answers on a separate sheet of paper.

1. What is the most important task of top-level service managers?

2. How are general business objectives expressed?

3. What are the elements of a SWOT analysis?

4. What are the steps in the strategic planning process?

5. List the fundamental issues that must be addressed before implementing strategies.

6. Describe an example of a "moment of truth."

2.3 Service Strategies

AFTER STUDYING SECTION 2.3, YOU SHOULD KNOW HOW TO:

♦ Describe the strategies used for managing supply

♦ Manage demand at hospitality properties

♦ Control payroll expenses

Since service firms cannot finish and store services, their financial success depends on how efficiently they match their productive capacity—their staff, equipment, and resources such as operating inventories—to consumer demand at any given moment. This is very difficult. When demand is low, production capacity will be wasted because there will be an oversupply of workers to serve the customers; when demand is higher than production capacity, there will be more guests than the workers or the building can serve and business will be lost. In other words, hotels are **capacity-constrained businesses** and therefore must constantly manage both supply (production capacity) and demand.

Managing Supply

Let's first look at strategies for managing supply. In the case of hotels and restaurants, the ability to supply the products manufactured in the service factory is fixed. A hotel has a fixed number of beds; a restaurant has a fixed number of seats. These cannot be altered to increase capacity whenever demand is greater than capacity—that is, when there are more guests than there are hotel beds or restaurant seats. That means that a good part of the time hotels and restaurants must follow a **level-capacity strategy** in which the same amount of capacity is offered no matter how high the demand.

However, some hospitality firms can follow a **chased-demand strategy,** in which capacity can be varied to suit the demand level—in a limited way. For example, there is a measure of flexibility in some parts of a hotel, such as the space set aside for meetings and conventions. Another common tactic in hospitality firms is to have a certain

Happily Ever After

Disneyland Hotel is a popular destination for weddings. Their Fantasy Weddings Office serves guests who crave the Disney flair for their weddings. The office provides such services as Cinderella's glass coach (for $2,500), pairs of trumpeters (for $1,550), and appearances by costumed characters for $675 each.

Taking reservations is one way restaurants and hotels can manage demand.

number of part-time employees who work only when the demand is high. Sometimes firms such as caterers can rent extra equipment and thus increase their capacity as needed. Finally, companies can cross-train employees so that they can be shifted temporarily to other jobs as needed. In the long run, a hotel or restaurant can increase its capacity by enlarging its property or building a new one.

Managing Demand

Because hotel and restaurant capacity is limited, it is important to put most of the strategic planning emphasis on managing demand. One of the goals of managers in a service business is to shift demand from periods when it cannot be accommodated (because the hotel is already filled) to peri-

ods when it can be. One way to do this is to encourage business during slow periods. Some restaurants offer early-bird specials to increase demand early in the day, and lounges have happy hours to increase demand early in the evening.

While supply cannot be inventoried, sometimes demand can. This happens when managers or employees encourage guests to stand in line or sit in the restaurant's lounge until the next table becomes available. Reservations systems also are an example of demand inventorying.

The most common method used to influence demand in the hotel industry is price. Using pricing strategies to control demand is risky unless the strategies are thoroughly understood. Hotels are faced with pricing decisions every day, such as whether to accept meeting and convention reservations at low group rates, or hold on to those rooms for later sale at higher rates to individual business travelers. One tool managers use is yield management.

Sometimes the product itself can be varied to help balance supply and demand. Restaurants routinely change their menus and level of service between lunch and dinner. Cruise ships reposition themselves to call on ports in the Caribbean in the winter and Alaska in the summer. Sometimes different services can be offered at the same time to accommodate the demand levels of different groups as with first-class, business-class, and economy-class airline seats—all on the same plane—or concierge floors in hotels.

Payroll Control

Controlling payroll and other costs involved in providing service is part of controlling the quality of service. Hotels could have enough employees around to give good service all the time. But they would not be profitable. Every operation must provide good, if not superior, service within its own economic constraints. Companies that do the best job of controlling service quality also excel at controlling labor and other costs, since clearly they are closely connected. Payroll control can be achieved by employee training and careful scheduling, a combination that almost always produces higher productivity and better service.

Apply Your Learning 2.3

Please write all answers on a separate sheet of paper.

1. Explain how hotels manage supply.

2. Explain how hotels manage demand.

3. How does job restructuring and payroll control affect service?

Match the following concepts with their definitions.

capacity-constrained business   chased-demand strategy
level-capacity strategy   demand inventorying

4. A management strategy in which the same amount of capacity is offered, no matter how high the consumer demand.

5. A management strategy in which capacity can, to a limited extent, be varied to suit the level of demand.

6. Businesses that produce "products" or services that cannot be inventoried or stored for future use. Success depends on their ability to efficiently match productive capacity to consumer demand at any given moment.

7. A process by which managers or employers encourage customers to wait for an available service.

2.4 Delivering Service

AFTER STUDYING SECTION 2.4, YOU SHOULD KNOW HOW TO:

◆ Target a market segment

◆ Set service standards

◆ List the tangible things a hotel can do to provide good service

To deliver outstanding service, a hospitality operation must determine its targeted markets and set service standards.

Targeting a Market Segment

A hotel is actually a series of businesses that cater to a number of different markets. The hotel's guestrooms may appeal primarily to leisure travelers on the weekends and to business travelers during the week.

Hotel managers are placing guests in narrower market segments and targeting more of those segments than ever before. This **market segmentation** consists of viewing a market as a number of smaller market segments, each segment a group of consumers with similar product and service preferences.

Markets can be segmented in a number of ways:

• Demographically (senior citizens, young marrieds)

• Purpose of trip (business, leisure)

• Benefits sought (security, wake-up and message service)

• Geographically (by zip code)

• Lifestyle (sports-minded, culture seekers)

• Usage (frequent business travelers, occasional business travelers)

• Intermediary (travel agent, tour operator, meeting planner)

It is impossible, however, to be all things to all people. Properties must realistically define their product in terms of the major market segments they can best satisfy. A property should determine the segments for which it is best suited, the areas of least competition, and modifications (if any) necessary to reach its **target markets**.

In Like a Lion

The Red Lion is believed to be the oldest hotel in Britain. The original part of the building was built more than 750 years ago to house the draughtsmen working on Salisbury Cathedral. By the 1700s the hotel had become a flourishing coaching inn and was the main stop for regular mail coach services linking London and the West Country.

Service Standards

Successful hospitality companies focus a good deal of management attention on establishing service quality standards, communicating them to employees through training programs, and measuring performance. For example, one service standard that is frequently established and easy to measure is waiting time. Many hotels with busy telephone reservation systems have set time limits for how long guests can be kept on hold before their call is handled.

Providing consistent services is extremely complex where guest contact is involved, especially when some of the lowest-paid employees make the most contacts. A former Marriott executive, G. Michael Hostage, described one strategy he used to deal with the problem:

The *Marriott Bellman* booklet is designed to convince our uniformed doormen that they represent an all-important first and last impression for many of our guests, that they must stand with dignity and good posture, and that they must not lean against the wall or put up their feet when sitting.... Bellmen are often looked at subconsciously by guests as being "Mr. Marriott himself" because many times a guest will speak to and deal with a bellman more often during a visit than with any other employees of the hotel.... They are coached to smile often and to do all they can to make the guest feel welcome and special.

Marriott is known for setting exact standards—including service standards—for all of its jobs and for communicating them clearly in writing as well as in training sessions. The company continually measures how well standards are being met with frequent inspections, and it encourages its employees to provide good service through profit sharing, stock options, and other bonus programs.

Making the Delivery

The bottom line for students of hospitality management is delivering on the promise that a company makes to its owners, employees, and guests. It is easy enough to write a mission statement that says, "We are a premier and progressive lodging company" or, "We deliver the best service of any restaurant chain in our class"—but how do you do it? What makes it really happen?

Everyone understands that guests want superior service and that better service leads to better profits. Understanding it is one thing; doing it is another. There are a number of tangible things that any organization that cares about good service can do. Here are four of them.

Don't forget who you are. Companies who succeed have a single service strategy for each market segment. They stick to it. They make certain that everyone who works for them understands what they are selling and who they want to sell it to. They don't confuse or anger consumers by offering something they don't deliver.

Encourage every employee to act like a manager. Managers understand the need for repeat business; employees may not. Service-oriented companies motivate, train, and empower their employees to act like it's their business. That means really caring when anyone has a problem, whether it's another employee or a guest. It also means making sure that they can solve problems they run into, which in turn requires that they be given the authority to make the necessary decisions. Embassy Suites uses an upside-down organization chart to dramatize the idea that the front-line employees, the ones who deal with guests, are the most important people in the organization. It's not easy to find hotel managers who will accept the idea that when it comes to pleasing the guests, the front desk clerks may be more important than they are. Embassy Suites does that by hiring managers who have the right attitude and then training them to help the people who work for them.

Hire good people and keep them happy. Turnover is the worst enemy superior service has. New people don't know what is expected of them and may have inadequate training or the wrong training. They are often unprepared to give the kind of service that is expected of them. Superior companies make every effort to recruit, hire, and hold onto people who have the right personalities. (Many companies today hire for attitude rather than skill. Skills that are learned on the job are often more easily upgraded than attitudes that employees bring with them.) They regard their people as being as important as their customers. That means training them well, motivating them, and rewarding them. This strategy is inevitably more cost efficient and more successful than constantly finding and training new employees.

Be responsive. Guests don't like to wait. It is, a hallmark of poor service. At limited-service establishments even five minutes may seem too long. No one likes to hold the phone to make a reservation for a hotel room. Long check-in and check-out lines spell disaster. Excellent companies are constantly monitoring the waiting time of their guests and looking for ways to decrease it, or at least make it less stressful.

Every organization and every situation is unique. Managers need to develop their own lists of key criteria and ways to implement them. It's the difference between wining and losing the battle for satisfied customers.

Apply Your Learning 2.4

Please write all answers on a separate sheet of paper.

1. List target markets that a hotel might have.

2. What is a service standard?

3. List things that a hotel can do to show that it cares about good service.

4. Which of the following is *not* a service standard?

    a. Guestrooms overlook the ocean.
    b. Four body towels will be placed in each guestroom.
    c. Guests can be kept on hold for only two minutes.
    d. Employees must not lean against the wall.

Quick Hits

Chapter 2

SECTION 2.1—WHAT IS SERVICE?

- Because obvious physical and product differences have faded, consumers look for other ways to **differentiate** one brand from another. The biggest difference in the minds of many consumers is **service.**

- Good service is defined as meeting guest needs in the way that they want and expect them to be met. **Superior service** results from exceeding guest expectations.

- Hospitality operations, which often deal in **intangible products,** have very different management and marketing problems than companies that deal exclusively in tangible products.

- The nature of an intangible product is different than a tangible product.

- Customers are more involved in the production process, people are part of the product, it's harder to maintain quality control standards, there are no inventories, the time factor is more important, and distribution channels are different for intangible products than for tangible ones.

SECTION 2.2—SUPERIOR SERVICE

- Broad, long-range planning is called **strategic planning.**

- Companies must form general business objectives for themselves, otherwise there is bound to be confusion about where they are going and how they intend to get there.

- Broad general business objectives are most commonly called a company's mission and are expressed as a mission statement.

- Once a mission has been clearly established, there are steps a company must take: Perform a **SWOT analysis,** formulate strategies, implement strategies, and monitor and evaluate results.

- Some companies focus on "moments of truth." These are the times when employees come in contact with guests.

SECTION 2.3—SERVICE STRATEGIES

- Hotels and restaurants are **capacity-constrained businesses** and must constantly manage supply and demand.

- Supply can be managed to some extent by using a **level-capacity strategy or a chased-demand strategy.** It is more productive to focus on managing demand. Demand can be shifted, inventoried, and controlled by varying price, changing service levels, or using communications strategies such as advertising.

- Payroll controls are an essential part of delivering service at levels that make economic sense.

SECTION 2.4—DELIVERING SERVICE

- Successful service companies share a "strategic service vision"—a blueprint for service managers.

- **Target markets** are groups of customers with similar product and service preferences.

- Successful hospitality companies focus a good deal of management attention on establishing service quality standards, communicating them to employees through training programs, and measuring performance.

- There are many things organizations can do to demonstrate that they care about service. They include sticking to service strategies, encouraging employees to act like managers, hiring good people and keeping them happy, and being responsive.

Profile

Nancy Johnson

Executive Vice President, Select Service Hotels, Carlson Hotels Worldwide

When she was a college student working in a full-service hotel, Nancy Johnson had little idea she would be training for a career in lodging that would take her to the highest rungs in the industry. At St. Cloud State University in Minnesota, Johnson worked in nearly every department of the hotel to help pay her tuition. Her interest in the real estate led her to working on the development side of a construction company.

The Brutger Cos. designated Johnson its hotel specialist by virtue of her college jobs. "During my 10 years there, we built 48 hotels, and that is where I got my love of hotels," she says.

From there, she worked for two years as vice president and COO at Hospitality Development Co., then made the leap to franchise sales at Carlson Hotels Worldwide. Johnson thrived in the corporation's aggressive growth culture, and she quickly became vice president of development for Country Inns and Suites by Carlson. Still, she was surprised that Jay Witzel, president of Carlson Hotels Worldwide, approached her about being executive vice president and brand leader for the Country Inn and Park Inn brands.

"I had been in franchise sales for 13 years, so personally, it was quite a leap," Johnson says. "It's very unusual to take someone from franchise sales development and put them back in operations."

As Johnson enters her third decade in lodging, thoughts of legacy mean much more to her. Last year, she began groundwork for founding an AH&LA industry council of women in lodging.

"The intent is to create a visible role model for women within the industry," Johnson says. "We want to make sure we understand what is 40 percent of our customer base—women travelers—and we want to make sure that the women executives we do have coming up through the industry have their voices heard."

Excerpted with permission from Lodging Magazine, March 2005

Safety and Security

Sections

3.1 Workplace Safety

AFTER STUDYING SECTION 3.1, YOU SHOULD KNOW HOW TO:

♦ Describe safe methods for lifting, moving, and carrying items

♦ Handle ladders and electrical equipment safely

♦ Conduct a job safety analysis

Managers and employees must work together to keep all job functions—no matter how routine or difficult—from becoming hazardous. The key is to identify a hazardous condition before it threatens employees, guests, and the property. An alert and careful employee can be a property's best defense.

Wet floors and slippery walkways are accidents waiting to happen. Cluttered floors or cleaning equipment left out and in the way are invitations for injury. Improper lifting techniques and lifting or moving too much at once can threaten employee health. Such hazards result in the most common forms of employee injury: sprains, strains, and falls.

Accidents and injuries do not have to occur. By following three simple rules, employees can contribute to a safe, accident-free work environment.

1. Take adequate time. No job is so urgent that you must do it in an unsafe, hurried manner.

2. Correct unsafe conditions immediately. If you cannot correct an unsafe or hazardous condition yourself, report it at once to your supervisor.

3. Do it safely the first time. Every employee must do his or her job in a safe and correct manner. This is the best way to prevent accidents.

All lodging properties should have a list of safety rules encouraging employees to develop and practice safe work habits.

Lifting

Many tasks around the hotel involve lifting heavy objects. Employees may also need to move furniture. Incorrectly lifting heavy objects such as bags, luggage, boxes, and containers may result in strained or

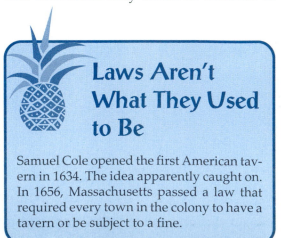

Laws Aren't What They Used to Be

Samuel Cole opened the first American tavern in 1634. The idea apparently caught on. In 1656, Massachusetts passed a law that required every town in the colony to have a tavern or be subject to a fine.

Exhibit 1
Guidelines for Safe Lifting

1. Inspect the object before lifting. Do not lift any item that you cannot get your arms around or that you cannot see over when carrying.
2. Look for any protrusions, especially when lifting trash or bundles of linen. Quite often, these items can contain pointy objects or broken glass. Exercise special care to avoid injury.
3. When lifting, place one foot near the object and the other slightly back and apart. Keep well balanced.
4. Keep your back and head straight. Because the back muscles are generally weaker than the leg muscles, do not use the back muscles to lift the object.
5. Bend slightly at the knees and hips but do not stoop.
6. Use both hands and grasp the object using the entire hand.
7. Lift with the leg muscles.
8. Keep the object close to the body. Avoid twisting your body.
9. If the object feels too heavy or awkward to hold, or if you do not have a clear view over the object, set it down.
10. When setting an object down do not use your back muscles. Use the leg muscles and follow the procedures used to lift objects.

pulled muscles and back injury. In turn, these injuries can result in loss of work and long-term pain and suffering.

Employees can also receive cuts and scratches when lifting trash or dirty linens that contain pointy objects or broken glass. Employees should know what conditions to look for and the special precautions to take. Exhibit 1 outlines safe lifting techniques.

Ladders

When selecting a ladder for a particular cleaning job, inspect its condition, height, and footing. Check the ladder for stability and examine crosspieces for sturdiness. If the ladder is broken or defective, do not use it. Rather, tag the ladder, place it out of service, and report it to the appropriate supervisor or the maintenance department.

A ladder must also be high enough so that an employee can stand on it and do the job without overreaching. Never stand on the top step of the ladder; if the area cannot be reached while standing on the step below the top step, the ladder is too short for the job. Metal ladders should never be used working near or on electrical equipment. Ladders with rubber footings should be used and tile floors or in kitchen areas to prevent slipping. In all instances, the floor should be dry and clean.

Before climbing, make sure the ladder is well balanced and secure against the wall and floor. Ladders should be placed so the footing is at least one fourth of the ladder length away from the wall. For example, if the latter is twelve feet tall, the footing should be three feet away from the wall. Never place the ladder against a window or an uneven surface. When possible, have another employee stabilize the ladder while you are aloft by bracing the footing with his or her feet and studying the ladder with his or her hands.

Always be sure to face a ladder when climbing, and have clean and dry hands and feet. Do not hold any items or tools that may prevent the use of one or both hands. Mark the area underneath the ladder with caution signs so that guests or employees do not walk under the ladder. Walking under a ladder may be considered unlucky by the superstitious, but it is also a very unsafe practice.

Electrical Equipment

Extra care must be taken when operating electrical equipment. Even, common appliances like vacuum cleaners can be harmful or deadly if operated improperly or unsafe conditions. Electrical equipment and machinery used at a lodging property should be approved by the Underwriters Laboratories.

The Underwriters Laboratories is an independent, nonprofit organization that tests electrical equipment and devices. The purpose of such testing is to ensure that electrical equipment is free of defects that can cause fire or sparks. Approved equipment bears the initials "UL" in a circle on the packaging, instructional material, or tag.

Employees should never operate electrical equipment when standing in water or when his or her hands or clothing are wet. It is also unsafe to operate electrical equipment near flammable liquids, chemicals, or vapors as sparks from the equipment could start a fire. Equipment that sparks, smokes, or flames should be turned off immediately. If it is possible and safe to do so, equipment should be unplugged. In no instance should

an employee attempt to restart the equipment. The malfunction should be reported to an appropriate supervisor.

Equipment wires and connections should be checked periodically. Do not use equipment with loose connections or exposed wires. Never unplug an appliance by pulling or yanking the cord. This will loosen the connection between the cord and plug and cause sparks and shorts. Instead, unplug by grasping the plug and pulling gently away from the outlet.

When using electrical equipment, the cord should be kept out of traffic areas such as the centers of aisles or doorways. This is not always possible, particularly with such tasks as vacuuming corridors. In such situations, keep the cord close to the wall and post caution signs in the work area. If the appliance will be stationary and in use for a lengthy period, tape the cord to the floor and place caution signs over the taped cord.

Extension cords are sometimes required—particularly when an electrical outlet is not near the work area. Extension cords should be inspected for exposed wire before use, just like any other electrical cord. There are many types of extension cords; not all are acceptable for use in the hospitality operation. The local fire department can pinpoint which types of cords meet the local, state, or federal fire codes and regulations.

Job Safety Analysis

Safety information is often best communicated through orientation and ongoing training. The design and use of a safety manual is also an excellent communication vehicle. The manual should detail the different jobs and instruct employees on the safe and proper way to perform each job. The first step in designing such a manual is to perform a job safety analysis.

A **job safety analysis** is a detailed report that lists every job function performed by all employees. This is often performed on a department-by-department basis. The job list provides the foundation for analyzing the potential hazards of a particular position. The format for each analysis can parallel that of job breakdowns, with safety tips and potential hazards being cited in the third column.

Apply Your Learning

Please write all answers on a separate sheet of paper.

1. What are some of the potentially hazardous conditions that employees should be aware of?

2. What are the three simple rules that employees can follow to contribute to a safe accident-free work environment?

3. Why must electrical equipment and machinery be approved by the Underwriters Laboratories?

4. What is a job safety analysis and what should it include?

Fill in the following blanks regarding the proper use of ladders.

5. A _____ ladder should never be used when working near or on electrical equipment.

6. A ladder must be high enough so that an employee can stand on it and do the job without _____.

7. When selecting a ladder for a particular job, inspect its condition, height, and _____.

8. When possible, have another employee _____ the ladder while you are aloft.

9. If the ladder is eight feet tall, the footing should be _____ feet away from the wall.

3.2 Chemicals and OSHA

AFTER STUDYING SECTION 3.2, YOU SHOULD KNOW HOW TO:

- Use cleaners and chemicals safely
- List the safety equipment needed when handling chemicals
- List the five steps needed to comply with the HazComm standard.
- Obtain MSDSs from chemical suppliers
- Label chemical containers

Rita is cleaning a badly stained toilet bowl with an ammonia-based cleaner. She scrubs vigorously at the stains, but they will not come out. She pours more of the ammonia cleaner into the bowl, but the stains are still there. Finally, she reaches for a container of chlorine bleach, dumps some into the bowl, and leans over to scrub again.

This scenario underscores a vital element of chemical use in the housekeeping department: proper training in the safe and effective use of chemicals. Rita does not know that mixing ammonia and chlorine will produce a deadly gas that will very probably result in her death.

Safety Equipment

Hospitality employees, especially those in the housekeeping department, may use chemicals that require wearing protective gear. Personal protective gear may be used for covering the eyes, face, head, hands, and, in some cases, the entire body. Protective gear should be worn when using hazardous or toxic chemicals.

Gloves, goggles, or face shields may be required when diluting chemicals for cleaning purposes or when mixing chemicals for treating swimming pools. When cleaning very dusty areas or overhead areas such as ceiling vents, goggles and dust/mist respirators may be needed. These respirators fit over the employee's mouth and nose and prevent dust and other small airborne particles from being inhaled.

HazComm Standards

OSHA is a broad set of rules that protects workers in all trades and professions from unsafe working conditions. The federal government often revises or expands these regulations and notifies employers when they must comply with new rules.

OSHA regulations require hotel employers to inform workers about the risks posed by chemicals they may use to do their jobs. The rule also requires that employers provide training in the safe use of these chemicals. This regulation is called the **Hazard Communication** (often shortened to **HazComm) Standard.** In order to comply

Exhibit 1
Form for Listing Hazardous Chemicals and Indexing MSDSs

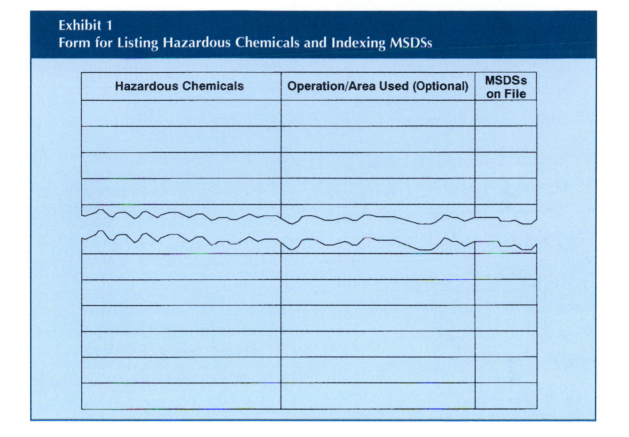

Hazardous Chemicals	Operation/Area Used (Optional)	MSDSs on File

with the HazComm Standard, OSHA requires that hotels must:

1. Read the standard.

2. List the hazardous chemicals used at the property. This includes doing a physical inventory of chemicals used, checking with the purchasing department to make sure the list is complete, setting up a file on hazardous chemicals, and developing procedures for keeping the file current.

3. Obtain **material safety data sheets (MSDSs)** from the suppliers of the chemicals used at the property, and make them available to employees.

4. Make sure all chemical containers are properly labeled.

5. Develop and implement a hazard communication program that explains MSDS information and labeling procedures to employees and informs them about hazards and protective measures.

Listing Hazardous Chemicals

Properties may assign one person to inventory all the chemicals used by the property, or department heads may be responsible for inventorying chemicals used in their specific areas. Exhibit 1 shows the inventory sheet provided by OSHA that can be used to compile a list of hazardous chemicals.

The name of each chemical that appears on the MSDS and on the label should be included on the inventory sheet. The common or trade name for the chemical can also be included. Some substances on a list of hazardous chemicals might be:

- Substances in aerosol containers

- Caustics such as laundry alkali

- Degreasing agents used in the laundry

- Detergents

- Flammable materials such as cleaners and polishes

- Fungicides and mildewcides used on carpets or in the laundry

- Floor sealers, strippers, and polishes

- Pesticides

The MSDS will indicate whether a chemical is hazardous—look for words such as *caution, warning, danger, combustible, flammable,* or *corrosive* on the label. If an MSDS for a particular chemical is not available, or if the MSDS does not indicate whether the chemical belongs on the list, OSHA recommends treating the substance as if it were a hazardous chemical.

Obtaining MSDSs from Chemical Suppliers

Once the inventory of hazardous materials is completed, the person in charge of the inventory should check to see if MSDSs are on file for each of the materials listed. If the property has an MSDS for a chemical, the person in charge of the inventory can put a check in the last column of the inventory sheet presented in Exhibit 1. If there is no MSDS for the chemical, the property must contact the chemical manufacturer to obtain one. A sample request letter is presented in Exhibit 2.

MSDSs can be filed by hazard, ingredients, or work areas—whatever way will make it easy for employees to find MSDSs in case of emergencies. MSDSs must be available during *all* work shifts.

All MSDSs should be examined carefully to make sure they are complete and clearly written. If data on MSDSs provide an insufficient basis for training employees on the chemical's hazards, the person in charge of the inventory should contact the manufacturer for additional information or clarification. MSDSs must include the following information:

- Chemical identity

- Hazardous ingredients

- Physical and chemical characteristics

- Fire and explosion hazard data

- Reactivity data

- Health hazards

- Precautions for safe handling and use

- Control measures

Chemical Identity. OSHA requires that manufacturers list the chemical and common name(s) for the substance. The form must also include the manufacturer's name, address, and telephone number so information can be obtained in case of an emergency.

Hazardous Ingredients. The manufacturer must list certain hazardous substances in the chemical.

Physical and Chemical Characteristics. The physical and chemical properties of the

**Exhibit 2
Sample Letter Requesting an MSDS**

Orange Grove Motel
1234 Leisure Avenue
Vacationland, FL 12345

Acme Hotel Products
5678 Industrial Park Way
Chemical City, NJ 54321

Dear Sir/Madam:

As you are aware, OSHA requires employers to provide training to their employees concerning the hazards of chemicals or other hazardous materials.

To properly train our employees, we need a material safety data sheet (MSDS) for one of your products, _____.

Your prompt attention is necessary to maintain a proper level of safety for our employees. Please send the MSDS for _____ no later than _____.

Sincerely,

Catherine Smith
Executive Housekeeper

chemical can help workers identify the chemical by sight or smell. This increases workers' understanding of the chemical's behavior and alerts them to take necessary precautions.

Fire and Explosion Hazard Data. Knowing if and under what circumstances the chemical could catch fire and/or explode is extremely important when training employees to handle chemical emergencies. OSHA requires manufacturers to recommend fire-fighting procedures and the substance (extinguishing media) to be used to extinguish the fire. The manufacturer must also note any unusual fire or explosion hazards.

Reactivity Data. The chemical manufacturer must provide information about the

chemical's stability. A stable chemical is one that will not burn, vaporize, explode, or react in some other way under normal conditions. The MSDS should describe the circumstances under which the chemical could become unstable. Temperature extremes or vibrations, for example, could cause some chemicals to ignite.

Health Hazards. How the chemical could enter the body (routes of entry) and its acute and chronic hazards must be listed on the MSDS. **Acute hazards** are those which could affect the user immediately; **chronic hazards** are those that could affect the user over repeated, long-term use of the chemical. In addition, the manufacturer must list whether the chemical is a carcinogen according to the National Toxicity Program (NTP), the International Agency for Research on Cancer (IARC), or OSHA; whether it will aggravate any other medical conditions; and what emergency and first aid procedures should be taken if dangerous exposure to the chemical occurs.

Precautions for Safe Handling and Use. Chemical manufacturers must provide advice on handling, storing, and disposing of chemicals. Information on the proper handling of spills must also be included.

Control Measures. How to use the chemical safely must be outlined. Manufacturers may recommend that users wear protective gloves, goggles, or clothing—or that they use protective equipment. A section on good work/hygiene practices must also be included.

Labeling All Chemical Containers

Chemical manufacturers, in addition to providing MSDSs, must provide proper labels for chemicals. OSHA requires employers to check these labels for completeness and accuracy. The label must contain the name of the chemical, hazard warnings, and the manufacturer's name and address. If no label is provided, the employer must prepare a label from the MSDS or ask the manufacturer to provide one.

The point of the labeling requirement in the HazComm regulations is to provide an "early warning system" for users of the chemical. Labels must note the chemical's physical and health hazards *during normal use* to comply with OSHA regulations. (It is nearly impossible to list all the hazards that could occur during accidents or improper use.) For example, the label may not simply state, "avoid inhalation." It must explain what effects inhaling the chemical could have. However, if the label is too detailed, employees may not see important cautions.

To make the label quick to read and easy to comprehend, some properties use a labeling system with color, letter, and number codes. For example, a red label might indicate that the chemical poses a physical hazard; the letter F might indicate that the chemical is flammable; and the number four (on a scale of one to four) might indicate that the hazard is relatively severe. Employees must be trained to read and understand whatever labeling system is used at the property.

The OSHA labeling provision also requires employers to ensure that employees properly label containers into which they pour chemicals. In some states, the portable containers into which chemicals are poured for immediate use *by the person pouring them* do not need to be labeled. Other states require labeling of all portable containers. Labeling requirements should be ascertained on a state-by-state basis.

Apply Your Learning 3.2

Please write all answers on a separate sheet of paper.

1. What is the purpose of the HazComm Standard and what are the five steps OSHA requires hotels to take to comply with the standard?

2. What words help determine whether a chemical is hazardous?

3. MSDSs must be on file for:
   a. each chemical listed on the inventory.
   b. the most commonly used chemicals.
   c. training purposes only.
   d. emergency purposes only.

For numbers 4–11, identify which MSDS information category would provide the answer.

Chemical identity   Reactivity data
Hazardous ingredients   Health hazards
Physical and chemical characteristics   Precautions for safe handling and use
Fire and explosion hazard data   Control measures

4. "Can I identify the chemical by any certain smells?"

5. "What's the best way to clean up a spill of this chemical?"

6. "What is the common name for the substance?"

7. "Will this chemical aggravate any certain medical conditions?"

8. "Are there any other hazardous chemicals in the substance?"

9. "Will this chemical catch fire or explode under normal circumstances?"

10. "Do I need to wear protective clothing or equipment when using this chemical?"

11. "How stable is this chemical? Could vibrations cause it to ignite?"

3.3   Front Office Security

AFTER STUDYING SECTION 3.3, YOU SHOULD KNOW HOW TO:

♦ Describe the role of the front office in security

♦ Explain how key control measures protect guests

♦ Outline the ways that locking systems protect guests

♦ Create a plan for front desk surveillance and access control

♦ Describe how to protect hotel funds

♦ Control access to a safe deposit box and limit liability

Providing security in a hotel means protecting people (guests, employees, and others) and property. The responsibility for developing and maintaining a property's security program lies with its management. The information in this section introduces elements that apply to the front office.

The Role of the Front Office

A security program is most effective when *all* employees participate in the hotel's security efforts. Exhibit 1 addresses the role hotels played during a national emergency.

Front office staff play a particularly important role. Front desk agents, door attendants, bellpersons, and parking attendants can observe all persons entering or departing the premises. They can report suspicious activities or circumstances involving a guest or a visitor to the hotel's security department or a designated staff member.

Some security procedures include front desk agents never giving keys, room numbers, messages, or mail to anyone requesting them without first requiring appropriate identification. Similarly, front desk agents do not announce an arriving guest's room number.

Guests may be further protected if front office employees withhold guest information from callers or visitors. People calling guests at the hotel should be directly connected to the guestroom without being told the room number. Conversely, someone asking for a specific room number over the telephone should be connected only after the caller identifies whom he or she is calling and the hotel employee verifies the identity of the person in the room requested. A person inquiring at the front desk about a guest may be asked to use the house phone to contact the guest.

A hotel also helps protect its guests' personal property. The front office may move luggage and other guest items to a secured area when it is given to the bellperson; guests later recover their belongings by presenting a receipt. Other hotel employees can help protect the guests' property. A valet parking attendant, for example, can secure the keys of all parked vehicles.

Exhibit 1
Hotels in Their Communities

A hotel is part of a larger community. This became very apparent after September 11, 2001 in New York City. Manhattan Island, where the tragedy occurred, was cut off from the rest of the area. To get home, many people in Manhattan had to walk, sometimes for miles because the subways, trains, some bridges and automobile tunnels were closed. People turned to hotels for shelter and in some cases protection. Yet, hotels were not part of New York's master plan for emergencies. Hotel managers responded well to the emergency, and accommodated many guests, whether they could pay or not, during the crisis. This example is proof of emergency plans that consider a hotel to be isolated from the vitality of the city and region may be inadequate.

Since September 11, 2001, coordinating with emergency management agencies has taken on special importance as hotel managers and government officials came to realize that terrorists can strike anywhere. Hotel managers are involved in emergency notification planning, so that hotel guests and employees can be notified of the need to evacuate. In some cases, hospitals may not be large enough to handle emergencies and may ask hotels to serve as emergency medical treatment centers.

Front office staff are also important to asset protection. Failure to collect payment from guests may represent a more significant loss than, for instance, a guest's theft of towels or ashtrays.

Verifying Guest Identity

Many hotels require positive identification to complete the registration. This is a common practice in Europe, especially for foreign guests. It is very common to have the frong desk agent ask for guest passports for positive identification of the name, address, signature, and photograph. Since September 11, 2001, this has become more common at American hotels. Hotel managers want to be sure they know who is staying at their property.

For domestic guests, a driver's license or other form of photo identification is usually enough. Foreign guests are usually asked for their passports. In both cases, the type of identification and identification number on the card or passport is recorded in the guest record. As an additional security measure, if the guest does not speak the local language, it is also noted in the guest's record. This is intended to assist hotel personnel in identifying guests requiring foreign language translation in emergency matters.

Key Control

Most lodging properties use at least three types of guestroom keys: emergency keys, master keys, and individual guestroom keys. An **emergency key** (E-Key) opens all guestroom doors, even when they are double-locked—that is, locked with both a standard door lock and a deadbolt from within the guestroom. It can be used, for example, to enter a room when the guest needs aid and is unable to reach or open the door. Emergency keys are highly protected and stored in a secure place, such as the hotel safe, safe deposit box, or a special cabinet which only the general manager or the hotel security chief controls. Authorized staff use a log book to sign out the key, noting the time, date, and reason for the key's removal. Removal of the key is witnessed by at least one other authorized staff member, who also signs the log book. The key is returned to the secure area as quickly as possible. The return time is noted in the log and a witness also signs the log book confirming that the key was returned as recorded. An emergency key should never be removed from the hotel property.

A **master key** opens all guestroom doors that are not double-locked. When not in use, a master key should be secured in a designated place. Only authorized personnel should have access to master keys. Keys are issued to personnel based on their need to use the key. For example, housekeeping room attendants have floor or section master keys. Hotels maintain a written record of employees who have been issued master keys. Hotel employees sign keys out at the beginning of their shift in a key log book. At the end of the shift, the keys are signed back in.

A guestroom key opens a guestroom door so long as it is not double-locked. Front desk agents should not give a guestroom key to anyone not registered to the room. The front desk agent should check appropriate identification to ensure that the person requesting the key is the guest registered to the room.

Front office staff should not remove hotel keys from the property. Whenever there is any known or suspected compromise of a key, an unauthorized entry by key, or any loss or theft, every lock affected should be changed (or rotated to another part of the property).

Electronic Locking Systems. An **electronic locking system** replaces traditional mechanical locks with computer-based guestroom access devices. Electronic locking systems, which eliminate the need for emergency and master keys, operate through a master control console at the front desk that is wired to every guestroom door. The ability to change the data on an electronic key card with every new registration means the card, issued to the guest, is the only working guestroom key.

Centralized electronic locking systems provide improved security and help reduce employee theft. Many of these systems keep track of which keys or cards opened which doors, by date and time. Employees tempted to steal may be discouraged by the fact that an entry record may be used to incriminate them.

Surveillance and Access Control

Although open to the public, a hotel is a private property. An innkeeper has the responsibility to monitor and, when appropriate, to control the activities of people on the premises. All hotel employees should be trained to recognize suspicious people and situations. Discouraging or stopping suspicious or unauthorized individuals from entering the property relies on responding to the observations of employees.

Most lobbies are designed so front desk agents can view the property's entrances, elevators, escalators, and stairways. Mirrors may be placed in strategic locations to aid visibility. Observing elevators and escalators is important for both security and safety reasons; front office staff should know how to stop both in an emergency.

In many hotels, someone is stationed at the front desk at all times. In a smaller property, a front desk agent may be the only staff member on the premises during late night hours. Under such circumstances, some properties limit late night access to the lobby and reception areas and give the front desk agent the authority to deny admittance. If the front desk agent needs to leave the desk area for any reason, many properties advise the agent to lock the front door. With the door locked, no one can enter the hotel until the agent returns to the front office area.

Although successful surveillance techniques rely on hotel personnel, proper equipment can enhance the surveillance function. Closed-circuit television cameras and monitors can be an effective surveillance system in multiple-entry properties. Employees are assigned to watch the monitors and respond to incidents picked up by surveillance cameras.

Protection of Funds

The accounting division is primarily responsible for the protection of hotel funds. However, other departments, particularly the front office, contribute by protecting certain financial assets.

The amount of cash in a front office cash register is limited through a **cash bank** sys-

tem. At the start of a workshift, each cashier is given the smallest amount of cash that will allow him or her to transact a normal business volume. The cashier is responsible for this cash bank and for all changes to it during the workshift. Ideally, only one person has access to each cash bank, and each cash bank should be in a separate cash drawer.

All front office transactions are immediately recorded. The front office cashier needs to close the cash drawer after each transaction. A cashier working with an open cash drawer may fail to record a transaction, either accidentally or deliberately. Front office cashiers must complete a transaction in process before changing currency into different denominations for guests; each request for change should be handled as a new transaction to avoid confusion. A supervisor or a member of the accounting division staff should occasionally conduct an unscheduled audit of front office cash registers.

Safe Deposit Boxes

Laws in most states limit a property's liability for the loss of a guest's valuables if the property has safe deposit boxes or a safe for the storage of guest valuables. Liability also depends on whether the hotel notifies the guest that safe deposit boxes or safes are available for their use. The required notice usually takes the form of public postings within guestrooms and in the front desk area.

Safe deposit boxes are located in a limited-access area. Such a location may be near the front desk, where the safe deposit boxes may be secured while still visible to guests.

Strict safe deposit box control includes the storage, issuance, and receipt of safe deposit box keys. Only front office staff responsible for safe deposit boxes have access to unissued keys. Two keys are required to open any safe deposit box. The front office's *control key* must be used with the *guest's key* to open the box. The control key is always secured. Under no circumstances should there be more than one guest key for each safe deposit box, even when more than one guest is using the same box. If a guest key is lost, the box is drilled open in the presence of a witness and a second staff member.

Access. Controlled access is the most critical of all safe deposit box responsibilities. The guest's identity should be verified by signature each time access is desired. Under no circumstances should a guest be granted access unless signatures match.

Front office policies may vary on how to maintain the guest's privacy regarding the contents of the safe deposit box. Only the guest should place items into or remove items from a safe deposit box. The front desk agent should never be alone with the guest's valuables. Once the box has been opened, the front desk agent should leave the area with the control key and the guest should be left alone until he or she summons the front desk agent. When the guest is finished, the front desk agent locks the box in view of the guest and returns the guest's key. The front desk agent then returns the control key to its secured location. When the guest relinquishes the safe deposit box and returns the key, the guest and the front desk agent both sign the safe deposit box record.

An in-room safe is another popular option for storing guest valuables. Guest convenience is the main advantage of in-room safes. In most states, in-room safes are not considered by law to offer the same level of protection for guest valuables as safe deposit boxes. This means that if guest valuables are lost after being placed in an in-room safe, the hotel cannot be held liable since the item was not in the care, custody, or control of the hotel.

Lost and Found

One employee or department should be assigned the lost and found responsibilities. No one but the authorized employee or department should handle lost and found items or discuss them with the guest. All telephone calls about lost or found items should be directed to the appropriate personnel; callers should be asked to provide a description of the item and to estimate where and when it was lost. The employee should record this information, as well as the guest's name and address, in a lost and found log (Exhibit 2). This log is also where items discovered by employees are noted.

Lost and found personnel should store a found item until it is claimed by the owner—or for the length of time designated by law. Under no circumstances should a found article be mailed to a guest at the address on a registration card without the guest's explicit permission. The front office may send a letter to the guest that asks him or her to contact the hotel to identify a found item. Once ownership of the item is established, the item can be mailed to an address specified by the guest. The department in charge of lost and found should keep records of all such actions.

Exhibit 2
Sample Lost and Found Log

LOST AND FOUND LOG

Item No. (optional)	Date and Time Found	Description of Article (include color, size, brand, etc.)	Area/Room No. Where Found	By Whom Found	How Disposed Of (Enter address if mailed)	By Whom	Date

Apply Your Learning 3.3

1. What role does the front office play in hotel security?

2. What form of identification is often used to verify guest identity?

3. What is the difference between a master key and an emergency key?

4. What type of system is used to limit the amount of cash in a front office register?

5. Who should have access to safe deposit keys?

3.4 Housekeeping Security

AFTER STUDYING SECTION 3.4, YOU SHOULD KNOW HOW TO:

♦ Identify activities that are suspicious

♦ Minimize guest and employee theft

Providing security in a hospitality operation is the broad task of protecting both people and assets. Security efforts may involve guestroom security, key control, perimeter control, and more. Each lodging property is different and has unique security needs.

Suspicious Activities

Hotel housekeeping employees can be part of an effective security force—particularly in guestroom areas.

The individuals allowed in guestroom areas are guests, their visitors, and on-duty employees who are performing their jobs in the authorized area. The housekeeping staff is trained to spot suspicious activities and unauthorized or undesirable persons. If an individual is seen loitering, checking doors, knocking on doors, or looking nervous, he or she should be considered suspicious and approached with caution. If an employee feels threatened or in danger, he or she should not approach the person but rather go to a secure area such as a storage room, lock the door, and call the front desk or security.

If the employee does approach such an individual, he or she does so politely. If the individual claims to be a guest, the attendant asks to see a room key or other type of verification. If the person says that he or she is not a guest, or does not have a room key, the attendant explains the hotel policy and directs the individual to the front desk. The attendant then watches to see whether that person proceeds to the directed area and then call the front desk or security.

Employees themselves can present similar security problems. Employees who are not in their designated work area should

A Matter of Security

Hotel security was largely an afterthought at U.S. lodging operations until 1974, when famous 1960s singer Connie Francis was attacked while staying at a Howard Johnson's Motor Lodge. Francis and her husband successfully sued the hotel, proving that inadequate security made it possible for her attacker to gain access to her guestroom. A key point in the jury's decision was that the property knew their security was lax and had not taken appropriate steps to correct it. The case was settled for $1,475,000 while Howard Johnson's appeal was pending.

be stopped and asked if they need help. Depending on the individual's response and manner, he or she should be reported to security or the housekeeping supervisor. Also, friends and visitors of employees should not be allowed in guestroom areas or employee locker rooms.

Theft

Management can reduce the volume of furniture, fixtures, equipment, and soft goods stolen from a property by reducing the opportunities to steal. Opportunities present themselves as unlocked doors, lack of inventory control, and plain carelessness.

Guest Theft. Unfortunately, guest theft is all too common in hotels. Some guest theft is considered a form of marketing; other guest theft is not. Most hotels assume that guests will take items which prominently display the hotel logo such as matches, pens, shampoo, ashtrays, and sewing kits. For the most part, these items are provided for the guest's convenience and are actually a form of advertising used by the hotel. However, towels, bathrobes, trash bins, and pictures are not part of the marketing strategy and are not meant to be taken by guests. When these items turn up missing, it can add up to a large expense.

To reduce theft, some properties keep count of the number of towels placed in the room. When the guest requests additional towels, it is noted at the front desk. The room attendant, too, notes how many towels are in the room when cleaning the next day. The room attendant's ability to spot missing items may allow the hotel time to charge the guest for items that have been taken.

As another strategy, some hotels place items such as towels, bathrobes, and leather

stationery folders on sale in their gift shops. This may reduce the likelihood of theft since guests have the option of purchasing these items. Other helpful ideas to reduce guest theft are:

- Use as few monogrammed items as possible. Most guests are looking for a souvenir. The use of fewer items with logos reduces temptation.

- Keep storage rooms closed and locked. Do not allow guests to take any items from storage rooms. Also, amenities stored on carts should be stocked in a secure place or in a locked compartment.

Employee Theft. Management must set the standards for reducing employee theft—and act as a good example. A manager who takes hotel steaks home to barbecue will not be effective when asking employees not to steal food, linen, and other hotel property. The employee handbook should spell out the consequences of stealing hotel property. If the rules state that employees who are caught stealing will be prosecuted and fired then the hotel should follow through. It is important that management not discriminate against or in favor of any employees when enforcing these rules.

Managers should screen applicants before making a job offer. A thorough background check should be conducted, including a check for any criminal convictions.

Records should be kept of stolen or missing items—including those from guestrooms. The record should include the name of the room attendant and any other hotel employee who had access to the room. For example, if a room service employee delivers a meal, that employee's name should be entered into the log.

Keep all storeroom doors locked. Storerooms should be equipped with automatic closing and locking devices. Locks on store-rooms should be changed periodically to reduce the opportunity of theft.

If the property's design permits, management should designate employee entrances and exits. These entrances should be well lighted, adequately secured, and provided with round-the-clock security. Employee en-trances may include a security staff office that monitors arriving and departing employees.

Employees should know what items they may bring onto or remove from the property. Management may establish a claim-checking system for bringing items onto the premises and a parcel-pass system for taking items off the premises.

Apply Your Learning Section 3.4

Please write all answers on a separate sheet of paper.

1. How should suspicious, unauthorized, or undesirable persons be approached and handled?

2. Explain why some guest theft is considered a form of marketing. What items are generally included in this category?

3. What are some strategies for minimizing theft by hotel guests?

4. What are some strategies for minimizing employee theft?

3.5 Emergency Response

AFTER STUDYING SECTION 3.5, YOU SHOULD KNOW HOW TO:

- Demonstrate techniques for handling fires
- Describe procedures for handling power failures
- Handle elevator malfunctions
- Explain how lodging employees respond to weather emergencies
- Name actions employees may perform during a medical emergency
- Explain what to do if an employee or guest dies
- Describe how to respond to civil unrest
- Identify ways to respond if weapons are found at the property

Emergency Planning

Because emergencies don't usually happen often at a property, there is no way to fully prepare for them. That's why properties conduct emergency drills and create a disaster action and recovery plan. By simulating emergencies, everyone at the property can become familiar with the procedures for handling various situations. The more familiar employees are with procedures, the more prepared they will be to handle a real emergency. A prepared property is a safer property.

There are many types of disasters that can threaten properties. They can range from power failures to computer failures, floods, fires, weather, criminal activities and terrorism. While not every disaster can be anticipated, many can and plans help the hotel respond to them.

Unfortunately, one of the most common issues facing a hotel is criminal activity, whether it is at the front desk, a revenue outlet, in a guestroom, or elsewhere. Managers prepare for this by clearly documenting procedures and teaching staff how to conduct themselves during such events.

Fires

Fire alarms and power failures are the most common emergencies experienced in the lodging industry. The key to providing good responses when these types of emergencies happen is to be prepared, stay calm, and act quickly.

Lodging properties are encouraged to have written emergency plans which outline what needs to be done to protect people and property in a specific emergency. These plans can help each employee know exactly what he or she is expected to do in an emergency.

When you know in advance how to respond to a fire emergency or power failure, you not only make better decisions, but you

True Hotel Heroes

While most of the news reports on the September 11, 2001 terrorist attacks focused on the loss of the twin towers, another building was destroyed that day: The Marriott WTC hotel.

While most guests and employees were able to escape the Marriott WTC hotel before it collapsed, about 50 people inside the hotel were killed, including at least 41 firefighters and two hotel employees.

Joseph Keller, the hotel's executive housekeeper, stayed to help guide people out of the hotel and was last seen trapped in the lobby with two firefighters. Abdul Malahi, an audiovisual engineer, was working with an economists' meeting and also stayed to help people evacuate.

After the attacks, the Marriott Financial Center worked with the Red Cross to be a respite center for recover workers. They opened up their banquet rooms to use as meals and a rest place for those working at the World Trade Center Site.

Marriott continues to honor those who were lost in the attacks, especially the two employees who died after helping guests out of the hotel. The flag that was recovered from the hotel is now on permanent display at the Marriott headquarters. In 2003, they held a tree-dedicating ceremony for the two trees planted as a memorial to the employees who died. There were also two pillar candles displayed in the New York Marriott Marquis in their memory.

can save time making the decisions. And when you save time, you have a better opportunity to manage the situation effectively.

If a fire does break out at a property, every second counts. Fires can double in size every 60 seconds. Even a small fire can quickly rage out of control unless immediate action is taken.

Fire alarms may be triggered automatically by heat or smoke detectors, or manually.

Although some fire alarms turn out to be false alarms, lodging employees respond to every alarm as if it were the real thing. Every alarm should be treated as valid until a manager or emergency personnel confirm that it's a false alarm.

Initial actions should depend on the answers to these questions:

1. Where is the fire?

2. Are people in immediate danger?

3. How big is the fire?

4. Has the fire department been called?

If people are in immediate danger, lodging employees evacuate them at once if possible. If the fire does not pose an immediate threat to lives, they notify the fire department first. If possible, they notify the fire department and guests at the same time. Lodging employees usually notify the fire department in one of three ways:

- Trigger a pull station fire alarm.

- Radio or call the front desk or PBX operator and have someone call the fire department.

- Call the fire department themselves.

After lodging employees evacuate the area, they can try to keep the fire from spreading, but only if it's safe to do so. Their safety is as important as that of the people around them, so they are discouraged from trying to be a hero if it puts them at risk.

Lodging employees must use common sense when deciding whether it's safe to try to put out a fire. They consider the equipment they have on hand, how quickly the fire is growing, and the possibility of something in the area exploding. They attempt to put out only small, contained fires, and then only if they feel comfortable doing so. They make sure they have a safe escape route to use if they can't put out the fire. They also always make sure the fire department has been called before trying to put out a fire.

If it's not safe to put out the fire, there are still some things lodging employees can do as they leave the area to prevent the fire from spreading:

- Close windows, doors, and fire doors behind them.

- Remove **combustible** materials, such as gasoline or oily rags, from the area, but only if they have time.

- Shut off fans, air conditioners, or air circulators.

- If possible, shut off fuel to gas–powered equipment.

- If they think the fire is electrical, shut off electric current to the area.

If they do decide it's safe to try extinguishing the fire, they use the right equipment. Different types of fire extinguishers will put out specific types of fires.

Fires are generally classified by the type of fuel that is burning, and fire extinguishers correspond to these classifications. For example, a wood fire can be put out with water. However, spraying water on a grease fire will only cause the grease (and the fire) to spread.

Lodging properties need to be concerned mainly with Class A, B, and C fires. Today many lodging properties use fire extinguishers that have been developed to put out fires in either Class A, B, or C. These extinguishers are clearly marked with the symbols "A–B–C" and can be used to put out all fires except those fueled by combustible elements.

When lodging employees find themselves in a fire area, they can protect themselves by:

- Making sure they always have an escape route and trying not to get cut off from an exit.

- Staying low in smoky conditions. Smoke rises and the air will be clearer close to the floor.

- If they get cut off, going into a guestroom and closing the door. They can seal around the door and vent openings with damp towels. They can try the phone to let someone know they are cut off. They can also fill the bathtub and sink with water to dampen towels and to keep the room door wet.

When firefighters arrive, lodging employees can help them as much as possible.

- Have master keys and a list of guests with disabilities available.

- Direct them to the fire.

- Answer any questions that they might have.

- Alert them to any potential dangers, such as hazardous materials, that might affect how they fight the fire.

- Follow their directions and obey their commands immediately — they are the experts in these situations and should have total command.

- Be prepared to leave the property if firefighters instruct them to do so.

Power Failures

Power failures are often triggered by some other emergency, such as severe weather, vandalism, or acts of terrorism. Since the massive power failure of 2003 where several states lost power for days and the multiple hurricanes that hit Florida and the East Coast in 2003 and 2004, most lodging managers view power failures as a "when" not an "if" scenario. During a power failure, lodging employees have three major responsibilities:

1. Protect the safety of people at the property

2. Minimize vandalism

3. Secure money and valuable assets

The first priority is always the safety of the people at the property—including employees. Each property has a predesignated emergency command center (usually the front desk). Lodging employees should head to this command center. If they notice anyone trying to get around in the dark, they can help them get back to the main areas of the property, such as the lobby or evacuation areas.

If the problem is only in one area of the property, maintenance can try to fix it. Then other employees can concentrate on protecting the people around them.

- Post employees with flashlights at all ramps, escalators, and especially at stairways. The property may have battery–powered lamps that can be used as well.

- Notify guests about the problem. The front desk or PBX operator may do this by telephone or public address system, but if the systems are out, someone may be asked to go to guestrooms to give personal notice.

- Ask guests to remain in their rooms unless it is absolutely necessary that they leave. The more guests roaming around in the dark, the greater the chance that someone will get hurt. However, some situations, such as a fire, might justify the added risks of guests evacuating the guestroom areas.

- Some properties may advise guests to call the front desk for an escort if they need to leave their rooms.

- Be calm when speaking with guests. Reassure them that the situation is being taken care of and remind them of the danger of tripping or falling in the dark. The employees' attitudes will help keep them calm.

- Don't spend a lot of time talking to any one guest. There will probably be a lot of ground to cover and employees can't afford to waste time. Give guests only the information they need to know.

- Remind guests about the potential fire hazards of using matches, lighters, or candles for light. Tell guests to open drapes for external lighting during daylight.

Vandalism can be a big problem during power failures. The confusion in an emergency plus the poor lighting provide an excellent environment for wrongdoers, so employees need to maintain a visible presence on the property.

A power failure provides a perfect opportunity for criminals to try stealing property assets. Some employees will be asked to secure property valuables such as cash or important records.

Elevator Malfunctions

Most multiple–floor properties have elevators to provide access to upper floors for people with disabilities and to make it easier for guests and employees to move themselves, their belongings, and equipment throughout the building. In high–rise properties, elevators are obviously a necessity.

Elevator malfunctions can be caused by power failures, mechanical problems or equipment failures. When an elevator isn't working correctly, it causes inconvenience and creates potential safety and security problems for a property.

If an elevator malfunctions, lodging employees try to find out what floors the car is trapped between. Then they try to communicate with anyone trapped inside.

- If the elevator's phone or intercom doesn't work, they call up the elevator shaft from below without entering the elevator shaft. Sound rises and will make it easier for passengers to hear.

- Reassure them of their safety. It can be frightening to be stuck in a small, enclosed space for even a short time.

- Ask them what happened when the elevator stopped. Try to find out anything that could help maintenance or the elevator company identify how to fix the elevator, such as sounds, strange vibra-

tions or motions, or whether the emergency switch was accidentally activated.

- Tell the passengers what is being done to fix the problem and ask them to remain calm. Don't try to get them out of the elevator. Leave evacuation for the elevator company or the fire department.

Lodging employees then stay in communication with the passengers. Someone calls the maintenance department and gives them details about the problem so they can determine how to fix it. If the problem will take some time to fix, an employee updates the people trapped about any progress or lack of progress. If they are not kept posted, they may feel abandoned and start to panic.

Lodging properties must then keep people from using the elevator until it has been checked out and repaired. If possible, they lock the elevator with a key and place "Out of Service" signs near elevator doors until the elevator is fixed.

Weather Emergencies and Natural Disasters

Hurricanes. Floods. Tornados. Blizzards. Earthquakes. Ice and rain storms. All properties eventually experience some kind of weather emergency or natural disaster. Its location determines the type of weather it is most likely to experience. For example, hurricanes usually affect coastal areas, earthquakes happen more frequently on the West Coast, while tornados usually occur inland. The chances of a property in Kansas experiencing a hurricane are pretty slim. However, it has been known to snow in Florida, so you never know when or where a weather emergency may arise.

Properties may not get much advance notice of a potential weather emergency. Some weather situations such as hurricanes and floods usually take time to develop to danger stages, but others such as tornados develop quickly. No matter what type of weather emergency a property might experience, the key to handling it is planning.

- Know where emergency supplies are kept and when to get them out.

- Secure money, important papers, and other valuables in weather tight areas.

- Prepare all hazardous materials. Be prepared to shut off gas if necessary.

- Carry out responsibilities using a property's emergency plan. This may include evacuating people from the property.

- Make sure everyone has taken shelter in designated safe locations if appropriate.

- Remain at assigned posts, as long as it's safe, until ordered to seek shelter, or until relieved.

- Keep people in shelters until the danger has passed.

Medical Emergencies

When confronted with medical emergencies, lodging employees need to make decisions quickly. In many cases, lives are at stake.

The first minutes in any emergency are critical. Lodging employees must quickly evaluate the situation by finding out what the problem is and trying to identify all important symptoms. Are the victims injured? Are they sick? They then send for emergency medical help immediately. This may mean contacting the front desk, security office, or PBX operator to call emergency medical numbers, or it may mean any employee on the scene making the call themselves.

Sometimes lodging employees will need to provide first aid immediately. If the situation is life–threatening, they start first aid procedures at once if they have proper training, but have another employee or a bystander call for help as soon as possible.

They try to help the injured as much as possible without further endangering their condition. This means:

- Talk to them. Tell them that you've called for medical help.

- Render whatever first aid you can.

- Keep them calm.

- Make them as comfortable as possible.

- Keep the victims still. Don't try to move them unless it's dangerous to stay in that area.

- Ask them if they have a relative or friend that should be called.

- Keep bystanders away from the scene. The victims need some breathing room and probably won't want people staring and hovering over them.

- While your primary concern is for the well–being of the injured, you also need to protect the property from liability in these situations. What you say or do at the scene can reinforce a case against the property. So follow these tips:

  - Don't apologize to the injured for the accident. An apology can look like an admission of guilt.

  - Don't take responsibility for the accident. For example, if you say something such as, "Mrs. Jackson,

I've told them to fix that broken railing on the stairs," the victim could use your comment against the property in a lawsuit.

- Don't discuss the property's insurance or reimbursement for medical expenses. A victim might consider this an agreement and the property might be obligated to pay.

- Discuss the cause of the accident only with people who need to know. Don't talk to bystanders or employees unless they are involved.

Medical emergencies may require first aid. Under OSHA, lodging properties are required to have someone trained in first aid at the property at all times, unless medical services are easily accessible on or near the property.

Some common first aid procedures that lodging employees can learn to help them in life–threatening situations are:

- The **Heimlich maneuver** — used when someone is choking

- Mouth–to–mouth resuscitation — used to restore breathing when the victim is not choking

- **Cardiopulmonary resuscitation** (CPR) — used to restore breathing and heartbeat

Handling the Death of a Guest

It's uncommon for guests to die at a property, but if they do, it can be very difficult to handle. Usually deaths at lodging properties happen with little or no warning, so there's no way to fully prepare.

Each property has its own procedures for handling a guest's death. Here are some tips that apply to most cases:

- Immediately alert property management and police.

- Notify emergency medical help and call the local law enforcement. A supervisor or PBX operator may make the calls.

- Find out if the guest is really deceased. Check for a pulse or heartbeat, or breathing. Any death is unfortunate, but it is even more tragic if the death could have been prevented. A person who is "almost dead" may still be able to survive if medical help is brought in quickly.

- Try to disturb the scene as little as possible. Touch only what is absolutely necessary and leave everything exactly as found. Local police will try to determine a cause of death and details about how the guest died from clues in the room. These clues can easily be destroyed.

- Secure the area until police arrive. Only allow authorized people in the room until police arrive. Usually guests die in their own room. If this is the case, the room is double–locked so no one can get in without authorization. If a guest dies in a public area, the property attempts to lock the area if possible. If not, they block off the area so no one can disturb the scene.

Handling an Employee Death

Freak accidents, crime, and unknown health problems can cause an employee's death. Most of the techniques used to handle a guest's death are used when an employee dies at the property. Someone needs to notify property management and the police, call emergency medical help, and secure the area.

Some additional problems might develop when responding to an employee death. When the property seals off the area in which the death occurred, it might affect guest service. For example, if a kitchen steward dies in the kitchen, sealing off the area will probably hinder meal preparation for room service and restaurant guests.

Employees who are distressed over a co–worker's death may not be capable of using equipment or performing their job responsibilities safely.

Civil Unrest and Terrorist Threats

In today's society, the lodging industry has an increased chance of being threatened by civil unrest and terrorism. Arson, bombings, hostage–taking, and riots have become more common. Unfortunately, there is no way to prevent these situations — all a property can do is be prepared and act to prevent injuries and damages.

Terrorism has grown as a concern since September 11, 2001. Lodging properties have begun taking new precautions to help prevent terrorist acts at their properties. Some of these actions include:

- Watching unattended baggage.

- Increasing security training.

- Locking all entry doors except lobby entrances.

- Do not allow any non-guest or non-hotel vehicles to park near the premises.

- Suspending valet parking during code-red or code-orange alerts.

- Hiring extra security officers.

Probably the most common type of threat experienced in the lodging industry is a bomb threat. Lodging properties are attractive targets for bomb threats because:

- The public nature of the lodging industry provides easy access for bombers.

- There is a potential for huge losses in life and property.

- The potential for publicity is great.

The majority of bomb threats are hoaxes. It's easy for pranksters to call up a business and claim to have placed a bomb. The number of bombs found is small compared to the number of threats received. Despite this, every threat must be taken seriously. No property wants to take the chance that the threat is a prank. It could be endangering lives if it does.

Most bomb threats are received by phone. Often the threats are called into the security office or a PBX operator.

Other Threats of Violence or Damage

Political situations, court rulings, and even a controversial VIP can quickly turn a quiet protest or peaceful street into a riot. For example, an angry crowd of students protesting against a religious dignitary speaking at your property might quickly turn violent when the dignitary disagrees with their opinions.

Properties that could be most vulnerable to civil unrest or riots are:

- In large cities, downtown, or urban areas

- Near federal buildings or embassies

- Doing a large banqueting business

- Union properties or where union meetings are held

When a property is the target of such a threat, it follows these general rules:

- Try to get as much information as possible. The more information available, the easier it will be to decide on a course of action.

- Notify the proper authorities. Start with a supervisor or the manager on duty. Then follow instructions for notifying other authorities such as local police, fire department, Homeland Security, or FBI.

- Follow the instructions of the security supervisor or the manager–on–duty.

- Stay calm.

- Don't take any unnecessary risks.

- If a riot does start at or near the property, the employees' main concern is to follow police orders. Police will be involved and know more about handling any riot scene, so follow their directions. Usually those directions will involve keeping rioters out of the property buildings.

To protect the property:

- Secure all entrances except the main entrance to the lobby. Everyone, including employees, should use this door to enter and leave the building. Monitor this entrance to make sure rioters don't enter the building.

- Secure ground level windows and vulnerable windows or entrances on other floors. For example, windows near overhanging tree limbs might allow rioters to enter the property. Windows are often broken by objects rioters throw.

- Lock up alcoholic beverages and any valuables, such as cash or important papers.

- Patrol guest floors. Your presence on guest floors reassures guests and allows you to prevent them from further inciting the crowd.

- Check fire equipment.

Demonstrations

Demonstrations may occur when people want to protest against something or someone at the property. For example, animal rights activists may protest against a convention of medical scientists who use animals for experimentation. Strikes, on the other hand, happen when an employee contract is unresolved and bargaining breaks down. Either situation is an unusual security challenge for the property.

Both strikes and demonstrations can be highly emotional. People protest because of what they feel is right. The property becomes the symbol of the opposing side, whether because of its employment practices or because it shelters a controversial figure or group. Any situation where people have conflicting beliefs has the potential to explode into violence.

Keep in mind that people who protest are not criminals, and the property cannot keep them from protesting. Strikes and demonstrations are protected by law, and the property could be sued for interfering with First Amendment or labor law rights. However, the property does have the right to keep protestors from coming onto the property.

Communication is a key to preventing peaceful demonstrations from becoming ugly riots. A property needs to make sure the crowd knows the limits that it will enforce and that appropriate people are kept informed of developments. But it can't be too heavy–handed or it will generate hostility among the protestors.

Demonstrators may ask to use the rest rooms or telephones, or to be allowed to get something to eat from a property restaurant. The reason they give may be legitimate, but it could also be a cover for some other action. They may try to cause damage to property assets or to confront or assault a person against whom they are protesting. If they get onto the property they become an even bigger security risk. For example, an angry striker may try to damage valuable machinery in order to force the property management to agree to the union's demands. Property staff should try to keep protestors off the grounds. If any protestor tries to trespass, they can notify the police to enforce trespassing laws.

Weapons at a Property

Guns and knives are sometimes found at lodging properties. Some properties ask guests carrying weapons to secure them in a safe deposit box at the front desk. Other properties have policies that employees will not be allowed to service guestrooms while a weapon is in the room.

Usually employees are directed to call security when they see a weapon on the property. State and federal laws about carrying weapons, especially guns, vary widely. These laws also can change frequently.

Apply Your Learning 3.5

Please write all answers on a separate sheet of paper.

1. What type of basic emergency procedures should lodging employees know?

2. What are some types of emergency equipment that lodging employees might use?

3. What type of emergency drills might a property conduct?

4. What are some ways that lodging employees notify the fire department of a fire?

5. What are the three major responsibilities of lodging employees during a power failure?

6. From where should employees try to communicate with guests stuck in an elevator if the phone or intercom doesn't work? Why?

7. When should a lodging employee start first aid immediately on an injured guest?

8. When is mouth-to-mouth resuscitation used on a guest?

9. What are some actions properties are taking to reduce the opportunity for terrorist acts?

10. What is a key to preventing peaceful demonstrations from becoming riots?

Quick Hits

Chapter 3

SECTION 3.1—WORKPLACE SAFETY

- Potentially hazardous conditions include wet floors, slippery walkways, cluttered floors, cleaning equipment left out and in the way, improper lifting techniques, and lifting or moving too much at once.

- The best way to prevent accidents is to take adequate time, correct unsafe conditions immediately, and do it safely the first time.

- When selecting a ladder, inspect its condition, height, and footing. Also inspect the stability and sturdiness. If possible, have another employee help stabilize the ladder.

- Extra care is needed when operating electrical equipment.

- A **job safety analysis** is a detailed report that lists every job function performed by all employees in a department. The job list provides the basis for analyzing the potential hazards of a particular position.

SECTION 3.2—CHEMICALS AND OSHA

- Ammonia- and chlorine-based cleaning compounds should never be used together when cleaning because they form a highly toxic gas when combined.

- OSHA is a broad set of rules that protects all workers from unsafe working conditions.

- The **Hazard Communication (HazComm) Standard,** an OSHA regulation, requires employers to inform workers about the risks posed by the chemicals they may use to do their job.

- To comply with the HazComm Standard, hotels must read the standard; list the hazardous chemicals used at the property; obtain **material safety data sheets (MSDSs)** from the suppliers of the chemicals and make they available to employees; make sure all chemical containers are properly labeled; and develop a program that explains MSDS information, labeling, and protective measures.

- An MSDS must include the following information: chemical identity, hazardous ingredients, physical and chemical characteristics, fire and explosion hazard data, reactivity data, health hazards, precautions for safe handling, and use control measures.

SECTION 3.3—FRONT OFFICE SECURITY

- Front office staff play an important role in hotel security. They are responsible for key control measures, front desk surveillance, access control, protecting hotel funds, controlling safe deposit box access, and following lost and found procedures.

- Key control measure involve the use of three kinds of keys. **Emergency keys** open all guestroom doors even when they are deadbolted. **Master keys** open all guestroom doors that are locked but not deadbolted. A guestroom key opens a guestroom door as long as it's not double-locked. All keys should be highly protected and stored in a secure place.

- Electronic locking systems with computer-based access devices eliminate the need for emergency and master keys while providing improved security.

- Successful front desk surveillance and access control rely on hotel personnel, but proper equipment, such as closed-circuit television cameras and monitors, can enhance the surveillance function.

- The front office protects certain financial assets by limiting the amount of cash in the register per shift **(cash bank)**, recording all transactions, and conducting unscheduled audits.

- Because safe deposit boxes provide access to guest valuables, strict control procedures exist for the storage, issuance, and receipt of safe deposit box keys.

- One employee or department should be assigned lost and found responsibilities. These including maintaining the lost and found log, answering guest calls regarding lost items, and returning found items.

SECTION 3.4—HOUSEKEEPING SECURITY

- Providing security in a hospitality operation is the broad task of protecting both people and assets.

- Hotel housekeeping employees can be part of an effective security force—particularly in guestroom areas. Staff should be trained to spot suspicious activities and unauthorized or undesirable persons.

- Management can reduce the volume of furniture, fixtures, equipment, and goods stolen from a property by reducing the opportunities to steal.

- While some guest theft of convenience items is considered a form of marketing, larger items not meant to be taken can add up to a large expense for the hospitality operation. Theft reduction strategies include keeping track of towels distributed, keeping storage rooms locked, using as few monogrammed items as possible, and placing popular items in the gift shops.

- Management should detail explicit regulations concerning employee theft. Theft reduction strategies include screening applicants, good inventory control procedures, monthly supply inventories, recording stolen or missing items, and keeping storeroom doors locked.

SECTION 3.5—EMERGENCY RESPONSE

- All employees need to know basic emergency procedures for such things as evacuations, first aid, basic firefighting, power failure response techniques, crowd control, and emergency equipment use.

- Fire alarms and power failures are the most common emergencies experienced in the lodging industry.

- Power failures have grown more common and are often triggered by some other emergency. Lodging employees have three major responsibilities: protect people at the property, minimize vandalism, and secure money and valuable assets.

- If an elevator malfunctions, lodging employees should try to find out where the car is and communicate with anyone trapped inside.

- Lodging properties have to be prepared for weather emergencies and natural disasters since they may get very little warning.

- During a medical emergency, the response of employees could save a life. Common first-aid procedures include the Heimlich maneuver, mouth-to-mouth resuscitation, and cardiopulmonary resuscitation.

- When someone dies at the property, the police and management must be called immediately and the area secured.

- Properties are taking extra measures to reduce the chance of terrorist acts and respond to civil unrest.

- Demonstrations can be managed by communicating and controlling access to the property.

- Employees are usually asked to call security when they see a weapon on the property.

The importance of the front office cannot be overemphasized. This department represents the single largest profit center for the hotel, which is room sales. The front office is the hotel's nerve center and the liaison between the guest and the property. It is often said that, to the guest, the front office *is* the hotel. During the guest's stay, the front office is the focus of requests for information and services. Check-in and check-out activities are usually the guest's first and last impressions of the property, its staff, and its philosophy of guest service.

First impressions are very important. If a guest begins a visit in a pleasant frame of mind because of front office courtesy and service, chances are good that he or she will view other hotel services favorably as well. However, let the front office err, delay, or be indifferent, and the guest's dissatisfaction may spread to all aspects of his or her stay.

The three main functions of the front office are to:

- Sell rooms, which includes registering and assigning rooms
- Keep accounts, determine credit, render bills, receive payments, and provide for proper financial and credit accommodations
- Provide services such as handling mail, telegrams, and messages for guests and furnishing information about the hotel, the community, and any special attractions or events

Unit

2

Rooms Division

Valerie Ferguson

*Regional Vice President, Loews Hotels and
Managing Director, Loews Philadelphia Hotel*

When Valerie Ferguson moved from San Francisco to Atlanta to attend law school in 1977, she went looking for a part-time job. She found a career—and it wasn't as a lawyer.

Ferguson, a regional vice president of Loews Hotels and the first African-American to become chairman of the American Hotel & Motel Association, began her hospitality career as a night auditor at the Hyatt Regency in Atlanta. She had wanted a job at the downtown federal building, but when she learned she would have to wait six months for an application, she turned to the hotel next door.

"I fell in love with the industry and I found an opportunity to grow," she says. "I absolutely loved working in a hotel. Every day was different, every day was a challenge. Everything that happens in a city happens in a hotel."

Ferguson's career took her up through the ranks of the rooms division. She held management positions at Hyatt hotels in Chicago; Flint, Mich.; and Atlanta, where she returned to the Hyatt Regency as general manager. She became general manager of the Ritz-Carlton Atlanta in 1995. In 1998, she became chairwoman of the AH&MA; during her year in office, she joined Loews Hotels as a regional vice president and managing director of the Loews Philadelphia Hotel.

In her high profile role as AH&MA chairwoman, Ferguson worked diligently to promote hospitality as a career and to support minorities and women as they seek greater opportunities in the lodging industry. In fact, her platform was titled, "The Opportunity of a Lifetime."

"We have to let people know that we are an industry of opportunity, that you can become a manager, a general manager—that in fact there are 172 career options for employees so that they can become part of the leadership and meet their desires and aspirations," she says.

Ferguson believes, "This is the industry that epitomizes the American Dream. Hard work, dedication, and sincere commitment to service is not only acknowledged by corporate advancement, but by the warm smiles and thank-you's you receive each day—because you were a part of making that day special for those you serve and those you serve with."

The Guest Cycle

Sections

4.1 Stages in the Guest Cycle

AFTER STUDYING SECTION 4.1, YOU SHOULD KNOW HOW TO:

♦ List the events that occur during pre-arrival

♦ Outline the activities occurring during the arrival stage

♦ Describe the tasks performed during the occupancy stage

♦ Protect the guest's right to privacy while at the hotel

♦ Explain what the guest and hotel do during the departure stage

---

The financial transactions a guest makes while staying at a hotel determine the flow of business through the property. Traditionally, the flow of business can be divided into a four-stage **guest cycle.** Exhibit 1 diagrams these four stages: pre-arrival, arrival, occupancy, and departure.

Front office employees can efficiently serve guest needs when they clearly understand the flow of business through the hotel. Exhibit 2 indicates which front office personnel are most likely to serve the guest during each stage of the guest cycle.

Pre-Arrival

The guest chooses a hotel during the *pre-arrival stage* of the guest cycle. In reality, the

reservations department is the sales office for the hotel's non-group business. Its employees must be "sales-oriented" and present a positive, strong image of the hotel. The attitude, efficiency, and knowledge of the front office staff may influence a caller's decision to stay at a hotel.

A reservations agent must be able to respond quickly and accurately to requests for future accommodations. If a reservation can be accepted as requested, the reservations agent creates a reservation record. The creation of a reservation record initiates the hotel

guest cycle. This record lets the hotel personalize guest service and schedule needed staff and facilities. Using the information collected during reservations, a property management system (the term used for a hotel's main computer system) may be able to initiate pre-registration applications. Such activities include automatically assigning a specific room and rate to guests and creating an electronic **guest folio.** A guest folio is a record of the charges incurred and credits acquired by the guest during the guest cycle.

Arrival

The *arrival stage* of the guest cycle includes registration and rooming functions. It is the front office staff's responsibility to monitor the financial transactions between the hotel and the guest.

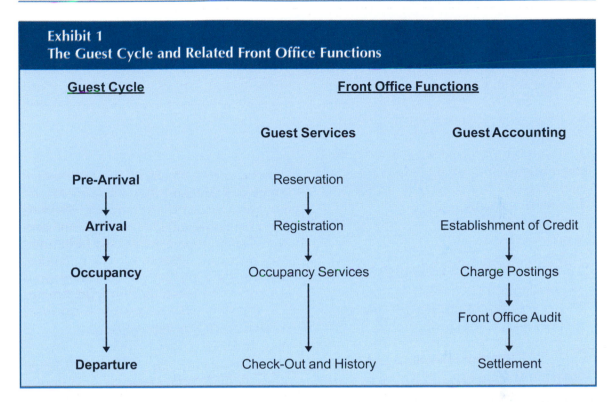

Exhibit 1
The Guest Cycle and Related Front Office Functions

Guest Cycle	Front Office Functions	
	Guest Services	Guest Accounting
Pre-Arrival	Reservation	
↓	↓	
Arrival	Registration	Establishment of Credit
↓	↓	↓
Occupancy	Occupancy Services	Charge Postings
		↓
		Front Office Audit
↓	↓	↓
Departure	Check-Out and History	Settlement

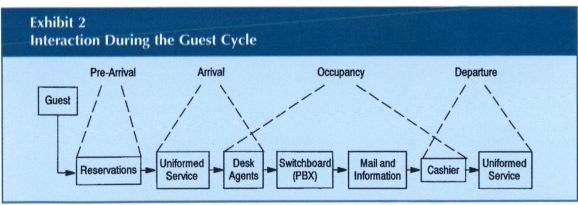

Exhibit 2
Interaction During the Guest Cycle

The front desk agent should determine the guest's reservation status before beginning the registration process. Guests with reservations may have already undergone pre-registration activities. Guests without reservations, termed walk-in guests, present an opportunity for front desk agents to sell guestrooms.

Often, the hotel's property management system can be used to quickly identify available rooms and amenities. An electronic reservation record, created during the pre-registration application or at the time of check-in, is essential to efficient front office operation. It includes information about the guest's intended method of payment, the planned length of stay, and any special guest needs such as a rollaway bed, or a child's crib. It should also include the guest's billing address, e-mail address, and telephone number. In this world of higher security concerns, the front office also needs to confirm that the guest has proper identification.

Gathering information during registration enhances the front office's ability to satisfy special needs, forecast occupancies, and settle accounts.

Front desk agents must also be sensitive to accessibility issues for guests with physical impairments. The Americans with Disabilities Act requires new and renovated properties to be barrier-free in design. *Barrier-free* means that facilities and accommodations must be designed with the disabled guest and visitor in mind. Some of the more prevalent features of barrier-free guest-rooms are extra-wide doorways for wheelchairs (both entry doors and bathroom doors), extra-large bathrooms, grab bars beside the toilet and inside the bathtub area, roll-in showers for wheelchairs, lowered vanity countertops and extra knee space under the sink, handles on doors and bathroom fixtures instead of knobs, and strobe lights and pillow shakers as part of the smoke and fire detection systems (for the deaf).

Once the guest decides to rent a room, the front desk identifies the guest's method of payment. Whether the guest uses cash, personal check, credit card, or some other method of payment, the front office must take measures to ensure eventual payment. A proper credit check at the outset of a transaction greatly reduces the potential for subsequent settlement problems.

Registration is complete once payment methods and the departure date are established. The guest may be given a room key and a map of the property and allowed to proceed to the room without assistance, or a uniformed service person may escort the guest to the room. When the guest arrives at the room, the occupancy stage of the guest cycle begins.

Occupancy

The manner in which the front office staff represents the hotel is particularly important throughout the *occupancy stage*. As the center of hotel activity, the front desk coordinates guest services. The front office should respond to requests in a timely and accurate way to maximize guest satisfaction.

A variety of transactions during the occupancy stage affect guest and hotel financial accounts. Most of these transactions will be automatically processed through property management system interfaces to revenue centers according to established posting and auditing procedures.

The room rate of the guestroom is usually the largest single charge on the guest's folio. Additional expenses can be charged to a guest's account if he or she established acceptable credit at the front desk during registration. Goods or services purchased from the hotel's restaurant, lounge, room service department, telephone department, transportation areas, gift shop, spa, and other revenue outlets may be charged to guest accounts. Many hotels set a high balance on the amount which guests can charge to their accounts without partial settlement. This amount is usually referred to as the **house limit** and can be automatically monitored by the property management system.

Front desk accounting records must be periodically reviewed for accuracy and completeness. This need is met through a system audit.

Departure

Guest services and guest accounting are completed during the guest cycle's fourth phase: *departure.* The final element of guest service is processing the guest out of the hotel and creating a guest history record. The final element of guest accounting is settlement of the guest's account (that is, bringing the account to a zero balance).

At check-out, the guest vacates the room, receives an accurate statement of the settled account, returns the room keys, and leaves the hotel. Once the guest has checked out, the front office updates the room's availability status and notifies the housekeeping department.

During check-out, the front office staff should determine whether the guest was satisfied with the stay and encourage the guest to return to the hotel (or another property in the chain). The more information the hotel has about its guests, the better it can anticipate and serve their needs and develop marketing strategies to increase business. Hotels often use expired registration records to construct a **guest history file.** A guest history file is a collection of guest history records.

The purpose of account settlement is to collect money due the hotel before the guest leaves. Depending on the guest's credit arrangements, the guest will pay cash, use a credit card, or verify pre-established direct billing instructions. Account balances should be verified and errors corrected before the guest leaves the hotel. Problems may occur in guest account settlement when charges are not posted to the guest's account until *after* the guest checks out. These charges are called **late charges.** Even if the charges are eventually collected, the hotel usually incurs additional

UNDER THE GAVEL

A Guest's Right to Privacy

A hotel owes a guest the rights of privacy and peaceful possession while the guest is in the guestroom. However, the hotel does have access to occupied guestrooms for routine housekeeping and during emergencies.

Police officers must usually have a search warrant to enter guestrooms. The U.S. Supreme Court has made it clear that when the hotel guest has paid for the room, the guest is entitled to constitutional protection against unreasonable search and seizure, and the hotel would generally have no authority to permit the search of the guest's room without a search warrant. This would violate the hotel guest's right to privacy.

costs through billing the gust. In addition, this can be an irritation to the guest, who may have to submit an incomplete expense account to their employer. Settling accoutns with outstanding balances for departing guests is generally transferred to a back office system to be handled by the accounting department, not the front office. However, the front office system is responsible for providing complete and accurate billing information to help collection efforts.

Once the guest has checked out, the front office can analyze data related to the guest's stay. System generated reports can be used to review operations, isolate problem areas, indicate where corrective action may be needed, and highlight business trends. Daily system reports typically contain information about cash and charge transactions and front office operating statistics.

Apply Your Learning 4.1

Please write all answers on a separate sheet of paper.

1. What are the four stages of the guest cycle?

2. What information should a registration record contain?

3. What is typically the largest charge on the guest's folio?

At what stage in the guest cycle are each of the following tasks performed?

4. Determine whether the guest was satisfied with her stay.

5. Create a reservation record.

6. Assign a room rate and room type for the guest.

7. Respond to guest requests.

4.2 Communications

AFTER STUDYING SECTION 4.2, YOU SHOULD KNOW HOW TO:

♦ Use a transaction file to record activities

♦ Consult an information directory to answer questions

♦ Handle guest mail and packages

Communication involves more than memorandums, face-to-face conversations, and electronic messages. Effective front office communication also involves the use of transaction files, information directories, internal and external networks, search engines, and mail and telephone procedures. The complexity of front office communication tends to be directly related to the number of guestrooms and the size and extent of the hotel's public areas and facilities.

Transaction File

The front desk may keep a **transaction file** (or log book) so that front office staff can be made aware of important events and decisions that occurred during previous workshifts. A typical front office transaction file is a chronolgoical journal that chronicles unusual events, guest complaints or requests, and other relevant information.

Front desk agents make entries to the transaction file throughout a work shift.

Before beginning their shift, front desk supervisors and agents should review the transaction file, noting any current activities, situations that require follow-up, or potential problems. For example, a front desk agent on the morning shift might record that a guest phoned requesting maintenance services. The agent might also note what action was taken. The front office transaction file should detail what happened, why, and when. By reviewing these notes, the front desk agent on duty can respond intelligently if the guest contacts the front desk for follow-up.

The front office transaction file is also important to management because it helps them understand the activity of the front desk and it records any ongoing issues. For example, if there are recurring problems with housekeeping issues, the front office transaction file can identify them. Also, should there be any guest complaints, compliments, or unusual activity, the transaction file helps management understand what happened and how it was handled.

Information Directory

Front office staff must be able to respond in a knowledgeable way when guests contact the front desk for information. Common guest reqests involve:

- Local restaurant recommendations

- Contacting transportation companies, including taxis, limousines, and airport shuttles

- Directions to a business or office building

- Directions to a shopping center, drugstore, or gas station

- Directions to a place of worship

- Directions to a bank or automated teller machine

- Directions to a theater, stadium, or ticket agency

- Directions to universities, libraries, museums, or other points of interest

- Directions to a federal building, capitol, district court, or city hall

- Information about hotel policies (for example, check-out time or pets)

- Information about the hotel's recreational facilities or those near the hotel

Some front offices accumulate such data in a bound guide or electronic file called an **information directory.** The front office information directory may include simplified maps of the area; taxi and airline telephone numbers; bank, theater, church, store locations; area restaurants and menus; and special event schedules.

Some hotels have installed automated information terminals or kiosks in public areas. Information kiosks are the electronic equivalent of the front office information directory. Because guests can easily access

information kiosks, front desk agents are free to attend to other guest needs.

In addition, many hotels provide a schedule of daily events through the television system or information display panels. A common industry term for displaying daily events is the **reader board.** Reader boards may be placed near the front desk, in elevators, in the lobby area, and in the meeting room section of the hotel, as well as channels on guestroom televisions. Interfacing the electronic reader board with the hotel's sales and catering system allows the information to be updated automatically by the sales and catering system.

In convention hotels, it is also common to have a **group résumé** book or electronic file at the front desk. Each group staying in the hotel has a summary of its activities, billing instructions, key attendees, recreational arrangements, arrival and departure patterns, and other important information. Some hotels prefer to store the résumés by group name. Many hotels make the group résumé book or file required reading for front desk and uniformed staff at the beginning of each work shift.

Mail and Package Handling

Registered guests rely on the front office to deliver mail and packages quickly and efficiently. In general, the front office is expected to time-stamp all guest mail when it arrives. This helps answer any question that might arise about when the mail arrived or how quickly the guest was notified of its arrival. When mail and packages arrive, front office records should be checked immediately to verify that the guest is currently registered, due to check in, or has already checked out.

The front desk should promptly attempt to notify a guest that mail has been received. Some properties notify guests by turning on an in-room message light on the guestroom telephone; others deliver a printed form to the guestroom. If mail arrives for a guest who has not yet registered, a notation should be made on the guest's reservation record and the mail held until the guest arrives. Guest mail that is not picked up or has arrived for a guest who has already checked out should be time-stamped a second time and returned to its sender or sent to a forwarding address if the guest has provided one.

Packages are usually handled as mail. If the package is too large to store at the front desk, it should be taken to a secure room. The package and its location should be recorded in the front office mail signature book.

Apply Your Learning 4.2

Please write all answers on a separate sheet of paper.

1. What sort of information is recorded in a guest transaction file?

2. What sort of information is recorded in an information directory?

3. What is one standard procedure for handling guest mail?

Where would the following information be found?

4. Check-out time policy

5. Guest complaint about the food

6. Conference room for a training session

7. Directions to a gas station

4.3 Guest Services

AFTER STUDYING SECTION 4.3, YOU SHOULD KNOW HOW TO:

♦ List the types of equipment and supplies loaned to guests

♦ Explain how split folios and master folios meet guest needs

♦ Identify who meets special guest needs

As the center of front office activity, the front desk is responsible for coordinating guest services. Typical guest services involve providing information, special equipment, and supplies. Guest services may also include accommodating guests through special procedures. A guest's satisfaction with the hotel hinges in part on the ability of the front desk to respond to special requests.

A growing number of hotels employ a concierge to handle guest requests. A concierge should embody the warmth and hospitality of the entire property.

Equipment and Supplies

Guests may request special equipment and supplies while making a reservation, at the time of registration, or during occupancy. Reservations agents record special requests to ensure that they are properly met. After registration, a guest who needs special equipment or supplies will almost always contact a front desk agent. The front desk agent, in turn, follows through by contacting the appropriate service center or hotel department. Equipment and supplies commonly requested by guests include:

• Roll-away beds and cribs

• Additional linens/pillows

• Irons and ironing boards

• Additional clothes hangers

• Audiovisual and office equipment

• High-speed Internet connectors—cable or wireless adaptors

• Special equipment for visually impaired, hearing impaired, or physically challenged guests

Front desk agents should have ways to meet guest requests when the department that normally provides the equipment or service is closed or inaccessible.

Special Procedures

Guests may make special requests that represent exceptions to standard front office procedures. Front desk agents should be allowed to use their judgment when attempting to satisfy guest requests.

Procedural requests may require more time and effort to fulfill than equipment and supply requests. Typical procedural requests include:

• Split account folios

- Master account folios
- Transportation arrangements
- Entertainment reservations
- Newspaper delivery
- Bonded child care services
- Secretarial services

A knowledgeable front desk agent usually can fulfill a special request involving guest folios. **Split folios** are most often requested by business travelers. These folios separate guest charges onto two or more separate folio accounts. One folio account records the charges billed to the guest's company or to a group master account. Another folio account may track incidental charges that the guest will pay for, such as telephone calls, food, and beverages; this part of the folio will most likely be paid by the guest.

A convention group meeting in the hotel may request a **master folio.** Typically, only authorized charges incurred by the group are posted to the master folio and subsequently billed to the convention's sponsor. Each group member may be held responsible for other charges posted to his or her individual folio account.

A concierge may handle other procedural requests. Hotels not employing a concierge may have front desk agents use the front office information directory as a resource for referrals and outside services.

Some hotels operate a guest service center. When guests have a question or special request, they may not know whom to call. Often the call goes to front desk agents, who must then act upon the requests or refer them elsewhere. A guest service center makes it easier for guests.

Apply Your Learning 4.3

Please write all answers on a separate sheet of paper.

1. What are some typical equipment and supplies that guests request?
2. What type of procedural requests do guests make?
3. What are the advantages to a guest service center?

Match the following guest services with the guest most likely to request it.

Roll-away crib	Master account folio
Audiovisual equipment	Split account folio
A TDD phone connection	Newspaper delivery
Secretarial services	Transportation arrangements

4. A family with three children, including a newborn
5. A tourist in a wheelchair
6. A trainer holding a session in a conference room
7. Convention planner who wants a separate account for each member
8. A stock broker traveling on business
9. Account representative who is combining his vacation with a business trip

4.4 Guest Complaints

AFTER STUDYING SECTION 4.4, YOU SHOULD KNOW HOW TO:

♦   Categorize the types of complaints guests make

♦   Identify guest complaints

♦   Handle guest complaints

♦   Follow up on guest complaints

Guests will occasionally be disappointed or find fault with something or someone at the hotel. The high visibility of the front office means that front desk agents are frequently the first to learn of guest complaints. The front office should anticipate these complaints and devise strategies that help staff effectively resolve the situations. Front desk agents should be especially attentive to guests with complaints and should seek a timely and satisfactory resolution to the problem.

When guests find it easy to express their opinions, both the hotel and the guests benefit. The hotel learns of potential or actual problems and can resolve them. When problems are quickly resolved, a guest often feels that the hotel cares about his or her needs—and this can mean a more satisfying stay. Guests who leave a hotel dissatisfied may never return. A popular axiom in the lodging business is that it takes $10 to attract a guest for the first time, but only $1 to keep the guest coming back. By handling guest relations positively, the investment pays off many times.

Types of Complaints

Guest complaints can be separated into four categories of problems: mechanical, attitudinal, service-related, and unusual.

Most guest complaints relate to hotel equipment malfunctions. *Mechanical complaints* usually concern problems with climate control, lighting, electricity, room furnishings, ice machines, vending machines, door keys, plumbing, television sets, elevators, and so on.

Guests may make *attitudinal complaints* when they they have been poorly treated by hotel staff members. Guests who overhear staff conversations or who receive complaints from hotel staff members may also express attitudinal complaints.

Guests may make *service-related complaints* when they experience a problem with hotel service. These complaints may be about such things as long waits for service, no help with luggage, untidy rooms, phone difficulties, missed wake-up calls, cold or ill-prepared food, or ignored requests for additional supplies. The front office generally receives more service-related complaints when the hotel is operating at or near full occupancy.

Guests may also complain about the absence of a swimming pool, lack of public

Exhibit 1
Guest Perception Detail

Quantitative Details:

1 Name of report and date of survey.

2 The specific department or area the report is detailing.

3 All questions are grouped by the specific departments/categories.

4 Response Option—Guests are given the choice of options from which to mark their opinion.

5 Response Percentages—This number represents the percentage of guest responses per response option.

6 Guest Response—The number of guests who responded to the specific question.

7 Comparison of the overall rating by question for the current month, last month and year-to-date.

8 Response Option Averages—The average of all respondents per response option.

9 Overall Favorability Average—Overall average for all questions compared to current month, last month and year-to-date for the entire department/category.

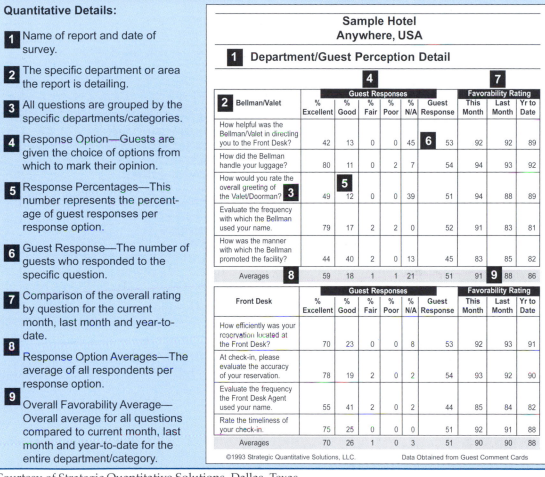

Sample Hotel
Anywhere, USA

1 Department/Guest Perception Detail

2 Bellman/Valet	Guest Responses **4**						Favorability Rating **7**		
	% Excellent	% Good	% Fair	% Poor	% N/A	Guest Response	This Month	Last Month	Yr to Date
How helpful was the Bellman/Valet in directing you to the Front Desk?	42	13	0	0	45	**6** 53	92	92	89
How did the Bellman handle your luggage?	80	11	0	2	7	54	94	93	92
How would you rate the overall greeting of the Valet/Doorman? **3**	49	**5** 12	0	0	39	51	94	88	89
Evaluate the frequency with which the Bellman used your name.	79	17	2	2	0	52	91	83	81
How was the manner with which the Bellman promoted the facility?	44	40	2	0	13	45	83	85	82
Averages **8**	59	18	1	1	21	51	91	**9** 88	86

Front Desk	Guest Responses						Favorability Rating		
	% Excellent	% Good	% Fair	% Poor	% N/A	Guest Response	This Month	Last Month	Yr to Date
How efficiently was your reservation located at the Front Desk?	70	23	0	0	8	53	92	93	91
At check-in, please evaluate the accuracy of your reservation.	78	19	2	0	2	54	93	92	90
Evaluate the frequency the Front Desk Agent used your name.	55	41	2	0	2	44	85	84	82
Rate the timeliness of your check-in.	75	25	0	0	0	51	92	91	88
Averages	70	26	1	0	3	51	90	90	88

©1993 Strategic Quantitative Solutions, LLC.   Data Obtained from Guest Comment Cards

Courtesy of Strategic Quantitative Solutions, Dallas, Texas

transportation, or bad weather. Although hotels generally have little or no control over the circumstances surrounding *unusual complaints*, guests sometimes expect the front office to resolve or at least listen to such situations.

Identifying Complaints

All guest complaints deserve attention. An excited guest complaining loudly at the front desk requires immediate attention. A guest making a more discreet comment deserves no less attention, although the need for action may be less immediate.

Transaction files can help identify complaints, as can the evaluation of guest comment cards or questionnaires. Exhibits 1 and 2 demonstrate the detail and sophistication that can be expected of a thorough analysis of guest responses to well-designed comment cards. Exhibit 1, "Guest Perception

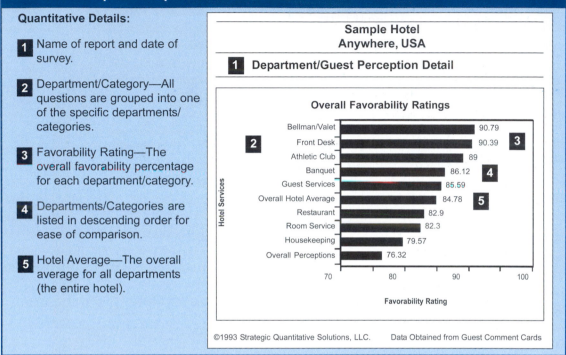

**Exhibit 2
Guest Perception Graph**

Quantitative Details:

1 Name of report and date of survey.

2 Department/Category—All questions are grouped into one of the specific departments/categories.

3 Favorability Rating—The overall favorability percentage for each department/category.

4 Departments/Categories are listed in descending order for ease of comparison.

5 Hotel Average—The overall average for all departments (the entire hotel).

Sample Hotel
Anywhere, USA

1 Department/Guest Perception Detail

Overall Favorability Ratings

Hotel Services	Favorability Rating
Bellman/Valet	90.79
Front Desk	90.39
Athletic Club	89
Banquet	86.12
Guest Services	85.59
Overall Hotel Average	84.78
Restaurant	82.9
Room Service	82.3
Housekeeping	79.57
Overall Perceptions	76.32

©1993 Strategic Quantitative Solutions, LLC.   Data Obtained from Guest Comment Cards

Courtesy of Strategic Quantitative Solutions, Dallas, Texas

Detail," groups comment card questions by specific hotel departments. Within each department, it lists the specific questions guests are asked, with their individual responses tabulated. Exhibit 2, "Guest Perception Graph," shows the overall favorability ratings of all hotel departments, in descending order for ease of comparison. The overall hotel average ("Overall Perceptions") is also shown on the graph. Departments falling below the overall average generally signal areas that need to be improved.

Handling Complaints

It is usually counterproductive to ignore a guest complaint. In many hotels, front desk agents are instructed to refer complaints to supervisors or managers. But front desk agents may not always be able to pass the complaint on, especially when the complaint demands immediate attention. The front office should have a contingency plan in place and be empowered to deal with such situations.

Front office management and staff should keep the following resolution guidelines in mind when handling guest complaints:

- Because a guest may be quite angry, do not go alone to a guestroom to investigate a problem or otherwise risk potential danger.

Exhibit 3
Guidelines for Handling Complaints

1. Listen with concern and empathy.
2. Isolate the guest if possible, so that other guests won't overhear.
3. Stay calm. Avoid responding with hostility or defensiveness. Don't argue with the guest.
4. Be aware of the guest's self-esteem. Show a personal interest in the problem. Use the guest's name frequently. Take the complaint seriously.
5. Give the guest your undivided attention. Concentrate on the problem, not on placing blame. Do NOT insult the guest.
6. Take notes. Writing down the key facts saves time if someone else must get involved. Also, guests will tend to slow down when they are speaking faster than you can write. More important, the fact that a front office staff member is concerned enough to write down what they're saying is reassuring to guests.
7. Tell the guest what can be done. Offer choices. Don't promise the impossible, and don't exceed your authority.
8. Set an approximate time for completion of corrective actions. Be specific, but do not underestimate the amount of time it will take to resolve the problem.
9. Monitor the progress of the corrective action.
10. Follow up. Even if the complaint was resolved by someone else, contact the guest to ensure that the problem was resolved satisfactorily. Report the entire event, the actions taken, and the conclusion of the incident.

- Do not make promises that exceed your authority.

- If a problem cannot be solved, admit this to the guest early on. Honesty is the best policy when dealing with guest complaints.

- Some guests complain as part of their nature. Have an approach for dealing with such guests.

Exhibit 3 lists guidelines for handling guest complaints in a professional manner. Front office staff members should anticipate how they might resolve some of the hotel's most common complaints. Role playing can be an effective method for learning how to deal with guest complaints.

Follow-Up Procedures

Front office management may use the front office transaction files to initiate corrective action, verify that guest complaints have been resolved, and identify recurring problems. This comprehensive written record may also let management contact guests who may still be dissatisfied with some aspect of their stay at check-out. After the guest has departed, a letter from the front office manager expressing regret about the incident is usually sufficient to promote goodwill and demonstrate concern for guest satisfaction. It may be good policy for the front office manager to telephone a departed guest to get a more complete description of the incident. Chain hotels may also receive guest complaints channeled through chain headquarters. Cumulative records of guest complaints about hotels in the chain may be compiled and sent to each manager. This method of feedback allows the chain's corporate headquarters to evaluate and compare each hotel's guest relations performance.

Apply Your Learning 4.4

Please write all answers on a separate sheet of paper.

1. What are some methods for identifying guest complaints?

2. What should an employee do if he or she cannot solve the problem for the guest?

Categorize each of the complaints listed in questions 3–9 using the following: mechanical, attitudinal, service-related, or unusual.

3. "Where was my wake-up call?"

4. "Why don't you have a stationary bike in your fitness room?"

5. "The vending machine is out of ice."

6. "The bellperson kept staring at my chest."

7. "The traffic in this town is deplorable."

8. "My door key isn't working right."

9. "I've asked for extra towels three times and still haven't gotten them."

Quick Hits

Chapter 4

Section 4.1—Stages in the Guest Cycle

- The four-stage **guest cycle,** which makes up the flow of business, includes pre-arrival, arrival, occupancy, and departure.

- The guest chooses a hotel during the pre-arrival stage of the guest cycle. Other activities that follow could include creating a reservation record, assigning a specific room and rate, and preparing a **guest folio,** which is a record of the charges incurred and credits acquired by the guest during occupancy.

- The arrival stage of the guest cycle includes registration and rooming functions. The information the front desk agent gathers during registration enhances the hotel's ability to satisfy special guest needs. The front desk agent uses the registration information to assign a room and room rate. Registration is completed once a guest's method of payment and the departure date have been established.

- The occupancy stage begins when the guest arrives at the room. It is during this stage that front office staff plays an important part in the guest's stay. They should respond to requests in a timely and accurate way to maximize guest satisfaction. It is also during this stage that a variety of financial transactions are posted to the guest folio.

- Guest services and guest accounting are completed during departure, the guest cycle's fourth stage. At check-out, the guest vacates the room, receives an accurate statement of his or her settled account, and leaves the hotel.

Section 4.2—Communications

- A **transaction file** contains a listing of important events and decisions that occurred during previous workshifts. Such entries might include unusual events and guest complaints or requests. The information noted in the transaction file allows the front desk staff to respond intelligently if a guest contacts the front desk for follow-up.

- An **information directory** contains information that can be used to answer frequent guest questions. The directory allows the front office staff to respond in a knowledgeable way when guests contact them for information. Some hotels have installed computer information terminals to provide such data.

- All mail and packages should be time-stamped upon arrival. Depending on the registration status of the guest, mail should be delivered immediately, held until the guest's arrival, or returned to sender or forwarded. If a package is too large to keep at the front desk, it should be taken to a secure room; the package and its location should be recorded.

SECTION 4.3—GUEST SERVICES

- Typical guest services involve providing information, special equipment, and supplies. This may also include accommodating guests through special procedures. While generally provided by the front desk staff, a growing number of hotels are employing a concierge or other designated staff member to handle such requests.

- Guests may request special equipment and supplies while making a reservation, at the time of registration, or during occupancy. Hotel staff should take special care to make sure the requests are properly met by contacting the appropriate service center or hotel department.

- Special procedures are requests that guests may make that represent exceptions to standard procedures and take more time and effort to fulfill than equipment and supply requests. These might include split or master folios, transportation arrangements, entertainment reservations, newspaper delivery, or secretarial services.

- Split folios and master folios are two types of special request. **Split folios** separate guest charges onto two or more separate folio accounts; these are typically requested by business travelers. A convention group meeting may request a **master folio** that consolidates authorized charges incurred by the group; the convention's sponsor is subsequently billed.

SECTION 4.4—GUEST COMPLAINTS

- Guest complaints can be separated into four categories: mechanical, attitudinal, service-related, and unusual.

- Most guest complaints relate to hotel equipment malfunctions, or mechanical complaints, such as problems with climate control, lighting, vending machines, door keys, and plumbing.

- When guests feel they have been poorly treated by staff members, they may make an attitudinal complaint.

- Guests may make service-related complaints when they experience a problem with hotel service. This could include cold food, ignored requests for additional supplies, or a long waiting time for service. This type of complaint increases when the hotel is operating at or near full occupancy.

- Although hotels generally have little or no control over the circumstances surrounding unusual complaints such as bad weather or the lack of a swimming pool, guests sometimes expect the front office to resolve or at least listen to such situations.

- All guest complaints deserve attention. Identify them through log books, the evaluation of guest comment cards, or questionnaires.

- It is usually counterproductive to ignore a guest complaint. Although front desk agents in many hotels refer complaints to supervisors or managers, the front office should have a contingency plan in place when the complaint demands immediate attention and cannot be passed on.

- Follow-up procedures (such as a letter or phone call from the front office manager expressing regret about a guest complaint or incident) are a good way to promote goodwill and demonstrate concern for guest satisfaction.

H.P. Rama

CEO, JHM Enterprises, and 1999 chairman of AH&LA

By nearly any measure or standard, Hasmukh P. Rama has made it big.

Without any previous lodging experience, Rama, along with his four brothers, has built a mini hotel empire. A decade ago, he co-founded an association dedicated to improving and increasing opportunities for fellow Asian American hoteliers. In January 1999, he became the first Asian American to serve as chairman of the American Hotel & Lodging Association (AH&LA).

H.P., as virtually everyone knows him, stands tall in the lodging industry. Rama, 50, is CEO of JHM Enterprises.

Rama, who was born to Indian parents living in Malawi, earned a business degree in India, then came to the United States in 1969 "with only $2 in my pocket" to pursue an MBA at Xavier University. After graduation, he worked as an accountant for two years before buying his first lodging property, the 37-room Sunset Motel in Pomona, California, in 1973. Brothers J.P. and Manhar (M.P.) soon joined in H.P. in California (JHM takes its name from the initials of the Ramas' first names).

In the late 1980s, Rama, along with SREE Hospitality Group president Ravi Patel, founded what is now the Asian American Hotel Owners Association. He was also AAHOA's first chairman. AAHOA was founded to help Asian Americans become better hotel operators and "to create a position for ourselves in the lodging industry," Rama says.

As AH&LA chairman, Rama had two primary missions: increasing business opportunities for all hoteliers, and improving the image of lodging as a career.

From his efforts on behalf of AAHOA and AH&LA to serving as a mentor for the younger members of his own family, Rama has always stressed the value of education. In August 1998, during JHM's 25th anniversary celebration, he and his brothers announced the creation of the Rama Scholarship Fund for the American Dream. Endowed through the American Hotel Foundation, it provides scholarships for minority students enrolled in hotel management schools.

In 2004, Rama was the Executive in Residence at Cornell University. He was also selected as a Society of International Business Fellows member, which took him to Chile, Brazil, and Argentina.

Telecommunications

Sections

5.1 Types of Calls

AFTER STUDYING SECTION 5.1, YOU SHOULD KNOW HOW TO:

♦ Describe the way guests can make direct-dial calls

♦ Explain how operator assisted calls are placed

♦ Outline the concerns a hotel may have with premium price calls

---

There are many types of calls a guest may place during a hotel stay:

• Local

• Direct-dial long-distance

• Calling card/credit card

• Collect

• Third-party

• Person-to-person

• Billed-to-room

• International calls

• Toll-free

• 900 premium-price

• Internet access

Some of these calls require operator assistance while most are completed by the guest independently. In addition, a single call often fits into more than one category.

A direct-dial long-distance call could also be a credit card call; a person-to-person call could also be a collect call; and an international call could be a person-to-person credit card call. For many of these types of calls, the hotel can charge guests a surcharge for use of its telephone equipment.

Direct-Dial Calls

Local Calls. A local call typically is billed on a per-call basis rather than on a per-minute basis. Hotels may charge guests on a per-call basis or offer unlimited local calling for a flat daily charge. Some hotels do not charge guests at all for local calls.

Direct-Dial Long-Distance Calls. Direct-dial long-distance calls are the most common calls placed by hotel guests. Hotels may add a surcharge or charge a per-minute fee.

But No HBO...

The first commercial hotel was the Statler Hotel in Buffalo, New York, which opened its doors on January 18, 1908. It introduced many of the features that today's travelers take for granted—from a light switch just inside the door to a private bath, a large mirror, and running water.

Calling Card/Credit Card Calls. Calling card calls are typically billed to a code number on a card issued by either a local phone company or by a long-distance company. Calling cards are not credit cards; phone companies, not financial institutions, issue them. Whenever either is used, the hotel does not bill the guest for telephone charges.

Operator-Assisted Calls

Collect Calls. With collect calls, a guest first dials "0" and then the full telephone number, then waits for an operator or a computerized recording. The guest informs the operator or the recording that the call is to be billed to the receiving party. The operator or computer verifies that the receiving party accepts the charge. Most telephone companies pay a commission to the hotel for collect calls placed by guests.

Third-Party Calls. Third-party calls are similar to collect calls, except that the billed number is not the called number. In most cases, the operator may require that someone at the third-party number accept the charge before putting through the call. The hotel's telephone company bills the third party and the amount does not appear on the guest's folio.

Person-to-Person Calls. Person-to-person calls are not connected unless a specific party, named by the caller, verifies that he or she is on the line. This is an expensive call, unless the requested party is not available, in which case there is no charge. A person-to-person call is charged to the number initiating the call.

Billed-to-Room Calls. Billed-to-room calls are operator-assisted calls. An operator places the call for a guest and later informs the hotel of the amount of the charge. Billed-to-room calls can also be handled automatically by a call accounting system.

Other Calls

International Calls. International calls can be direct-dialed or placed with operator assistance. To direct-dial an international call, the guest typically dials an international access code, a country code, city code, and the telephone number. The hotel bills the guest for direct-dialed international calls, while the phone company bills the guest for calling card or credit card calls.

Toll-Free Calls. Toll-free calls can be direct-dialed from a guestroom. The guest receives access to an outside line and dials "1" plus the 800 or 888 number.

Premium-Price Calls. Calls made to businesses that charge callers a fee for the call (a fee separate from the one the telephone company charges for placing the call) are 900 or premium-price calls. Problems can arise when these types of calls are made from guestrooms. The businesses involved in 900 telephone services charge widely varying rates—from $1.50 per minute to a flat rate of $9.00 a call. Guests may be shocked and mistakenly blame the hotel upon receiving their charges. Another problem is that the hotel's telephone system may be able to track only the costs involved in placing the call and not the premium charged by the 900 service company. A guest could settle a phone charge of $2.50 at check-out and the hotel could later receive a bill of $39.50 for the same call.

Internet Access. An increasingly popular guestroom service is Internet access. Dial-up services may be offered on a transaction, fixed fee, or daily fee basis. Guests who use in-room telephones for Internet access may tie up phone lines for extended periods of time, thereby precluding other guests access. While some hotels have chosen to expand their telephone systems, others have elected to install alternate systems that do not rely on telephone switches or trunk lines. These systems involve high-speed Internet access data services via an Internet service provider.

Apply Your Learning 5.1

Please write all answers on a separate sheet of paper.

1. List the types of calls that can be made from a guestroom phone.

2. Which types of calls are usually operated-assisted?

3. Which types of calls are usually dialed directly by the guest?

Match the types of calls with the guest who is making them by drawing a line between the two:

4. Pierre is calling Paris   Toll-free call

5. Cherie dials 1-900-555-6423   Premium-price call

6. Taylor bills the call to the person she's calling   Person-to-person call

7. Keturah orders pizza for her room   Billed-to-room call

8. Gordon calls his agency's 800 sales line   International call

9. Maria calls home while traveling out of state   Local call

10. Cabot asks the operator to connect him to Wendy Long-distance call

11. Riley charges a call to her room while in a conference room   Collect call

5.2 Telecommunications Equipment

AFTER STUDYING SECTION 5.2, YOU SHOULD KNOW HOW TO:

♦ Explain the functions of a PBX system

♦ Define a call accounting system

♦ List the types of phones that might be found in a hotel

♦ Identify some of the sophisticated telecommunication systems sometimes found in hotels

Hotels need the right mix of telephone equipment and lines. There are many types of telephone lines or *trunks*. Each type of line is designed to carry certain types of calls. There are lines dedicated to incoming calls, lines dedicated to outbound calls, and two-way lines. Systems and equipment that hotels use for placing and pricing call include:

• PBX systems
• Call accounting systems
• Guestroom phones
• Pay phones
• Pagers and cellular phones

PBX Systems

Historically, an important piece of equipment controlling phone service at hotels was the switchboard or private branch exchange (PBX). This equipment takes inbound calls to the hotel's PBX operator's console. The hotel's operator sends these calls on to particular extensions or station lines. These might be at the front desk, guestrooms, offices, the kitchen, or other areas. This arrangement allows the hotel to have a large number of telephones sharing a limited number of telephone lines. Outbound calls are usually placed without the hotel operator's

Find Me a Find

You can hire a matchmaker to find yourself the perfect San Francisco hotel—as well as some attractions and local people.

Joie de Vivre Hospitality has created the Golden Gate Greeter service. Guests take a brief Hotel Matchmaker test and then "Yvette" matches them up with a volunteer based on their cultural preferences, suggests a handful of their 17 San Francisco hotels, and recommend things to do that match the guest's interests.

help. Some hotel PBX systems have advanced features enabling them to handle data as well as voice communications.

Call Accounting Systems

A **call accounting system (CAS)** is a set of software programs that initiate the placement, pricing, and posting of calls. The CAS interfaces with a hotel's computer system and electronically posts charges to guest folios. Some CASs have a least-cost-routing component that routes a call to the type of line that can carry the call at the lowest cost.

Types of Phones

Guestroom Phones. Guestroom phones are increasing in sophistication and capabilities. For example, guests can plug personal computers or portable fax machines into some guestroom phones. These phones have an input jack for standard computer or fax machines. An increasing number of hotels are providing two-line guestroom phones, so one line can accommodate a computer while the guest talks on the other line. Other features of some guestroom phones include:

- Conference calling
- Caller ID
- Speed dialing
- Hold buttons
- Call waiting
- Hands-free speakers
- Message-waiting alert
- Voice messaging

Some phones combine voice-mail, data, fax, and other technologies so guests can re-trieve messages, order room service, receive written documents, and place wake-up call requests.

Pay Phones. Hotels rarely purchase their own pay phones. These phones generally take a lot of abuse and are placed in public areas such as in or near the hotel lobby, meeting rooms, conference areas, banquet rooms, and restaurants. Many hotels have their pay phones supplied and maintained by a company other than their local phone company. Pay phones are not connected to the hotel's PBX system or CAS and so the hotel receives no direct revenue from their operation. Instead, most telephone carriers contract to pay the hotel a commission on operator-assisted long-distance calls placed from the pay phones. The carrier sets the rates, bills the guest directly, and sends the hotel an agreed-upon commission.

Pagers and Cellular Phones. Some hotels offer a pager or cellular phone rental service to guests at check-in. In the case of cellular phones, the hotel bills the guest for the number of minutes of recorded use, as indicated by the phone's usage meter.

Other Technology

Often, hotels install telephone systems with sophisticated features for reasons other than just cost effectiveness. Examples of these features include:

- Automatic call dispensing systems
- Telephone/room status systems
- Call detection equipment

In many cases, *automatic call dispensing* is limited to wake-up services. The operator enters the room number and time for each wake-up call into the computer. At the scheduled time, a telephone call is automatically placed to the guest's room. Once the guest answers the call, the computer may activate a synthesized voice that reports the current time, temperature, and weather conditions. Another variation on automatic call dispensing allows the hotel to call rooms in case of an emergency or to call all guests with a specific group to remind them of a meeting.

Telephone/room status systems can assist with rooms management and prohibit the unauthorized use of telephones in vacant rooms. Housekeeping or room service employees can use guestroom telephones to enter data concerning room service charges (for example, what was consumed from an in-room bar), maintenance information, or current room status information. These features lower payroll costs and help ensure a more efficient in-room bar restocking system.

Call detection equipment works with the hotel's telephone equipment and call accounting systems. Call detection equipment can pinpoint the exact moment a telephone call is connected. This helps improve billing accuracy and reduces guest account discrepancies since only answered calls will be billed.

Apply Your Learning 5.2

Please write all answers on a separate sheet of paper.

1. List the major types of telecommunication equipment that might be found in a hotel.

2. What features might a guestroom phone have?

3. What phones, other than the switchboard and guestroom phones, might be found in a hotel?

Complete the following sentences:

4. Hotels can keep unauthorized people from using telephones in vacant rooms by using a _____.

5. A system that automatically places a series of calls (usually wake-up calls) is called a _____.

6. Hotels may rent _____ or _____ _____ to guests. Hotels bill guests based on how long they use these devices.

7. Software programs that initiate the placement, pricing, and posting of calls are called _____ _____ _____.

5.3 Telephone Services

AFTER STUDYING SECTION 5.3, YOU SHOULD KNOW HOW TO:

♦ Take and deliver messages for guests

♦ Handle guest faxes

♦ Make wake-up calls properly

♦ Demonstrate how voice mail works

♦ Describe how hotels are providing e-mail and TDD technology to guests

Most hotels provide in-room local and long-distance telephone service 24 hours a day. All employees answering calls should be courteous and helpful (see Exhibit 1). Front office management may restrict the type of information the front office staff may furnish to callers because of guest privacy and security issues.

Front office staff should time-stamp telephone messages they record and place

them in the guest's mail and message rack slot. If guestroom telephones are equipped with a message indicator light, the front desk agent may turn on that light so the guest is alerted to a message waiting at the front desk. When the guest returns to the room, the flashing light on the phone informs the guest that mail or a message is waiting at the front desk. In some hotels, the guest may be able to display recorded messages on the guestroom television screen.

Faxes

Faxes are usually treated like mail, but with special care. Guests are often waiting for these documents. If the incoming fax has special delivery instructions, such as deliver immediately to a specific meeting room, the front desk should dispatch a bell attendant with the fax right away. If no special instructions are provided, the hotel may store the fax in the mail rack and turn on the message light in the guestroom. Some hotels deliver the fax in an envelope to the guestroom. Faxes are different from mail in that they do not need to be time stamped; the fax document usually contains the date and time of transmission on it. Confidentiality of the contents is essential. Front desk staff members should never read a fax.

Some front offices maintain a fax log or combined fax and mail log for tracking all received documents. Information recorded in the fax log book may list the recipient, the sender, the time the fax was received, and the total number of fax pages. Front desk agents may also record when the guest was notified and when the guest picked up the fax. A similar record is kept of outgoing faxes if the property offers public fax service. If a

Exhibit 1
Building Telephone Skills

Building Telephone Skills

Regardless of whom you talk with over the telephone, it's essential that you make a positive impression. Answering the telephone is an opportunity for you to portray a professional image as well as a positive image for the property.

During any business telephone conversation, you should:

1. **Smile even though you are on the telephone.**
   When you smile, you automatically improve your vocal quality. You'll sound pleasant and interested.

2. **Sit or stand up straight.**
   By sitting or standing up straight, you'll be more alert and pay better attention to what is being said.

3. **Use a low voice pitch.**
   A lower voice pitch will make you sound more mature and authoritative.

4. **Match your speaking rate to the caller's.**
   Let the caller set the tempo of the conversation. For example, he or she may be in a hurry; in that case, you should provide information more quickly.

5. **Avoid extremes in volume.**
   If you speak too loudly, you may sound rude or pushy. If you speak too softly, you may sound timid or uncertain.

6. **Avoid expressions such as "uh-huh" and "yeah."**
   Such expressions make the speaker sound dull, indifferent, and uninterested.

Front office staff often take phone messages for other employees or guests. Most front offices have a standard telephone message form. If you answer the phone, it's important that you listen carefully and take accurate written notes while speaking with the caller. When you take a telephone message, be sure to get the following information:

- Date
- Time of the call
- Name of the person being called
- Caller's full name
- Caller's department (if the call is internal)
- Caller's company (if appropriate)
- Caller's time zone (if out of state)
- Caller's telephone number (and area code, if needed)
- Message (do not abbreviate—provide a full message)

If the message is urgent, mark it as such. It is also a good practice to repeat the telephone number back to the caller for accuracy. Some front offices recommend that the message also be repeated. Finally, sign your name and follow front office procedures for storing or delivering the message.

Any telephone conversation can be improved by following these simple guidelines. Remember to treat all callers, guests, and employees with courtesy and respect.

fax is undeliverable, the hotel should immediately notify the party sending the fax. Most hotels charge guests to send faxes. Some hotels charge guests for received faxes. One of the more recent innovations in technology is the in-room fax, which is connected to a second telephone line in the room.

Wake-up Services

Since a guest may miss an important appointment, a flight, or simply a head start on a vacation by oversleeping, front desk agents must pay special attention to wake-up call requests. Front office mechanical devices or a front office computer system can remind front desk agents to place wake-up calls, or the systems can be programmed to place the calls and play a recorded wake-up message. Many hotels still prefer that front desk agents place wake-up calls; for the most part, guests appreciate this personal touch.

Quite often, the clock in the telephone department used for wake-up purposes is called the hotel clock. It is the official time of the hotel. Therefore, the clock should be checked daily to be sure it is correct. Other clocks in the hotel, such as front desk time stamps, should be synchronized with the hotel clock.

In many hotels, guests can simply dial a special extension on their telephone and follow the instructions to request a wake-up time. The hotel then can provide an automated wake-up call or prompt the hotel operator to place a personalized wake-up call. For example, hotels can also combine a wake-up call with room service, allowing the guest to order breakfast upon receiving a wake-up call.

Voice Mail

Voice mail is a message-recording system that allows several guests to receive messages at the same time, thereby freeing the hotel operator for other duties. Voice mail is a service most travelers are used to in their own offices and homes. A hotel voice mail system is like a private answering machine for each guestroom. This enables a guest to receive complete and accurate messages in the caller's own voice and in the privacy of the guestroom. Guests can also call into the system from outside the hotel and retrieve their messages. Some voice mail systems allow guests to record a personalized message for callers.

E-mail

Many hotel guests have e-mail capability, and an increasing number of hotel guests want to be able to send and receive e-mail at hotels. A hotel guest with a laptop computer can plug into the guestroom's data port (on the phone or wall jack) and communicate with a corporate office or various other networks both public and private.

Many hotels have added in-room high-speed Internet service to provide more effective guest e-mail service.

TDDs

A TDD is a telecommunications device for hearing- and/or speech-impaired travelers. A TDD is a specially designed piece of equipment for placing and conducting telephone calls. It looks like a small typewriter with a coupler above the keyboard for a telephone receiver. The Americans with

Disabilities Act requires that hotels make a TDD available upon request. Similarly, the front desk should have a TDD device to handle in-house calls from hearing- or speech-impaired guests. To use a TDD, the caller turns on the unit, places the telephone receiver into the coupler, dials the telephone number, and begins typing when the other party picks up. A small display screen shows what the caller is typing.

Apply Your Learning 5.3

Please write all answers on a separate sheet of paper.

1. What is one process for taking telephone messages?

2. What is one process for delivering fax messages?

3. How are wake-up calls delivered?

4. What additional telecommunications technology is being used to provide guest services?

Quick Hits

SECTION 5.1—TYPES OF CALLS

- Local calls are typically billed per call, rather than per minute, or are offered free to guests.

- Direct-dial long-distance calls are the most common calls made by hotel guests and may include an added surcharge or per-minute fee on the guest's folio.

- Calling card and credit card calls are charged to the guest's personal account and are not charged on the guest's folio.

- Collect calls involve operator assistance. Most telephone companies pay a commission to the hotel for guests' collect calls.

- Third-party calls are similar to collect calls, but the billed number is not the called number. Typically, the operator must get approval for the charges from someone at the third-party number. The bill does not appear on the guest's folio.

- Person-to-person calls include verification that the called party is the party on the line.

- With billed-to-room calls, calls are placed by an operator for the guest. The operator then informs the hotel of the charge.

- International calls may be direct-dialed or placed with operator assistance. Guests may choose to pay through their folio account or bill the call to their calling card.

- Toll-free calls are direct-dialed from a guestroom.

- Premium-price calls, also known as "900" calls, carry additional fees charged to the caller.

- Internet access, whether dial-up or high-speed, is being offered in more and more guestrooms.

SECTION 5.2—TELECOMMUNICATIONS EQUIPMENT

- PBX—or private branch exchange—systems control incoming and outgoing telephone service in most hotels, allowing many telephones to share a limited number of telephone lines.

- A **call accounting system (CAS)** is a set of software programs used to place, price, and post telephone calls.

- Modern guestroom phones often include such features as speed dialing, hold buttons, call waiting, hands-free speakers, and input jacks for computer modems or fax machines.

- Pay phones are often supplied and maintained by an outside vendor and are not connected to a hotel's PBX system or CAS.

- Pagers and cellular phones are becoming increasingly popular amenities for hotel guests.

- Call dispensing systems are used to place automated calls to a selected number of guestrooms. Uses include wake-up calls, emergency alerts, and meeting reminders.

- Telephone/room status systems allow employees to enter data into hotel computers via guestroom phones and prohibit unauthorized use of guestroom phones.

- Call detection equipment helps improve billing accuracy and reduce guest account discrepancies.

SECTION 5.3—TELEPHONE SERVICES

- Valuable telephone skills include smiling, sitting or standing straight, using a low-pitched voice, matching your speaking rate with the caller's, avoiding extremes in volume, and avoiding expressions such as "uh-huh" and "yeah," which may give the impression of being inattentive.

- Common hotel telephone services include fax handling, wake-up calls, voice mail, e-mail, and other message handling.

- Guests with disabilities may require the use of a TDD, a telecommunications device for hearing- and/or speech-impaired individuals.

Profile

Liz Erikson

Vice President of International Sales Network
Fairmont Hotel Management

Liz Erikson has earned a place among the luxury lodging industry's most savvy salespeople. But few are aware of the life-long devotion to innkeeping that has driven her phenomenal career.

At 15 years old, Erikson read letters from her grandmother and decided to pursue a career in hotels. She also listened to stories from her father about life in the residence of a hotel, and knew the hard-working, exciting lifestyle was right for her.

"I was supposed to go to Cal-Berkeley and get a nice liberal education," the fourth-generation San Francisco native says, adding that her father was appalled that she wanted a career in the stressful business of hotels. She had been inspired by the experience of her grandmother, who led a zestful life taking her everywhere from acting consulate for the territory of Alaska to manager of the inn inside the 1915 World's Fair in San Francisco. Erikson's grandmother was the first female general manager of a hotel in California.

Erikson felt a promise in the industry, and her father eventually came to her side. In 1966, Erikson went to San Francisco City College, California. She entered its hotel and restaurant program, in which out of 200 students, only four were women.

In her first job in the industry, she went to work for Handlery Hotels as a reservations manager. She was eventually named director of sales at the Hotel Mark Hopkins.

In 1975, Erikson joined the Fairmont. In 1979, the late Richard Swig—a legend in the luxury hotel business—relocated her to Philadelphia.

Swig was one of the most influential people in Erikson's life. "He was the greatest mentor I ever had. His passion for the hotel business was honestly contagious."

Erikson's accomplishments have grown from her desire to succeed as a hotelier and from her contemplative attitude about life.

"If you want to have a career in sales ... for the first five years let the pendulum swing to your professional life more than your personal life.

"First, make a commitment to your profession; make a conscious decision on your career objectives at that point."

Excerpted with permission from an article written by Christopher Cole in USAE, Weekly News of Associations, CVBs and Hotels, *January 12, 1999.*

Reservations

Sections

6.1 Types of Reservations

AFTER STUDYING SECTION 6.1, YOU SHOULD KNOW HOW TO:

Explain the functions of the following types of reservations:

♦ Prepayment

♦ Credit card guarantee

♦ Advance deposit guarantee

♦ Travel agent guarantee

♦ Voucher or MCO guarantee

♦ Corporate guarantee

♦ Non-guaranteed reservation

List the factors that make a binding agreement between a hotel and a potential guest.

The majority of hotel guests make reservations. Reservations may take many forms.

Guaranteed Reservations

A **guaranteed reservation** assures the guest that the hotel will hold a room until a specific time of the day following the guest's scheduled arrival date. This time may be check-out time, the start of the hotel day (that is, when the front office audit has been completed and the books are closed for the day), or any time the lodging company chooses. The guest, in turn, guarantees to pay for the room, even if it is not used, unless the reservation is canceled according to the hotel's cancellation procedures. Guaranteed reservations protect the hotel's revenue even in the case of a **no-show,** a situation in which a guest makes a reservation but does not register or cancel the reservation. Variations of guaranteed reservations include the following.

Prepayment. A **prepayment guaranteed reservation** requires that a payment in full be received before the guest's day of arrival. This type of guaranteed reservation is commonly used at U.S. resorts and at hotels outside the United States.

Credit/Debit Card. Unless a **credit/debit card guaranteed reservation** is properly canceled before a stated cancellation hour, the lodging property will charge the guest's account for the amount of the room's rate plus tax; the card company will then bill the card holder. Credit/debit

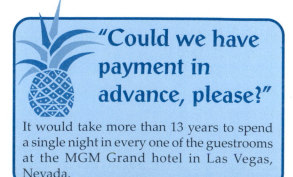

"Could we have payment in advance, please?"

It would take more than 13 years to spend a single night in every one of the guestrooms at the MGM Grand hotel in Las Vegas, Nevada.

card guaranteed reservations are the most common form of guaranteed reservation. Resorts may charge more room nights, since the length of stay at a resort is usually longer and it is more difficult to fill rooms due to advanced bookings.

Advance Deposit. An **advance deposit guaranteed reservation** (or partial prepayment) requires that the guest pay the hotel a specified amount of money before arrival. The amount of an advance deposit is typically enough to cover one night's room rate and tax. The pre-arrival amount may be larger if the reservation is for more than a one-night stay. If a guest holding an advance deposit guaranteed reservation fails to register or cancel, the hotel may retain the deposit and cancel the reservation for the guest's entire stay. This type of guaranteed reservation is more common at destination resorts and convention center hotels.

Travel Agent. **Travel agent guaranteed reservations** have become less common since both travel agents and hotels prefer the protection provided by credit card or advance deposit guarantees whenever possible. Under a travel agent guaranteed reservation, the travel agent guarantees the client's reservation. In the case of a no-show, the hotel generally bills the travel agency for payment and the travel agent must then collect from the guest.

Voucher or MCO. Another type of travel agent guarantee is the travel agency **voucher** or miscellaneous charge order (MCO). The MCO is a voucher issued by the Airline Reporting Corporation (ARC) and is controlled by many of the same travel agency regulations that control airline tickets. Many resorts prefer MCOs if they must accept vouchers because ARC guarantees payment if the travel agency defaults. With

UNDER THE GAVEL

Is Confirmation a Contract?

When a hotel and a person seeking to become a guest agree that the hotel is to reserve a room for a definite period of time at a specified price, if either the hotel or prospective guest breaches this agreement, that party may become liable to the other party for damages. This is general contract law. The agreement may be oral or may be written. To be binding, the agreement must be in definite terms indicating the intent of the parties and reciting the material points of the agreement, such as the dates of the reservation, the rate, the number of rooms, the nature of the accommodations, and the number of persons.

Confirmations should include an explanation that non-guaranteed reservations will not be held past the hotel's cancellation hour.

travel agency vouchers and MCOs, the guest has prepaid the amount of the deposit to the travel agent. Usually, with vouchers and MCOs, the travel agency deducts its commission before sending payment to the hotel.

Corporate. A **corporate guaranteed reservation** is a contractual agreement between the corporation and the hotel which states that the corporation will accept financial responsibility for any no-show business travelers the corporation sponsors.

Non-Guaranteed Reservations

In the case of a **non-guaranteed reservation,** the hotel agrees to hold a room for the guest until a stated reservation cancellation hour (usually 4 P.M. or 6 P.M.) on the day of arrival. This type of reservation does not guarantee that the property will receive payment for no-shows. If the guest does not arrive by the cancellation hour, the hotel is free to release the room, meaning that it can add the room to the list of other rooms available for sale. If the guest arrives after the cancellation hour, the hotel will accommodate the guest if a room is available.

It is common for hotels nearing full occupancy to accept only guaranteed reservations.

Apply Your Learning 6.1

Please write all answers on a separate sheet of paper.

1. What are the major types of reservations?

2. What is the difference between a confirmed reservation and a guaranteed reservation?

3. What methods can a guest use to guarantee a reservation?

For questions 4–8, use the words below to complete the following correct statements.

   credit/debit card   advance deposit   voucher   MCO   corporate

4. Widget, Inc. signed a contract with the Pleasantville Inn to accept financial responsibility for any no-show business travelers that it sponsors. They have made a(n) _____ reservation.

5. Cheyenne did not register for her reserved room or cancel it. The hotel charged her credit card for the first night's room and tax as she had made a(n) _____ reservation.

6. Nathan mailed a check to the Seaside Hotel that covered the first night's room charges. He reserved a room for a week. His reservation is a(n) _____ reservation.

7. The Airline Reporting Corporation issued vouchers to cover the reservations of an Irish tour group. The reservations agent recorded the reservation as a(n) _____ reservation.

8. A travel agent collects a prepaid deposit from the Johnson family for their upcoming vacation. He then deducts his commission and sends payment to the hotel. This reservation is considered a(n) _____ reservation.

6.2 Sources of Reservations

AFTER STUDYING SECTION 6.2, YOU SHOULD KNOW HOW TO:

♦ Describe how a global distribution system works

♦ Define an intersell agency

♦ List the ways properties directly receive reservations

♦ Make reservations through the Internet

♦ Contrast affiliate and non-affiliate reservation networks

♦ Outline the functions of a central reservations office

The more channels of distribution hotels have, the more opportunities guests will have to inquire and book their rooms. Reservation requests may be made:

• In person
• Over the telephone
• In the mail
• Via fax or telex
• Through an intersell agency
• Through the Internet
• Through a central reservation system
• Through a global distribution system (airline reservation system)

The reservations agent will collect information about the guest's stay through the reservation inquiry. The reservations agent should collect such information as the guest's name, address, and telephone number; company or travel agency name (if applicable); date of arrival and date of departure; and the type and number of rooms requested. The reservations agent should also try to establish the room rate, number of people in the party, method of payment or guarantee, and any special requests.

The reservations agents enters the data through a computer terminal. Simultaneous processing involves a **real time capability**. This means that the reservations agent receives the necessary feedback from the system to respond to a caller's requests during the telephone call.

Most of the information gathered during the reservation inquiry will be used to create the **reservation record**.

Global Distribution Systems

Most central reservation systems connect with one of the **global distribution systems (GDS).** The largest and best known GDSs include SABRE, Galileo International, Amadeus, and WorldSpan. GDSs provide worldwide distribution of hotel reservation information and allow selling of hotel reservations around the world. This is usually accomplished by connecting the hotel company reservation system with the GDSs.

Intersell Agencies

An **intersell agency** is a unique form of reservation system that contracts to handle reservations for more than one product line. Intersell agencies typically handle reservation services for airline companies, car rental companies, and hotel properties—a "one call does it all" type of approach.

Property Direct

Hotels handle many of their reservation transactions directly. A hotel may have a reservations department aside from the front desk. This arrangement is common in hotels of 250 rooms or more. A reservations department handles all direct requests for accommodations, monitors any communication links with central reservation systems and intersell agencies, and maintains updated room availability status information. Property direct reservation requests can reach a hotel in several ways:

- Telephone
- Mail
- Property Website
- Property-to-property
- Telex, cable, fax, e-mail, and other

Internet Distribution Systems

Many airlines, hotel companies, and car rental firms offer online reservations services through an **Internet distribution system (IDS)**. This lets travelers use their computers or hand-held units to book travel and accommodation needs. The variety of po-

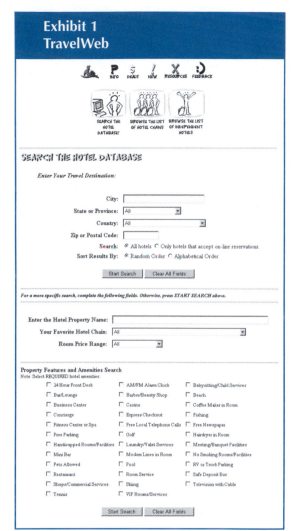

**Exhibit 1
TravelWeb**

TravelWeb's Internet booking service (at www.travelweb.com) enables travelers to directly access hotel's central reservations systems to check room availability and make online credit card guaranteed reservations. Other features on the site include airline flight reservations, hotel photos, maps, weather, and special discount programs.

tential guests accessing Internet sites to place reservations has prompted travel and hospitality companies to develop user-friendly reservation procedures.

Large and small hotels alike have a presence on the Internet. Chains often have

a Web site focusing first on the brand and its features, then on the individual properties. Most chain Internet sites allow visitors to the site to book reservations. Independent hotels also support Websites that may not be as sophisticated as chain sites, but normally provide similar information and allow visitors to make reservations.

Hotel Websites have adopted security procedures based on reliable encryption methods to protect against fraud. When users access online reservation systems, Web browsers automatically engage a high-level security feature.

E-commerce is an important force in reservation management. E-commerce extends the reach of hotels far beyond the traditional distribution channels of a hotel. Hotels have a presence in multiple distribution channels and direct access to the consumer through the Internet. Linking with guests is actually the easiest part of e-commerce. The more difficult part is knowing which sites provide the best opportunities, what hotel features to present, and what room rates to display.

E-commerce has become so important that a hotel may assign a dedicated manager to be responsible for managing electronic business transactions. Buyers who search for rooms do so for convenience as well as price. Many Web sites now combine air transportation and car rentals with hotel reservations into one booking engine for possible price discounts and bundled purchasing.

Central Reservation Systems

A majority of lodging properties belong to one or more **central reservation systems.** There are two basic types of central reservation systems: affiliate networks and non-affiliate networks.

An **affiliate reservation network** is a hotel chain's reservation system in which all participating properties are contractually related. Nearly every chain operates its own reservation network or outsources the central reservation function and technology to a reservation service company.

Chain hotels link their reservations operations to streamline the processing of reservations and reduce overall system costs. Also, one chain property can attract business for or refer business to another chain property. For group reservations, information may be shared among affiliate properties through a sales office automation program (SOAP).

Affiliate reservation networks that allow non-chain properties to participate in the reservation system are able to represent themselves to a broader market. Non-chain properties in an affiliate reservation system are referred to as **overflow facilities.** Reservation requests may be routed to overflow facilities only after all the available rooms in nearby chain properties have been booked.

A **non-affiliate reservation network** is a subscription system designed to connect independent or non-chain properties. Non-affiliate reservation networks enable independent hotel operators to enjoy many of the same benefits as chain-affiliated operators. Like an affiliate reservation network, a non-affiliate network usually assumes responsibility for advertising its service. Examples of non-affiliate reservation networks are Leading Hotels of the World, Preferred Hotels, and Distinguished Hotels. In many cases, these non-affiliate networks accept only hotels of a certain quality or a limited number of hotels in any geographical area to keep the value of service high to participating members.

Central Reservation System Functions

A central reservations office (CRO) typically deals directly with the public by means of a toll-free telephone number. Most large lodging chains support two or more reservation centers, with calls being directed to the center nearest the caller. Reservation centers often operate 24 hours per day, most days of the year. At peak times, reservation centers have a large number of agents on duty at the same time.

Central reservation services are provided by the central reservation office (CRO). The CRO receives room rate and availability information from participating properties. Information is typically sent over communication lines and enters the database directly. The responsibility and control of central reservation information lies with managers at the property level. The key to successful central reservation management is that the property and the central system must have access to the same room and rate availability information. When this is the case, reservationists at the CRO can directly confirm room rates and availability at the time of reservation.

The goals of a central reservation system are to improve guest service while enhancing profitability and operating efficiency. A CRO accomplishes these goals by:

- Providing access to special room rates and promotional packages
- Instantly confirming reservations
- Communicating with major airline, travel, and car rental agencies
- Building extensive guest files

Apply Your Learning 6.2

Please write all answers on a separate sheet of paper.

1. List the sources of reservations.
2. Contrast affiliate and non-affiliate reservation networks.
3. What are the ways that reservations arrive at a property?
4. What tasks do a central reservation system perform?
5. Which of the following is not a type of central reservations system?
   a. Preferred Hotels
   b. SABRE
   c. Affiliate reservation network
   d. Leading Hotels of the World

6. The Major City Hotel has 150 properties around the world. Reservations can be made by calling a toll-free number. What type of network do they have?

    a. Global distribution system

    b. Intersell agency

    c. Affiliate reservation network

    d. Non-affiliate reservation network

6.3 Reservation Computer Systems

AFTER STUDYING SECTION 6.3, YOU SHOULD KNOW HOW TO:

Access the reservations module and use it to perform the following tasks:

♦ Determine availability

♦ Create the reservation record

♦ Confirm the reservation

♦ Maintain the reservation record

♦ Generate reports

Property-level reservation systems are designed to meet the needs of the lodging industry.

A reservation module of a computer-based **property management system (PMS)** enables a reservationist to respond quickly and accurately to callers. The module reduces paperwork, physical filing, and other clerical tasks. This provides the reservationist with more time for giving personal attention to callers and for marketing the various services the hotel offers. Stored information can be accessed quickly, and many of the procedures for processing requests, updating information, and generating confirmations are simplified.

The reservationist's initial inquiry procedures create a **reservation record** that initiates the hotel guest cycle. Reservation records identify guests and their needs before their arrival at the property and enable the hotel to personalize guest service and appropriately schedule needed personnel. In addition, reservation modules can generate a number of important reports for management's use. The following sections describe typical activities associated with the use of a reservation module:

• Reservation inquiry (as discussed earlier in this chapter)

• Determining of availability

• Creating of the reservation record

• Confirming of the reservation

• Maintaining of the reservation record

• Generating of reports

Determining Availability

Once entered, the reservation inquiry is compared to rooms availability. The computer program is designed to sell rooms in a specified pattern (by zone, floor, block, etc.). Processing a reservation request may result in:

• Acceptance or rejection of the reservation request

Exhibit 1
Guestroom Control Log

Scheduler - Newmarket Hotel & Towers

File View Activity Reports Window Help

QuickBook...

March 2002

S	M	T	W	T	F	S
24	25	26	27	28	1	2
3	4	5	6	7	8	9
10	11	12	13	14	15	16
17	18	19	20	21	22	23
24	25	26	27	28	29	30

To Do List | Diary | GRC | Appointments

- Account
  - Merck Pharmecutical, Inc
  - Ernst & Young
  - American Express Travel
  - Avery Labels
- Booking
  - American Medical Association
  - Brown and Smith Consulting
  - Avery Labels
  - Merck Pharmecutical, Inc
- Contact
  - Mr. Richard Durgan
  - Ms. Janet Evans
  - Mr. Rick Fennimore
  - Mr. Jake Thompson

14 Bookings			2002	Tue 3/5	Wed 3/6	Thu 3/7	Fri 3/8	Sat 3/9	Sun 3/10	Mon 3/11
Total Available				175	190	30	170	190	330	390
Group Definite				175	155	170	40	40	0	0
Group Tentative				20	25	180	180	170	70	0
Trans Protected				130	130	120	110	100	100	110
MAR				110	120	110	90	90	90	110
Archer	D	BK	125	25	25					
Ernst & Young	D	BK	220	20						
Ambleside	D	BK	140	90	90	90				
Merck	D	BK	145	40	40	40				
Brown Co.	D	JRL	130			40	40	40		
AMA	T	LRH	125	20	25					
Exxon	T	CMK	225			180	180	170	70	
Avery Labels	P	BK	125	200	200					
Oceans, Inc	P	BK	120	90						
MPC Holdings	P	BK	45					45	45	
IBM	P		110							
Johnson & Co.	P	BK	123						45	45
Prudential	P	PH	230						100	100
Toyota	P	BK	120						100	

Source: Delphi for Windows/Newmarket International, Inc., Durham, New Hampshire. For more information, visit the company's Internet site at www.newmarketinc.com.

- Suggestions of alternative room types or rates
- Suggestions of alternative hotel properties

Exhibit 1 shows a guestroom control log from a hotel sales software package.

Creating Reservation Records

Once the reservation request has been processed and the room blocked, the system requires that the reservationist complete the reservation record by collecting and entering necessary data, such as:

- Guest's personal data (name, address, e-mail address, and telephone number)
- Time of arrival
- Reservation classification (advance, confirmed, guaranteed)
- Confirmation number
- Caller data (agency or secretary)
- Special requirements (handicapper, crib, no smoking, etc.)

Confirming the Reservation

Property management systems can automatically generate letters of confirmation at the time a reservation request is processed. Information can be retrieved from the reservation record and printed on a specially designed hotel form or into an electronic format for e-mail or fax distribution.

Reservation confirmations may be printed or e-mailed at any time. However, they are normally printed during system update. **System updates** are run daily to allow for report production, system file reorganization, and system maintenance, and to provide an end-of-day time frame.

Maintaining Reservation Records

Reservation records are stored in an electronic file and commonly segmented by date of arrival (year, month, day), group name, and guest name. File organization and the method of file retrieval are critical to an effective reservation module because callers frequently update, alter, cancel, or reconfirm their reservations.

Data from reservation records may be used to generate preregistration forms. Reservation records can also serve as preregistration folios. Prepayments, advance deposits, and cash payouts are examples of transactions that can be posted to the reservation record and later transferred to the guest's in-house folio.

The reservation module can interface with other front office functions. Reservation record data can be:

- Printed onto preregistration cards to facilitate faster check-in procedures.

- Used for creating electronic guest folios and information lists (alphabetical listings or sequential room number listings).

- Transferred to commission agent files for later processing.

- Formatted for eventual inclusion in a guest history file.

Generating Reports

The number and type of reports available through a reservation module are functions of the user's needs, software capability, and database contents. An in-house reservation module is designed to maximize room sales by accurately monitoring room availabilities and providing a detailed forecast of rooms revenue. A computer-generated **rooms availability report** lists, by room type, the number of rooms available each day (net remaining rooms in each category). A **revenue forecast report** projects future revenue by multiplying predicted occupancies by current house rates. The reservation module can also automatically compile and generate:

- Reservation transaction records

- Expected arrival and departure lists

- Commission agent reports

- Turnaway statistics (also called a refusal report)

Apply Your Learning 6.3

Please write all answers on a separate sheet of paper.

1. What tasks does the reservations module of the property management system perform?

2. When are reservation confirmations normally printed?

3. What reports can be generated from a reservation module?

6.4 Forecasting

AFTER STUDYING SECTION 6.4, YOU SHOULD KNOW HOW TO:

♦ Identify information needed for forecasting

♦ Calculate a no-show percentage

♦ Calculate the percentage of walk-ins

♦ Calculate the percentage of over-stays

♦ Calculate the percentage of understays

♦ Determine the forecasted number of rooms available for sale

♦ Create a 10-day and 3-day forecast

♦ Explain the importance of accurate room counts

The most important short-term planning performed by front office managers is **forecasting** the number of rooms available for sale for future reservations.

A room availability forecast can also be used as an occupancy forecast. Since there is a fixed number of rooms in the hotel, forecasting the number of rooms available for sale and the number of rooms expected to be occupied provides the occupancy percentage expected on a given date. The forecasted availability and occupancy numbers are very important to the daily operations of the hotel. Room occupancy forecasts can be used for scheduling the necessary num-

ber of employees and ordering the correct amount of inventory.

A forecast is only as reliable as the information on which it is based.

Forecasting is a skill acquired through experience, effective recordkeeping, and accurate counting methods. Experienced front office managers have found that several types of information can be helpful in room availability forecasting:

• A thorough knowledge of the hotel and its surrounding area

• Market profiles of the constituencies the hotel serves

• Occupancy data for the past several months and for the same period of the previous year

• Reservation trends and a history of reservation lead times (how far in advance reservations are made)

• A listing of special events scheduled in the surrounding geographic area

• Business profiles of specific groups booked for the forecast dates

• The number of non-guaranteed and guaranteed reservations and an estimate of the number of expected no-shows

• The percentage of rooms already reserved and the cut-off date for room blocks held for the forecast dates

- The impact of city-wide or multi-hotel groups and their potential influence on the forecast dates

- Plans for remodeling or renovating the hotel that would change the number of available rooms

- Construction or renovating plans for competitive hotels in the area

Forecasting Data

The process of forecasting room availability generally relies on historical occupancy data and business already committed. To facilitate forecasting, the following daily occupancy data should be collected:

- Number of expected room arrivals

- Number of expected room walk-ins

- Number of expected room stayovers (rooms occupied on previous nights that will continue to be occupied for the night in question)

- Number of expected room no-shows

- Number of expected room understays (check-outs occurring before expected departure date)

- Number of expected room check-outs

- Number of expected room overstays (check-outs occurring after the expected departure date)

Some hotels with a very high double occupancy percentage (more than one guest staying in a room) may be as concerned with guest counts as room counts.

These data are used to calculate various daily operating ratios that determine the number of available rooms for sale.

Ratios are a mathematical expression of a relationship between two numbers that results from dividing one by the other. Most statistical ratios that apply to

front office operations are expressed as percentages. Occupancy history data from the fictitious property shown in Exhibit 1 (the Holly Hotel) are used to illustrate the calculation for each front office ratio examined in this section.

Percentage of No-Shows. The percentage of no-shows indicates the proportion of reserved rooms that the expected guests did not arrive to occupy on the expected arrival date. This ratio helps the front office manager decide when (and if) to sell rooms to walk-in guests.

The percentage of no-shows is calculated by dividing the number of room no-shows for a specific period of time (day, week, month, or year) by the total number of room reservations for the same period. Using figures from Exhibit 1, the percentage of no-shows for the Holly Hotel can be calculated as follows:

$$\text{Percentage of No-Shows} = \frac{\text{Number of Room No-Shows}}{\text{Number of Room Reservations}}$$

$$= \frac{52}{288}$$

$$= .1806 \text{ or } \underline{18.06}\% \text{ of Reserved Rooms}$$

Percentage of Walk-Ins. The percentage of walk-ins is calculated by dividing the number of rooms occupied by walk-ins for a period by the total number of room arrivals for the same period. Using figures from Exhibit 1, the percentage of walk-ins for the Holly Hotel during the first week of March can be calculated as follows:

$$\text{Percentage of Walk-Ins} = \frac{\text{Number of Room Walk-Ins}}{\text{Total Number of Room Arrivals}}$$

$$= \frac{90}{326}$$

$$= .2761 \text{ or } \underline{27.61}\% \text{ of Rooms Arrivals}$$

Exhibit 1
Occupancy History of the Holly Hotel

Occupancy History
First Week of March

Day	Date	Guests	Room Arrivals	Room Walk-Ins	Room Reservations	Room No-Shows
Mon	3/1	118	70	13	63	6
Tues	3/2	145	55	15	48	8
Wed	3/3	176	68	16	56	4
Thurs	3/4	117	53	22	48	17
Fri	3/5	75	35	8	35	8
Sat	3/6	86	28	6	26	4
Sun	3/7	49	17	10	12	5
Totals		766	326	90	288	52

Occupied Rooms	Overstay Rooms	Understay Rooms	Room Check-Outs
90	6	0	30
115	10	3	30
120	12	6	63
95	3	18	78
50	7	0	80
58	6	3	20
30	3	3	45
558	47	33	346

Percentage of Overstays. Overstays represent rooms occupied by guests who stay beyond their originally scheduled departure dates. Overstay guests may have arrived with guaranteed or non-guaranteed reservations or as walk-ins. Overstays should not be confused with stayovers. Stayover rooms are rooms occupied by guests who arrived to occupy a room before the day in question and whose *scheduled* departure date isn't until after the day in question.

The percentage of overstays is calculated by dividing the number of overstay rooms for a period by the total number of *expected* room check-outs for the same period. The number of expected room check-outs equals the number of actual check-outs on the books minus understays plus overstays. Using figures from Exhibit 1, the percentage of overstays for the Holly Hotel during the first week of March can be calculated as follows:

$$\text{Percentage of Overstays} = \frac{\text{Number of Overstay Rooms}}{\text{Number of Expected Check-Outs}}$$

$$= \frac{47}{346 - 33 + 47}$$

$$= .1306 \text{ or } \underline{13.06\%} \text{ of Expected Check-Outs}$$

Percentage of Understays. Understays represent rooms occupied by guests who check out before their scheduled departure dates. Understay guests may have arrived at the hotel with guaranteed or non-guaranteed reservations or as walk-ins.

The percentage of understays is calculated by dividing the number of understay rooms for a period by the total number of expected room check-outs for the same period. Using figures from Exhibit 1, the percentage of understays for the Holly Hotel during the first week of March can be calculated as follows:

$$\text{Percentage of Understays} = \frac{\text{Number of Understay Rooms}}{\text{Number of Expected Check-Outs}}$$

$$= \frac{33}{346 - 33 + 47}$$

$$= .0917 \text{ or } \underline{9.17\%} \text{ of Expected Check-Outs}$$

Guests leaving before their stated departure date create empty rooms that typically are difficult to fill. Thus, understay rooms may represent permanently lost room revenue.

Forecast Formula

Once relevant occupancy statistics have been gathered, the number of rooms available for sale on any given date can be determined by the following formula:

	Total Number of Guestrooms
−	Number of Out-of-Order Rooms
−	Number of Room Stayovers
−	Number of Room Reservations
+	Number of Room Reservations x Percentage of No-Shows
+	Number of Room Understays
−	Number of Room Overstays
	Number of Rooms Available for Sale

Note that the above formula does not include walk-ins. They are not included because the number of walk-ins a hotel can accept is determined by the number of rooms that remain available for sale. If a hotel is full due to existing reservations, stayovers, and other factors, it cannot accept walk-ins.

Consider the Holly House, a 120-room property, where on April 1 there are three out-of-order rooms, 55 stayovers, and 42 guests with reservations scheduled to arrive. Since the percentage of no-shows has been calculated at 18.06 percent, the front office manager calculates that as many as eight guests with reservations may not arrive ($42 \times .1806 = 7.59$, rounded up). Based on historical data, six understays and 15 overstays are also expected. The number of rooms projected to be available for sale on April 1 can be determined as follows:

	Total Number of Guestrooms	120
−	Number of Out-of-Order Rooms	− 3
−	Number of Room Stayovers	− 55
−	Number of Room Reservations	− 42
+	Number of Room Reservations x No-Show Percentage	+ 8
+	Number of Room Understays	+ 6
−	Number of Room Overstays	− 15
	Number of Rooms Available for Sale	19

Therefore, the Holly Hotel is considered to have 19 rooms available for sale on April 1. Once this figure is determined, front office management can decide whether or not to accept more reservations and can determine its level of staffing. Front office planning decisions are subject to change as the front office learns of reservation cancellations and modifications.

Sample Forecast Forms

The front office may prepare several different forecasts depending on its needs Occupancy forecasts are typically developed on a monthly basis and reviewed by food and beverage and rooms division management to forecast revenues, project expenses, and develop labor schedules. Together, these forecasts help many hotel departments maintain appropriate staff levels for expected business volumes and thereby help contain costs.

Ten-Day Forecast. The ten-day forecast at most lodging properties is developed jointly by the front office manager and the reservations manager, possibly in conjunction with a forecast committee. A ten-day forecast usually consists of:

- Daily forecasted occupancy figures, including room arrivals, room departures, rooms sold, and number of guests

- The number of group commitments, with a listing of each group's name, arrival and departure dates, number of rooms reserved, number of guests, and perhaps quoted room rates

- A comparison of the previous period's forecasted and actual room counts and occupancy percentages

A special ten-day forecast may also be prepared for food and beverage, banquet, and catering operations. This forecast usually includes the expected number of guests, which is often referred to as the **house count.**

The ten-day forecast should be distributed to all department offices by mid-week for the coming period. A ten-day forecast form, as shown in Exhibit 2, is typically developed from data collected through front office sources.

Most automated systems provide a summary of recorded data in a report format for the front office manager to use. However, only revenue management systems are programmed to "forecast" business. Programming hotel property management systems to succesfully analyze historical trends and market conditions has been tried in the past with little success. Revenue management systems are much more sophisticated, with special trend analysis and regressional analysis programming. Even with revenue management system forecasting, it is the knowledge and skill of the front office manager that determines the accuracy of the forecast.

Three-Day Forecast. A three-day forecast is an updated report that reflects a more current estimate of room availability. It details any significant changes from the ten-day forecast. The three-day forecast is intended to guide management in fine-tuning labor schedules and adjusting room availability information.

Room Count Considerations. Control books, charts, software applications, projections, ratios, and formulas can be essential in short- and long-range room count planning. Each day, the front office performs several physical counts of rooms occupied, vacant, reserved, and due to check out, to complete the occupancy statistics for that day. An automated system may reduce the need for most final counts, since the systemcan be programmed to continually update room availability information.

It is important for front desk agents to know *exactly* how many rooms are available, especially if the hotel expects to operate near 100 percent occupancy. Once procedures for gathering room count information are established, planning procedures can be extended to longer periods of time to form a more reliable basis for revenue, expense, and labor forecasting.

Exhibit 2
Sample Ten Day Forecast Form

Ten-Day Occupancy Forecast

Location _____ # _____ Week Ending _____

Date Prepared: _____ Prepared By: _____

To be submitted to all department heads at least one week before the first day listed on forecast.

	Fri.	Sat.	Sun.	Mon.	Tues.	Wed.	Thur.	Fri.	Sat.	Sun.
1. Date and Day (start week and end week the same as the payroll schedule)										
2. Estimated Departures										
3. Reservation Arrivals—Group (taken from log book)										
4. Reservation Arrivals—Individual (taken from log book)										
5. Future Reservations (estimated reservations received after forecast is completed)										
6. Expected Walk-ins (% of walk-ins based on reservations received and actual occupancy for past two weeks)										
7. Total Arrivals										
8. Stayovers										
9. TOTAL FORECASTED ROOMS										
10. Occupancy Multiplier (based on number of guests per occupied room for average of the same day for last three weeks)										
11. FORECASTED NUMBER OF GUESTS										
12. Actual Rooms Occupied (taken from daily report for actual date to be completed by front office supervisor)										
13. Forecasted Variance (difference between forecast and rooms occupied on daily report)										
14. Explanation (to be completed by front office supervisor and submitted to general manager; attach additional memo if necessary)										

APPROVED: _____ DATE: _____

General Manager's Signature

Apply Your Learning 6.4

Please write all answers on a separate sheet of paper.

1. What information is important for room forecasting?

2. What information is needed to calculate the number of no-shows?

3. How are forecasts used throughout the property?

The Ivy Motel has 160 rooms. On Monday they had 75 room reservations, 5 no-shows, 3 walk-ins, 10 overstays, 9 understays, 40 expected check-outs and 73 room arrivals. There were 80 stayovers. Perform the following calculations:

4. Percentage of no-shows

5. Percentage of walk-ins

6. Percentage of overstays

7. Percentage of understays

8. Number of rooms available for sale

Quick Hits

SECTION 6.1—TYPES OF RESERVATIONS

- **Guaranteed reservations** keep a room for a guest until a specific time on the day after the guest was scheduled to arrive. The guest agrees to pay for the room, even if he or she doesn't use it, unless he or she cancels it in time.

- The most common types of guaranteed reservations are: prepayment, credit card, advance deposit, travel agent, voucher or MCO, and corporate.

- **Non-guaranteed reservations** are ones where the hotel will hold the room for the guest until the cancellation hour on the day of arrival. If the guest does not arrive by the cancellation hour, then the hotel can rent the room to someone else. The guest does not have to pay if he or she doesn't show up.

- Confirmations are considered a legal contract under general contract law. Once a reservation is confirmed, the hotel must provide accommodations for the agreed-upon date according to the terms of the confirmation.

SECTION 6.2—SOURCES OF RESERVATIONS

- Guests can make reservation requests in person, over the phone, in the mail, via fax or telex, over the Internet, through a central reservation system, through a global distribution system, or through an intersell agency.

- A **central reservation system** is a network that communicates reservations to each participating property. Each individual property must update the system's computer database with room availability data on a timely basis.

- An **affiliate reservation network** is a central reservation system in which all of the participating properties belong to the same chain or have the same ownership.

- A **non-affiliate reservation network** is a subscription system that links independent or non-chain properties.

- A **global distribution system** is owned by an airline or consortium of airlines and distribute hotel reservation information worldwide. Some common ones include SABRE, Galileo, Amadeus, and WorldSpan.

- An **intersell agency** handles reservations for hotels, airline companies, car rental companies, and other travel-related businesses.

- Most properties will take reservations at the property either through the front desk or, especially if the property has 250 rooms or more, through a reservations department. Reservations may arrive through the mail, telephone, property-to-property, telex, cable, fax, e-mail, or the Internet.

SECTION 6.3—RESERVATION COMPUTER SYSTEMS

- Reservation systems modules are part of the **property management system (PMS).** This software is specifically designed for the hospitality industry.

- A reservations agent initiates the guest cycle by creating a **reservation record.**

- A **reservations record** usually contains guest personal data, time of arrival, reservation classification, confirmation number, caller data, and any special requirements.

- Other tasks performed by the computer system include: determining availability, creating a reservation record, confirming a reservation, maintaining the reservation record, and generating reports.

- Confirmation letters can be sent at any time, but they are usually sent out during the **system update** that is run daily.

- Reservation record data can be printed onto preregistration cards, used for printing guest folios, transferred to commission agent files, and formatted for a guest history file.

- Some common reports that the reservations module generates includes a rooms availability report, revenue forecast report, reservation transaction records, expected arrivals and departure lists, commission agent report, turnaway statistics.

SECTION 6.4—FORECASTING

- Room availability forecasts are used to help manage the reservations process. It can also be used as an occupancy forecast.

- Accurate information is essential to good forecasting. Information might come from within the hotel, the community, economic data, or the world.

- Daily occupancy data is needed for forecasting room availability as the forecast relies on historical data. The most important data is room arrivals, walk-ins, stayovers, no-shows, understays, check-outs, and overstays.

- No-show percentage is calculated by dividing the number of no-shows by the number of reservations.

- Walk-in percentage is calculated by dividing the number of walk-ins by the number of arrivals.

- Overstay percentage is calculated by dividing the overstays by the expected check-outs.

- Understay percentage is calculated by dividing the understays by the expected check-outs.

- The forecast formula is used to determine how many rooms are available for sale.

- The 10-day forecast predicts occupancy figures, group commitments, and compares the actual room counts and forecasts from the previous period. It may also include the house count to help food and beverage and housekeeping departments plan inventory and staffing.

- The three-day forecast is an update of the 10-day forecast and lets people know about any major changes.

- Room counts need to be as accurate as possible for the hotel to earn maximum revenue.

Profile

Steve Belmonte
President, Hopitality Solutions

"I became very taken by the hotel industry at a very young age," said Steve Belmonte. "Every summer, our family would vacation throughout Wisconsin and Minnesota. I loved staying in the hotels and motels. Absolutely everything about them fascinated me. Checking in, the ice machine, the little bars of soap in the bathroom—everything."

Belmonte was taking college courses before he put his love of hotels and his love of sales together, grabbing a job as a desk clerk. He was studying hotel management by correspondence, and doing classroom work first at Wright Junior College, and then at Harper College, both in Illinois.

Belmonte eventually saw an ad placed by the Executive House Hotel in Wacker, Ill., seeking a front desk manager. In three months, he was named assistant manager and was still only 17.

"I lied about my age. Then I saw another ad for general manager at the Holiday Inn O'Hare," Belmonte said. "I got a three-piece suit, grew a mustache and told them I was 26. I got the job and stayed 14 years."

Belmonte said that property became the most profitable Holiday Inn in the Midwest.

He then became a regional vice president overseeing three other Holidays, but he was getting an ownership itch. He made an art out of managing, renovating, repositioning, and then selling properties.

Owning and operating several Ramadas, Belmonte developed a particular fondness for the brand. In 1991, he was offered the presidency of Ramada.

Under his leadership, the size of Ramada nearly doubled and Belmonte held the distinction of being the longest-running head of a hotel chain.

In 2002, Belmonte launched a consulting firm specializing in helping hotel owners work with franchise companies. That same year, he received a Lifetime Achievement Award. He also donated money to create the Steven Belmonte Scholarship Fund. All the better to improve an industry with which he has been in love as long as he can remember.

This article excerpted with permission from Hotel/Motel Management.

Registration

Sections

7.1 The Registration Cycle

AFTER STUDYING SECTION 7.1, YOU SHOULD KNOW HOW TO:

♦ Identify the functions and purpose of preregistration

♦ Use registration cards to collect information

♦ Explain the flow of registration information throughout the hotel

To the casual observer, the registration process might look as if it involves nothing more than efficiently filling in a few blanks on a computer screen and handing out room keys. Nothing could be further from the truth. At some hotels, the registration cycle begins even before the guest arrives— and continues until the guest checks out and settles the bill. Throughout the process, an attentive and informed front desk agent can make numerous choices that directly affect customer service, contribute to guest security, protect the hotel, and actually improve revenues.

UNDER THE GAVEL

A Hotel's Duty to Receive Guests

Under common law, hotelkeepers were obligated to take all travelers who applied to be received as guests. This requirement derived from the common law of England during a time when it was not safe to stay on the open road because there were highway robbers. The common law rule still applies unless it has been changed by legislative statute.

The federal Civil Rights Act of 1964 supplemented the old common law rule by providing that hotels could not discriminate against any person on the grounds of race, color, religion, or national origin when providing accommodations.

The common law as modified by federal, state, and local legislation and court decisions still governs hotel and guest relationships and business transactions in the United States. However, each state can reach decisions separate from court rulings of other states in similar cases.

Maintaining Guest Registers

U N D E R T H E G A V E L

State or local laws often require hotels to maintain guest registers, written records of the guest's name, address, date of arrival, and date of departure.

On occasion, an attorney will request permission to examine a hotel's register or other guest records on behalf of a client, who may or may not be the guest in question. In such instances, the hotel should require the attorney to obtain the guest's written consent to the examination. The hotel should not divulge any information with respect to the guest's registration without this written consent and the advice of hotel counsel. If the records are required in connection with a litigated matter between private parties, a subpoena or a court order should be issued requiring the hotel to produce the records, and the hotel's lawyer should be consulted.

If a request for examination of hotel records is made by a police officer or a duly authorized official investigator, the hotel should consult with its attorney before permitting the examination, especially if there is any reason to believe that the property may be involved as a party in a civil or criminal suit.

Preregistration

Preregistration (registration activities that occur before the guest arrives at the property) helps accelerate the registration process. It typically involves producing a registration card, recording the room and rate assignment, creating a guest folio, and other functions.

Preregistration helps plan for special requirements of guests as well as of the hotel. For example, frequent guests may have a special room they enjoy; guests with disabilities may need rooms outfitted to their special needs. By preregistering these guests, the front desk agent can be sure to satisfy them.

Preregistration also lends itself to innovative registration options. For instance,

Double Duty

The Hotel Stilwell building (built in 1880) served as the Kansas State Capitol in 1919. The Rice Hotel is built on the site of the old capitol of the Republic of Texas, which housed the Texas Congress from 1837 through 1839.

Exhibit 1
Flow of Guest Registration Information

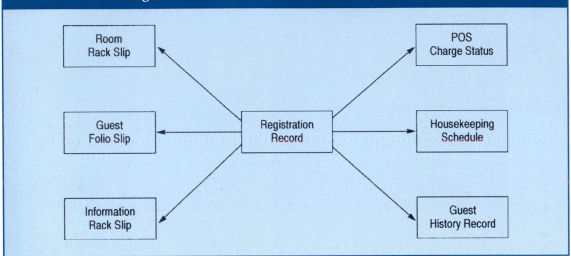

a hotel courtesy van might pick up a guest arriving at the airport who has been pre-registered. The driver could request the guest's signature on a prepared registration card or handheld computer, imprint the guest's credit or debit card, and issue a pre-assigned room key—all before the guest arrives at the hotel.

Registration Flow

Registration records facilitate the registration process. The registration record re-quires a guest to provide name, address, telephone number, company affiliation (if appropriate), and payment method. There is also space for the guest's planned departure date and room rate. These elements are critical to rooms and revenue management. Many registration cards also require the guest to acknowledge that he or she is personally responsible for payment in case the credit card or direct billing is not accepted.

Exhibit 1 shows the flow of guest registration information as it moves from the front desk to other areas of the hotel that can make use of it.

Apply Your Learning 7.1

Please write all answers on a separate sheet of paper.

1. What activities take place during preregistration?

2. What information can be found in a registration record?

Fill in the blanks:

3. Hotels have a duty to receive guests according to _____ law.

4. If an attorney asks to see a guest register, the hotel should ask him or her to get permission in writing from the _____.

5. _____ _____ facilitate the registration process.

7.2 Room Assignment

AFTER STUDYING SECTION 7.2, YOU SHOULD KNOW HOW TO:

- ♦ Determine when a room is available for sale

- ♦ Communicate changes in room status

- ♦ Interpret rate schedules

- ♦ List special room rate types

- ♦ Use floor plans to explain room locations

At most properties, the front desk agent is not allowed to assign guestrooms until the rooms have been cleaned, inspected, and released by the housekeeping department. Typically, rooms are recycled for sale according to the following process.

Each night, a front desk agent produces an **occupancy report** that lists rooms occupied that night and indicates guests who are expected to check out the following day. The executive housekeeper picks up this list early the next morning and schedules the occupied rooms for cleaning. As guests check out of the hotel, the front desk notifies housekeeping. Housekeeping ensures that these rooms are given top priority so that clean rooms are available for arriving guests.

At the end of the shift, housekeeping prepares a **housekeeping status report** (see Exhibit 1) based on a physical check of each

room in the property. This report is compared with the front desk occupancy report, and any discrepancies are brought to the attention of the front office manager. A **room status discrepancy** is a situation in which the housekeeping department's description of a room's status differs from the room status information being used by the front desk to assign guestrooms.

Knowing the condition of a room is important to rooms management. For example, if a guest checks out before the stated departure date, the front desk must notify the housekeeping department that the room is no longer a stayover but is now a check-out. Exhibit 2 defines typical room status terms.

Housekeeping and the front desk have instantaneous access to room status information. When a guest checks out, a front desk agent enters the departure into the computer system. Housekeeping is then alerted that the room needs cleaning through a terminal in the housekeeping department. Once the room is cleaned and inspected, housekeeping enters this information into the system. This informs the front office that the room is available for sale.

Room Rates

A **room rate** is the price a hotel charges for overnight accommodations. The cost

Exhibit 1
Sample Housekeeping Rooms Status Report

Housekeeper's Report

A.M.
P.M.

Date _____ , 20 _____

ROOM NUMBER	STATUS	ROOM NUMBER	STATUS	ROOM NUMBER	STATUS	ROOM NUMBER	STATUS
101		126		151		176	
102		127		152		177	
103		128		153		178	
104		129		154		179	
105		130		155		180	
106		131		156		181	
107		132		157		182	
108		133		158		183	
120						195	
121		146		171		196	
122		147		172		197	
123		148		173		198	
124		149		174		199	
125		150		175		200	

Remarks:
_____
_____
_____
_____

Housekeeper's Signature

Legend:

✓	-	Occupied
000	-	Out-of-Order
—	-	Vacant
B	-	Slept Out (Baggage Still in Room)
X	-	Occupied No Baggage
C.O.	-	Slept In but Checked Out Early A.M.
E.A.	-	Early Arrival

structure of the hotel dictates the minimum rate for a room, and competition helps the hotel establish its maximum rate. A hotel will usually designate a standard rate for each room, typically called the **rack rate,** somewhere between these two extremes.

Room rates are typically confirmed as part of the reservations process. Assigning rates for walk-in guests is left to the front desk agent, according to the hotel's policy.

Front desk agents may sometimes be allowed to offer a room at a lower price than its rack rate. Normally, this occurs only with managerial approval. Some hotels establish seasonal rate schedules in order to anticipate business fluctuations. The objective is to improve occupancy by offering lower prices during low demand periods and to maximize room revenue during high demand periods.

Exhibit 2
Room Status Definitions

Occupied: A guest is currently registered to the room.

Complimentary: The room is occupied, but the guest is assessed no charge for its use.

Stayover: The guest is not checking out today and will remain at least one more night.

On-change: The guest has departed, but the room has not yet been cleaned and readied for resale.

Do not disturb: The guest has requested not to be disturbed.

Sleep-out: A guest is registered to the room, but the bed has not been used.

Skipper: The guest has left the hotel without making arrangements to settle his/her account.

Sleeper: The guest has settled his/her account and left the hotel, but the front office staff has failed to properly update the room's status.

Vacant and ready: The room has been cleaned and inspected and is ready for an arriving guest.

Out-of-order: The room cannot be assigned to a guest. A room may be out-of-order for a variety of reasons, including the need for maintenance, refurbishing, and extensive cleaning.

Lock-out: The room has been locked so that the guest cannot re-enter until he/she is cleared by a hotel official.

DNCO (did not check out): The guest made arrangements to settle his or her account (and thus is not a skipper) but has left without informing the front office.

Due out: The room is expected to become vacant after the following day's check-out time.

Check-out: The guest has settled his or her account, returned the room keys, and left the hotel.

Late check-out: The guest has requested and is being allowed to check out later than the hotel's standard check-out time.

Other room rate schedules may reflect variations in the number of guests assigned to the room, service level, and room location. For example, room rates may cover billing arrangements for meals. Under the **American Plan,** room charges include the cost of the guestroom and three meals per day. Under the **Modified American Plan,** the daily rate includes charges for the guestroom and two meals per day (typically breakfast and dinner). Under the **European Plan,** meals are priced separately from guestrooms. American resorts frequently use either the American Plan or the Modified American Plan. Most nonresort hotels in the United States set their rates according to the European Plan.

Room rates may also vary based on the type of guest. Special room rates may include:

- *Commercial or corporate rates* for frequent guests

- *Complimentary rates (no charge)* for business promotion

- *Group rates* for a predetermined number of affiliated guests

- *Family rates* for parents and children sharing the same room

- *Day rates* for less than an overnight stay (usually check-in and check-out on the same day)

Exhibit 3
Simplified Hotel Floor Plan

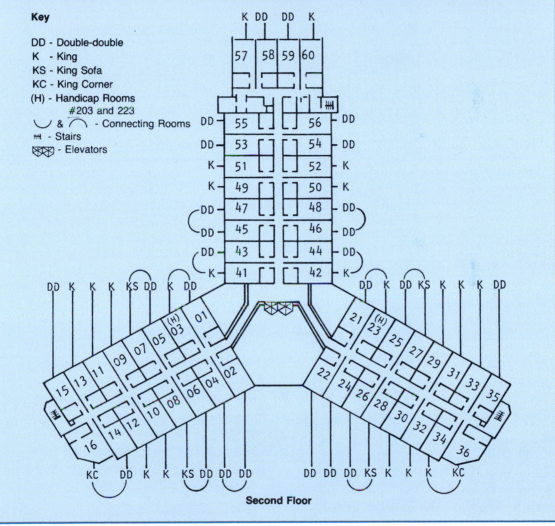

Key

DD - Double-double
K - King
KS - King Sofa
KC - King Corner
(H) - Handicap Rooms
        #203 and 223
⌣ & ⌢ - Connecting Rooms
⊢⊣ - Stairs
▨▨ - Elevators

Second Floor

Courtesy of The Sheraton Inn, Lansing, Michigan

- *Package-plan rates* for guestrooms sold in a package that includes special events or activities

- *Frequent traveler rates* for guests earning discounts through the hotel's frequent traveler program

Room Locations

A front desk agent must be aware of the characteristics of each room type. In most hotels built within the last 50 years, guestrooms within each room category tend to be approximately the same size; older hotels, due to different construction techniques and materials, often have rooms varying significantly in size and configuration. Differences between two guestrooms generally lie in their furnishings, amenities, and location. Front desk agents should be familiar with various guestroom configurations, as well as the hotel's floor plan, to satisfy guest rooming requests. Exhibit 3 contains an example of a simplified hotel floor plan.

Individual guests or groups may ask for certain rooms as part of their reservation requests. The front office system should contain specific data about each room—its type, rate, floor, view, bedding, and other pertinent information. It is the responsibility of the front desk to assign guestrooms from the preferred block of rooms at registration.

Apply Your Learning 7.2

Please write all answers on a separate sheet of paper.

1. What reports are generated to track room status?

2. What are the three main types of room rate plans and what do they include?

3. Why is a floor plan useful to a front desk agent?

Match the rates in column one with the guests in column two.

Commercial or corporate	Parents and child
Complimentary	Winner of a promotional pass
Group	Guest redeeming points for past visits
Family	Frequent business guest
Day	Member of convention
Package plan	Guest staying from 11 A.M. until 5 P.M.
Frequent traveler	Couple celebrating Valentine's weekend

7.3 Selling and Turning Away

AFTER STUDYING SECTION 7.3, YOU SHOULD KNOW HOW TO:

♦ Upsell a guest to a higher rate category

♦ Provide assistance to a walk-in guest who cannot be accommodated

♦ Handle guests with non-guaranteed reservations who must be turned away

♦ List the procedures to follow when there is no room for a guest with a guaranteed reservation

Selling the Guestroom

Front desk agents frequently have the opportunity to make individual sales presentations during registration, and they can substantially improve room revenue by using front office sales techniques.

 Upselling refers to the efforts of reservations agents and front desk agents to convince guests to rent rooms in categories above standard rate accommodations. These agents upsell rooms by knowing how and when to ask for a sale in a non-pressuring way and how to direct the sale from the guest's perspective.

Offering guestroom options is the key, and it requires thoughtful planning and prac-

tice. Some hotels, as a matter of policy, offer registering guests more than one room option and then let guests decide. Guests often provide clues about what they are looking for, and some information may already be available on a reservation record. Front desk agents must describe the hotel's facilities and services in a manner that makes them appealing. Exhibit 1 lists some general suggestions for upselling guestrooms.

As registration draws to a close, tell guests about the hotel's gift shops, restaurants, services, and facilities. Most guests appreciate this information. Before the guest

Welcome to the Igloo Inn

Imagine a hotel built entirely out of ice. That's what you'll find during the winter months in Jukkasjärvi, Sweden. Every year, the Ice Hotel is built from 10,000 tons of ice and 30,000 tons of fresh, natural snow.

The Ice Hotel can accommodate more than 100 guests. It includes an Ice Chapel, an ice art exhibition hall, a movie theater, and the "world famous" Absolut Ice Bar.

How could anyone get a good night's sleep in an oversize freezer? All Ice Hotel beds include a reindeer skin, sleeping mat, thermal sleeping bag, and sheets.

Exhibit 1
Suggestions for Upselling Guestrooms

- Always greet each guest with a smile in your voice as well as on your face. Be pleasant and businesslike. Remember: you are selling yourself as much as you are selling the hotel and its services.

- Establish and maintain eye contact with the guest.

- Find out the guest's name immediately and use it at least three times during the conversation. Always use courteous titles such as "Mr." or "Ms." when addressing the guest. Do not call a guest by his or her first name.

- Attempt to identify the needs of the guest since these needs may not have been identified during the reservations process. Match the guest's needs to the furnishings and/or amenities from among available rooms. For example, a guest staying at the hotel for three or four nights may appreciate and be more willing to pay for a larger or more isolated room than a guest staying only one night. Guests on a honeymoon or special vacation may be willing to pay for a room with a scenic view.

- Offer an upgraded room by pointing out its features and benefits first, then mention its rate. If the guest has a reservation, describe the differences between the reserved and the upgraded room. Walk-in guests provide the best opportunity for upselling. If two different types of rooms are available, mention the features, benefits, and rates of both. Do not risk losing the sale by mentioning only the higher-priced room.

- Complete the registration process.

- Thank the guest and wish him or her a pleasant stay.

---

leaves the desk, the front desk agent should thank the guest for choosing the hotel and express a personal interest in making his or her stay as pleasant as possible. Some hotels have front desk agents telephone the guest's room shortly after registration, to ensure that the accommodations are satisfactory.

Denying Accommodations

In general, a hotel is obligated to accommodate guests. Legitimate reasons for refusing to accommodate a guest may include a lack of available rooms, disorderly conduct, or unwillingness to pay for accommodations or services. State law may give other reasons that allow hotels to turn guests away. It is the responsibility of front office management to determine whether someone will be roomed.

Seldom, if ever, should a hotel be unable to accommodate a guest with a reservation, especially a guaranteed reservation. When this happens, most hotels will make other arrangements for the guest. In the case of a guaranteed reservation, most full-service hotels will pay for the guest's room at another property. However, the hotel may have no obligation to guests without guaranteed reservations, or to guests who arrive after the hotel's reservation cancellation hour (often 6 P.M.).

Walk-in Guests. A tired **walk-in** guest who has been traveling for an extended time may be disappointed to find that the hotel is fully occupied. However, hotels have no obligation to accommodate guests who arrive without a reservation when no rooms are available. If a walk-in guest cannot be

Refusing Guests

U
N
D
E
R

T
H
E

G
A
V
E
L

There are circumstances under which a hotel may refuse a guest, notwithstanding the general common law and statutory obligation to receive a person. In some jurisdictions, courts have indicated that a hotel can refuse to receive a guest if:

- the person is drunk or disorderly, creating a public nuisance
- the person is suffering from a contagious disease
- the person is bringing property into the hotel which it does not customarily receive, such as an animal, or property that may be dangerous to others, such as firearms or explosives
- the person is unwilling or unable to pay for hotel services
- the hotel has no accommodations to offer (though the hotel may be contractually liable if the person has a valid reservation)

A hotel cannot refuse accommodations merely because a person arrives at an unusual hour, such as the middle of the night. The hotel is presumed to be open to receive travelers at all times.

accommodated, front desk agents assist the guest by suggesting and providing directions to nearby hotels. The front desk agent may even offer to call another hotel to assist the guest.

The situation may be more difficult when a walk-in guest falsely believes he or she has a reservation. A hotel might take the following steps to clarify the situation:

- If the guest presents a letter of confirmation, verify the date and the name of the hotel; the guest may have arrived on a different date or at the wrong property. Some individuals have even shown up on the right day at the right property—but in the wrong city!

- Ask whether another person might have made the reservation for the

guest; the reservation may be at another property, or it may be misfiled under the caller's name, not the guest's name.

- Double-check the reservations file for another spelling of the guest's last name. For instance, B, P, and T may have been confused when the reservation was made during a telephone conversation. Also, check to see if the guest's first and last names were inadvertently reversed in the reservation file.

- If the reservation was made through a travel agency or representative, allow the guest to call the originating source for clarification.

- Verify no-show registration cards from the previous day just in case a no-show arrives a day late.

If there seems to be no alternative to **walking** (turning away) the guest, a manager should explain the matter in a private office. Registering one guest in view of another who cannot be accommodated can be extremely awkward and embarrassing.

Guests with Non-Guaranteed Reservations. A number of situations or circumstances can delay a guest's scheduled arrival. Guests frequently do not have the chance to change a non-guaranteed reservation to a guaranteed reservation by the time they realize they will arrive past the hotel's reservation cancellation hour. As a result, the hotel may not hold the room for the guest and may not have a room available when the guest arrives. If the hotel cannot provide a guestroom, front office management must be extremely tactful when informing the guest. Blame should not be placed on either party since the lack of accommodations is no one's fault.

Guests with Guaranteed Reservations. If reservations are carefully handled and sound forecasting procedures are followed, a hotel should not have to deny accommodations to a guest with a guaranteed reservation. If it does happen, the front office manager should take charge and make necessary decisions. The manager may:

- Review all front desk transactions to ensure full occupancy.

- Make an accurate count of rooms occupied, using all relevant data.

- Compare information int he rooms availability file, housekeeper's report, and guest folios for any discrepancy in occupancy status.

- Contact in-house **due-outs** (guests expected to check out today) who have not yet checked out and confirm their departure time. The guest may have left the hotel without stopping at the front desk or properly completing check-out. Finally, an early discovery of a **skipper** (a guest who leaves with no intention of paying for the room) will allow the guestroom to be assigned to another guest.

- Verify rooms listed as out-of-order, which may easily be readied for sale. If a guest is willing to occupy an out-of-order room, management may choose to adjust its rate accordingly.

- Identify rooms pre-blocked for one of two days in the future and preregister guests arriving today who will depart in time to honor the blocks.

Front desk staff must be consistent when discussing the lack of accommodations with arriving guests.

- Guests may be encouraged to return to the hotel at the earliest date of availability. Upon their return, they may be placed on a VIP list, given a complimentary room upgrade, or presented with a small gift as compensation for the inconvenience of being turned away.

- Management should prepare a follow-up letter for guests who arrived with a reservation but could not be accommodated, apologizing again for the inconvenience and encouraging the guest to consider returning to the hotel (with appropriate incentives).

- If a member of a tour group cannot be accommodated, the tour organizer should be notified immediately and the situation explained.

- The hotel may pay the transportation expenses associated with having the guest travel to an alternate property. The hotel may also notify its telephone department of the change to another hotel so that incoming calls and faxes can be redirected without confusion or concern on the part of the caller or the relocated guest.

Apply Your Learning 7.3

Please write all answers on a separate sheet of paper.

1. How can a front desk agent upsell a guest to a higher rate category?

2. When can a hotel legally turn away a guest?

3. How can a front desk agent help a walk-in guest that must be turned away?

On a separate sheet of paper, write whether the following statements are true or false:

4. Due-outs are guests who are expected to check out today.

5. Management should avoid apologizing to guests who were turned away with a guaranteed reservation so that they are not sued.

6. Walk-in guests must always be accommodated if there are empty rooms, even if a reservation is holding it.

7. If a member of a tour group cannot be accommodated, the front desk agent or manager should contact the tour organizer.

7.4 Completing Registration

AFTER STUDYING SECTION 7.4, YOU SHOULD KNOW HOW TO:

♦ List the methods that a guest can use to settle a bill

♦ Handle registration for a guest planning to pay in cash

♦ Describe hotel policies regarding checks

♦ Verify the validity of a credit/debit card

♦ Post bills for guests with direct-bill accounts

♦ Outline special programs that guests may use to pay for a hotel stay

♦ Describe policies governing the issuing of a room key

♦ Complete registration procedures

Methods of Payment

The hotel must take precautionary measures to ensure payment. Effective account settlement depends on taking steps during registration to determine the guest's payment method. Common methods of room rate payment include: cash, personal checks, credit cards, direct billings, and special programs.

Cash

Some guests prefer to pay guestroom charges during registration. Guests who pay cash for their accommodations are typically not extended in-house credit. Revenue-producing outlets—for example, the gift shop and in-house restaurants—are usually given **paid-in-advance (PIA)** lists of cash-paying guests who are not authorized to have charge purchases posted to their guestroom accounts (also known as "no post" status). At check-in, front desk agents may electronically capture credit card information for a cash-paying guest or require them to leave an imprint of a credit card before extending in-house charge privileges.

A hotel that accepts cashier's checks, traveler's checks, and money orders should require proper guest identification. Compare the picture and signature on the guest's identification with the appearance and signature of the person offering the payment. If there is doubt, verify the payment with the issuing bank or agency.

Personal Checks

Some lodging properties allow transactions to be paid by personal check, while others have a strict policy against it. Hotels may have different check-cashing policies relating to payroll checks, personal checks written on out-of-state and foreign bank

U
N
D
E
R

T
H
E

G
A
V
E
L

Evicting Guests

Evictions are rare, but they do happen. Before making an eviction, a hotel manager should consult with the property's attorney. The local police also should be present at any eviction.

A hotel generally has the right to evict guests for the following reasons.

Violation of Hotel Regulations

The hotel has the right to evict any guest who willfully violates a hotel's reasonable regulations governing the conduct of its guests, assuming no discrimination is involved. Regulations can be designed to prevent immorality, drunkenness, or any form of willful misconduct that may offend other guests or bring the hotel into disrepute.

Failure to Pay the Hotel Bill

A hotel has the right to evict a guest who has failed to pay the hotel bill when due. Ordinarily, a hotel makes a demand upon the guest for the amount of the bill and requests him or her to leave by a certain time if the bill is not paid. If the guest still fails to pay, the hotel can evict.

Contraction of Contagious Disease

When a hotel guest is taken ill with a contagious disease, the proprietor, after notifying the guest to leave, has the right to remove such a guest in a careful manner and at an appropriate hour to a hospital or place of safety, provided this does not imperil the guest's life.

accounts, government checks, and second- and third-party checks.

Some hotels allow guests to cash personal checks if they have a credit card that provides a check-cashing guarantee, and as long as the amount of the check is within the credit card company's established credit limit. When this is the case, imprint the credit card onto the back of the guest's personal check. Other hotels accept personal checks only during banking hours, when the front office can verify the check, if nec-

essary. Some hotels allow guests to write personal checks for the amount of the guestroom only. When this is the case, cash or a credit card payment is required for all other purchases.

When accepting checks, front desk agents must ask for proper identification. Record the guest's driver's license number, address, and telephone number on the face of a personal check. In some hotels, the amounts and dates of cashed personal checks also are recorded on the guest's registration card; this helps ensure that guests do not exceed the property's established check-cashing limits.

If front office cashiers are not authorized to accept personal checks, they must be aware of what procedures to follow when a guest attempts to write a personal check. Properties can also protect themselves against bogus checks by following some basic guidelines:

- Do not refund cash if the original transaction was settled by personal check. If possible, return the guest's original personal check and, when appropriate, require an alternate form of payment. Some properties do not write a refund check, even if a refund is warranted, until the guest's bank verifies that the personal check in question has cleared.

- Accept personal checks written only on the current day. Do not accept undated or post-dated personal checks.

- Require that personal checks written to settle an account be made payable to the hotel, not to "Cash." When a guest is allowed to write a personal check to obtain cash, not to pay a bill, that check should be made out to "Cash." This practice may prevent a nonpaying guest from later claiming that a personal check made out to "Cash" was used as payment against his or her hotel account.

Exhibit 1 suggests further steps to follow when accepting checks. A front desk agent may use a personal check guarantee service by telephoning the service or using a small, desktop terminal. He or she provides data from the tendered check and the amount of the transaction. The check guarantee service, in turn, determines the check writer's credit history and either guarantees or denies payment.

Credit and Debit Cards

There are two types of magnetic stripe cards used for payment of guest charges. Credit cards are plastic cards with a magnetic stripe that are assigned a line of credit with the issuer of the card. When a charge is made against the card, it is applied to the cardholder's credit line. Debit cards are attached to a savings or checking account. When a charge is made, it immediately reduces the balance in the debit cardholder's account. There is no credit extended. Debit card charges can be rejected if there is not enough money to cover the charge.

The front office usually compiles a set of steps for processing credit and debit card transactions. In addition, card payment companies often require explicit procedures to ensure transaction settlement. As shown in Exhibit 2, credit card companies also provide helpful tips for avoiding fraud and implementing sound processing procedures. Local banks may also provide procedural guidelines.

Expiration Date. When a guest presents a credit or debit card, check the card's expiration date. If the card has expired, point this out to the guest and request an alternate method of payment. Credit card companies are not required to honor transactions made with an expired card.

On-Line Authorization. Most hotels validate cards through an online clearinghouse service. The credit card verification service consults an account database and generates either an **authorization code** or a **denial code** for the transaction.

Invalid Card. Front desk employees should follow established front office and card payment company procedures when

Exhibit 1
Suggested Steps for Accepting Checks

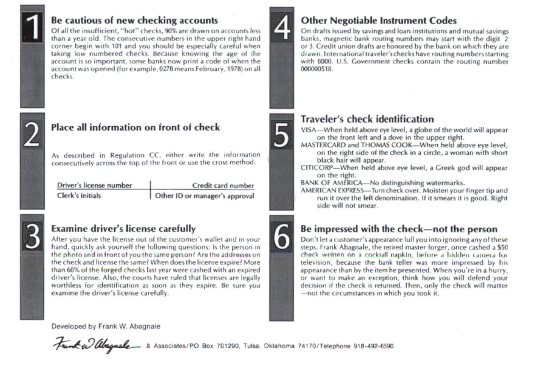

Steps to Follow when Accepting Checks

1 **Be cautious of new checking accounts**
Of all the insufficient, "hot" checks, 90% are drawn on accounts less than a year old. The consecutive numbers in the upper right hand corner begin with 101 and you should be especially careful when taking low numbered checks. Because knowing the age of the account is so important, some banks now print a code of when the account was opened (for example, 0278 means February, 1978) on all checks.

2 **Place all information on front of check**

As described in Regulation CC, either write the information consecutively across the top of the front or use the cross method.

Driver's license number	Credit card number
Clerk's initials	Other ID or manager's approval

3 **Examine driver's license carefully**
After you have the license out of the customer's wallet and in your hand, quickly ask yourself the following questions: Is the person in the photo and in front of you the same person? Are the addresses on the check and license the same? When does the license expire? More than 60% of the forged checks last year were cashed with an expired driver's license. Also, the courts have ruled that licenses are legally worthless for identification as soon as they expire. Be sure you examine the driver's license carefully.

4 **Other Negotiable Instrument Codes**
On drafts issued by savings and loan institutions and mutual savings banks, magnetic bank routing numbers may start with the digit 2 or 3. Credit union drafts are honored by the bank on which they are drawn. International traveler's checks have routing numbers starting with 8000. U.S. Government checks contain the routing number 000000518.

5 **Traveler's check identification**
VISA—When held above eye level, a globe of the world will appear on the front left and a dove in the upper right.
MASTERCARD and THOMAS COOK—When held above eye level, on the right side of the check in a circle, a woman with short black hair will appear.
CITICORP—When held above eye level, a Greek god will appear on the right.
BANK OF AMERICA—No distinguishing watermarks.
AMERICAN EXPRESS—Turn check over. Moisten your finger tip and run it over the left denomination. If it smears it is good. Right side will not smear.

6 **Be impressed with the check—not the person**
Don't let a customer's appearance lull you into ignoring any of these steps. Frank Abagnale, the retired master forger, once cashed a $50 check written on a cocktail napkin, before a hidden camera for television, because the bank teller was more impressed by his appearance than by the item he presented. When you're in a hurry, or want to make an exception, think how you will defend your decision if the check is returned. Then, only the check will matter —not the circumstances in which you took it.

Developed by Frank W. Abagnale

Frank W Abagnale & Associates/PO Box 701290, Tulsa, Oklahoma 74170/Telephone 918-492-6590

Courtesy of Frank W. Abagnale & Associates, Tulsa, Oklahoma

a card appears to be invalid. The card may appear to be invalid because it has been tampered with or the signature on the card does not match the signature on the hotel registration card. Normally, it is appropriate for staff to politely request an alternate form of payment. If the guest has no other acceptable means of payment, refer the situation to the front office credit manager or hotel general manager for resolution.

If a guest presents a card that appears invalid, the front desk agent might be advised to call hotel security. Although the federal government has made credit or debit card fraud a criminal offense, lodging properties should exercise care in detaining guests they suspect of theft or fraud. Such detention, especially if unjustified or improperly instituted, might expose the property to a lawsuit based on false imprisonment and slander.

Imprinting the Voucher. Although electronic verification and approval of credit and debit cards is becoming the industry standard, some hotels may not have online access to verification systems. In this case, front desk agents imprint valid cards onto approved card vouchers. Some

Exhibit 2
Tips from Credit Card Companies

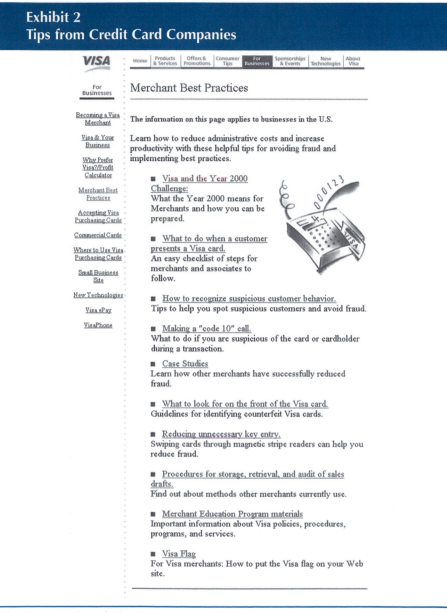

The Internet site of Visa International (http://www.visa.com) provides hotels with practical information to guide credit card processing procedures.

hotels require front desk agents to circle the card's expiration date and initial the validation number on the imprinted voucher as proof that procedures have been followed. The imprinted voucher is normally attached to the guest's registration card, to the guest folio, or placed in a voucher file for safekeeping. Usually, the guest is not asked to sign the voucher until account settlement or check-out time.

Exhibit 3
Suggestions for Resolving Credit Problems

When a credit card issuer refuses to authorize a transaction:

- Discuss the matter with the guest in private.
- Use care when describing the guest's unauthorized transaction (for example, do not call the guest's credit card "bad" or "worthless").
- Offer the use of a telephone to help resolve the matter with a credit card company representative.
- Allow the guest a chance to provide alternate, acceptable means of payment.

When a guest's personal check cannot be accepted:

- Explain the hotel's check cashing policy.
- Remain friendly and cooperative.
- Discuss alternative methods of payment with the guest.
- If local banks are open, direct the guest to a nearby branch, or extend the use of a telephone.
- Provide directions to the nearest ATM.

Direct Billing

Some hotels extend credit to guests by agreeing to bill the guest or the guest's company for charges. **Direct billing** arrangements are normally established through communication between the guest or company and the front office in advance of the guest's arrival. A list of approved direct billing accounts is usually maintained at the front desk for reference during registration. At check-out, a guest with approved credit simply signs his or her folio after approving its contents, and a statement is mailed for collection. The hotel assumes full responsibility for account collection.

Special Programs and Groups

During registration, guests may present vouchers, coupons, gift certificates, or special incentive awards received from businesses, airlines, or other authorized agencies. Front desk agents must be aware of hotel agreements to honor such items and know how to properly credit the bearer. Such documents may differ in value, conditions, or terms. Since vouchers represent a form of payment and may be the actual documents the front office uses to bill the issuing company, careful handling is warranted.

Group Registration

A group's coordinator or the front desk system can suppy front office staff with a rooming list that contains the names of members of an expected group. Registering group guests is different from registering individual guests. Guests attending corporate meetings often have their billing arrangements pre-established. In some cases, only the guest's room and tax charges are direct-billed to a group master account. Other charges—such as telephone, food, beverage, and laundry—may be the responsibility of individual guests. With a group master folio, credit for incidental charges may also need to be established for each member of the group. However, when the group agrees to pay for all of the charges made by its guests, it may not be necessary to estabish individual guest lines of credit. For example, VIPs or invited speakers for a group's meeting should sign a registration form and verify departure dates. In these cases, it may not be necessary to print the room rates on the registration form.

Denying a Credit Request

When a front desk agent discovers that a guest's credit has been denied by the issuing card comapny, he or she must exercise extreme care in notifying the guest of the problem. A person's credit involves more than money; it often involves self-esteem. In discussing problematic credit issues, be as diplomatic as possible. The agent's tone of voice should remain friendly and subdued, no matter how belligerent the guest may become. Exhibit 3 lists some suggested procedures for resolving credit problems.

Issuing the Room Key

By issuing a room key, the front desk agent completes the registration process. Guestroom key control policies should state who is authorized to issue keys, who re-ceives them, and where and how they are stored at the front desk. Nowadays, most room keys are actually keycards that are electronically coded at the front desk.

For security reasons, never announce the room number when handing a guestroom key to the guest. Instead, draw the guest's attention to the room number by writing it down or by pointing to the room on a hotel map.

If the hotel provides bell service, ask whether the guest would like assistance from a bellperson. If so, introduce the bellperson to the guest, hand the bellperson the guest's room key, and ask him or her to show the guest to the room. On the way to the room, the bellperson might explain the special features of the hotel and such things as restaurant locations, retail outlets' hours of operation, locations of ice and vending machines and emergency exits, emergency procedures, and other appropriate information. Once inside the guestroom, the bellperson can explain the features of the room, make the guest comfortable, answer any questions, and hand the key over. If the guest is displeased with the room, the bellperson should listen attentively and inform the front desk agent for immediate action.

Apply Your Learning 7.4

Please write all answers on a separate sheet of paper.

1. When can a hotel evict a guest?

2. What forms of payment are equivalent to cash?

3. How can a front desk agent verify the validity of a credit or debit card?

4. Which of the following is *not* a step in the procedure for verifying personal checks?

   a. Imprint a credit card onto the back of the personal check.
   b. Ask for proper identification.
   c. Require that personal checks be made out to "Cash" when settling an account.
   d. Call a check guarantee service.

7.5 Registration Computer Systems

AFTER STUDYING SECTION 7.5, YOU SHOULD KNOW HOW TO:

♦ Identify the features of a guest accounting computer module

♦ Create the following types of folios using the guest accounting module:

- Individual folios
- Master folios
- Non-guest folios
- Employee folios
- Control folios
- Semipermanent folios
- Permanent folios

♦ Describe the types of entries that can be made to accounts

Guest Accounting Module

The most critical component of a hotel front office system is the guest accounting module. This module is primarily responsible for online charge postings, automatic file updating (auditing) and maintenance, and folio display/printing on demand. In addition, guest accounting modules may provide electronic controls over such areas as folio handling, account balances, cashier reconciliation, food and beverage guest-check control, account auditing, and accounts receivable. Exhibit 1 shows the sequence of activities involved in the process of guest accounting.

Types of Accounts

Data elements needed to create a folio are referred to as header information. Common header elements include the guest name, address, e-mail address, folio number, and room number. If self-check-in terminals are available, guests may enter the necessary data themselves by responding to on-screen cues.

While not all hotel guest accounting modules offer the same folio formats, there are seven common types of **folios.**

Individual folios (also referred to as "room folios" or "guest folios") are assigned to in-house guests to chart their financial transactions with the hotel.

Master folios (or "group folios") generally apply to more than one guest or room and contain a record of transactions that are not posted to individual folios. Master

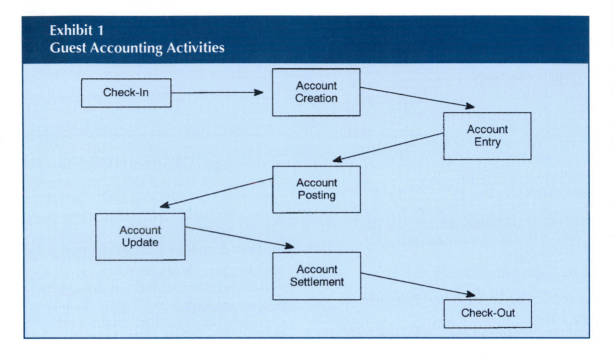

Exhibit 1
Guest Accounting Activities

folios are commonly created to provide the kind of billing service most groups and conventions require. For example, consider the needs of the International Gymnastics Conference. While attendees pay their own food and beverage expenses, the sponsoring organization pays all room charges. At checkout, each guest receives a folio documenting only the charges for which he or she is responsible, and the conference administrator receives the master folio containing the room charges.

Non-guest folios are created for individuals who have in-house charge privileges but are not registered as guests in the hotel, including health club members, corporate clients, special club members, political leaders, or local celebrities. Procedures for posting transactions to non-guest folios are similar to those required for online posting of transactions to individual folios. Instead of inputting a room number, the cashier, front desk

employee, or auditor inputs the designated account number.

When properties offer charge privileges to employees, transactions may be processed in a manner similar to non-guest accounts, using **employee folios** to record employee purchases, compute discounts, register expense account activity, and separate authorized business charges from personal expenditures.

Control folios may be created for each revenue center to track all transactions posted to other folios. They provide a basis for double-entry accounting and for crosschecking the balances of all electronic folios.

A **semipermanent folio** tracks "bill to" accounts receivable. A guest who establishes credit privileges before check-in may settle his or her folio balance by billing a sponsoring organization or individual. The hotel transfers the guest's folio balance to a semipermanent folio to track the billing and subsequent collection of payment from the approved third party (the "bill to" agency). Once the outstanding balance is paid, the semipermanent folio is closed and discarded.

A **permanent folio** is established for each entity with which the hotel has a contractual payment program. For example, a hotel could establish a permanent folio for each of the major credit card companies. When the guest charges a folio balance to an acceptable credit card, the guest accounting module transfers the balance to the appropriate permanent folio. Permanent folios exist as long as the hotel continues to maintain a business relationship with the entity.

Posting to Accounts

Account entries can be made from front desk terminals or from remote **POS** termi-nals that interface with the property management system (PMS). Account entries can also be made from within the guest accounting module itself. For example, during the system update routine, room charges and taxes may automatically be posted to all active guest folios.

After a room number (or account number) is entered, a guest accounting module may require that an identification code be entered. This is generally done by inputting the first few letters of the guest's last name. An **identification code** is used to post a charge when two separate accounts exist under the same room number.

Before a charge can be posted to a folio, the guest accounting module may also require that a **reference code** be entered. This is typically done by inputting the serial number of a departmental source document. Departmental **source documents** are usually numbered for internal-control purposes.

The final data entry requirement is the amount of the charge. However, before accepting a charge and posting it to a folio, the guest accounting module initiates a **credit monitoring routine.** This routine compares the current folio balance with a predetermined credit limit (also called a **house limit**) and it ensures that the outstanding balances do not exceed the account's credit limit.

Some PMS guest accounting modules allow guests to use their electronic keycards to make charges from remote POS terminals. If a guest presents a keycard for an unoccupied room, an account with a no-post status, or a guest account that already has been closed (settled), the system will not permit the cashier to post the charge.

Apply Your Learning 7.5

Please write all answers on a separate sheet of paper.

1. What types of folios can be used to post charges to guest accounts?

2. What information is needed to post an entry to an account?

Match the following types of folios with the person or account listed in questions 3–9.

Individual folios   Control folios
Master folios   Semipermanent folios
Non-guest folios   Permanent folios
Employee folios

3. Christine Conway is a front desk agent who is charging her lunch to her hotel account.

4. Receivables are posted to the Diner's Club account.

5. The mayor stops in to dine at the hotel restaurant and charges the meal to his account.

6. Jared Stroud checks out of the hotel and pays his bill.

7. The front desk agent bills the guest's business for her charges.

8. The night auditor opens this folio to crosscheck the balances of other folios.

9. The Faircity basketball coach pays for the room charges of everyone on the team.

Quick Hits

SECTION 7.1—THE REGISTRATION CYCLE

- Preregistration includes those registration activities that occur before the guest arrives at the property. Typically, that means producing a registration form, recording the room and rate assignment, and creating a guest folio, among other functions.

- **Registration forms** require a guest to provide name, address, telephone number, company affiliation (if appropriate), payment method, planned departure date, and room rate.

- Common law, as modified by federal, state, and local legislation and court decisions, still governs hotel and guest relationships in the United States.

- State or local laws often require hotels to maintain guest registers, records of the guest's name, address, and arrival and departure dates. Generally speaking, hotels should not divulge any information regarding a guest's registration without the written consent of the guest and the advice of hotel counsel.

SECTION 7.2—ROOM ASSIGNMENT

- The **occupancy report,** produced each night by a front desk agent, lists occupied rooms and indicates which guests are expected to check out the following day. The **housekeeping status report,** produced by the housekeeping department, is based on an actual physical check of each room.

- There are three common room rate schedules: the **American Plan** (a guestroom and three meals a day), the **Modified American Plan** (a guestroom and two meals a day), and the **European Plan** (guestroom and meals are charged separately).

- **Room rates** may also be based on the type of guest, including: commercial or corporate, complimentary, group, family, day, package plan, and frequent traveler.

- Differences between two guestrooms generally lie in their furnishings, amenities, and location. Front desk agents should be familiar with various guestroom configurations, as well as the hotel's floor plan, to satisfy guest rooming requests.

SECTION 7.3—SELLING AND TURNING AWAY

- **Upselling** refers to the efforts of reservations agents and front desk agents to convince guests to rent rooms in categories above standard rate accommodations. That means knowing how and when to ask for a sale in a non-pressuring way and how to direct the sale from the guest's perspective.

- A hotel may refuse to accommodate guests for a variety of reasons, including:

drunken or disorderly behavior, the presence of a contagious disease, inappropriate or dangerous belongings (such as an animal or firearms), an unwillingness or inability to pay for hotel services, and the lack of available accommodations.

- Hotels have no obligation to accommodate guests who arrive without a reservation when no rooms are available. Front desk agents can make the situation easier for the guest by suggesting and providing directions to alternate hotels nearby.

- If reservations are carefully handled and sound forecasting procedures are followed, a hotel should not have to deny accommodations to a guest with a guaranteed reservation. If it does happen, the front office manager should take charge and make necessary decisions.

SECTION 7.4—COMPLETING REGISTRATION

- Common methods of room rate payment include: cash, personal checks, credit or debit cards, direct billing, and special programs.

- To help prevent the acceptance of fraudulent credit or credit cards, front desk agents can check the card's expiration date, get online authorization, and process invalid cards according to the hotel's policy.

- Guestroom key control policies should state who is authorized to issue keys, who receives them, and where and how they are stored at the front desk. For security reasons, room numbers should not be announced when handing a key to a guest.

SECTION 7.5—REGISTRATION COMPUTER SYSTEMS

- The guest accounting module of the front office system is mainly responsible for online charge postings, automatic file updating and maintenance, and folio display/printing on demand.

- A variety of folio formats are available, including individual, master, non-guest, employee, control, semipermanent, and permanent.

- **Individual folios** are assigned to in-house guests to chart their financial transactions with the hotel.

- **Master folios** generally apply to more than one guest or room and contain a record of transactions that are not posted to individual folios. They are commonly created to provide the kind of billing service most groups and conventions require.

- **Non-guest folios** are created for individuals who have in-house charge privileges but are not registered as guests in the hotel—for example, health club members, corporate clients, special club members, political leaders, or local celebrities.

- **Employee folios** record employee purchases, compute discounts, register expense account activity, and separate authorized business charges from personal expenditures.

- **Control folios** may be created for each revenue center and used to track all transactions posted to other folios (individual, master, non-guest, or employee).

- A **semipermanent folio** is used to track "bill to" accounts receivable. Once the outstanding balance is paid, the semipermanent folio is closed and discarded.

- A **permanent folio** is established for each entity with which the hotel has a contractual payment program, such as credit card companies. Permanent folios exist as long as the hotel continues to maintain an ongoing business relationship with the entity.

- A module's **credit monitoring routine** compares the current folio balance with a predetermined credit limit (or **house limit**) set by management. It ensures that the outstanding balances during a guest's stay do not exceed the account's credit limit.

Profile

Joseph R. Kane, Jr., CHA
President & CEO, Days Inns Worldwide Inc.

Not many people know at the age of 16 what they want to do for the rest of their lives, but Joe Kane did.

"I'd read Arthur Hailey's novel *Hotel*, and it opened my eyes to a new exciting world," Kane says. "At 16, nothing seemed more glamorous than the chance to work at a hotel."

So Kane set out and found his first job at a small summer resort in New Hampshire, with 20 rooms and five housekeeping cottages.

While not exactly as glamorous as the New Orleans setting of *Hotel*, Kane loved the experience and worked every job—from raking the beach and landscaping to cleaning rooms and working the front desk.

"Getting to experience all aspects of hotel operations was invaluable, but the front desk was my favorite responsibility," Kane says. "From the very beginning, I loved interacting with guests."

Back at school, Kane asked his guidance counselor to help him investigate a career in hotel management.

"Back in the '60s, we didn't have resources like today that showed us the vast opportunities offered by our industry," Kane remembers. "But luckily, my counselor found a great book, *Your Future in Hotel Management* by Roger *Sonnabend of* Sonesta Hotels. This book also listed the few colleges in the U.S. that offered hotel management degrees."

After graduating from Paul Smiths College, Kane realized his aspirations when he became general manager of a 50-room hotel and conference center. At 28, he was elected the youngest president in the history of the Connecticut Lodging Association.

Over the next 35 years, Kane moved from GM, to area and regional managers, senior VP operations, and executive VP/COO.

Since 1996, Kane has led of the world's largest economy lodging franchise, Days Inns Worldwide, as its president and CEO, and will become chairman of American Hotel & Lodging Association in 2006.

"When I started out, all I ever wanted was to be an exceptional general manager," Kane says. "I had no idea just how many opportunities were available in this industry if you work hard, stay focused, and set goals. I've met exciting people—from celebrities to U.S. presidents—whose paths would not have crossed with mine, if not for the lodging business."

Check-Out and Settlement

Sections

8.1 Overview of Check-Out

AFTER STUDYING SECTION 8.1, YOU SHOULD KNOW HOW TO:

♦ Resolve outstanding account balances

♦ Update room status

♦ Create a guest history record

♦ List departure procedures

The front office performs at least three important functions during the check-out and settlement process before the guest departs:

• It resolves outstanding guest account balances.

• It updates room status information.

• It creates guest history records.

Guest Account Balances

Guest account settlement depends on an effective front office accounting system that maintains accurate guest folios, verifies and authorizes a method of settlement, and resolves discrepancies in account balances. Generally, the front office finds it most effective to settle a guest's account while the guest is still in the hotel.

A guest can settle an account by paying cash, charging the balance to a credit or debit card, deferring payment to an approved direct billing entity, or using a combination of payment methods.

Pre-settlement verification activities ensure that the hotel will be paid for the accommodations and services it provided during the guest's stay. When these verification activities are completed during check-in, they help minimize the guest's check-out time and may significantly improve the front office's ability to collect outstanding account balances.

Room Status Update

Effective front office operations depend on accurate room status information. When a guest checks out and settles his or her account, the front desk agent performs several important tasks. First, the agent changes the guestroom's status from *occupied* to *on-change* in the room status file. *On-change* is a housekeeping term that means that the guest has checked out of the hotel and that the room needs to be cleaned for the next guest. After making the room status change, the front office system may automatically notify the housekeeping department that the guest has departed. Some front office systems will also remind housekeeping of any equipment to be removed from a guestroom.

Guest History

Check-out and settlement also involve the creation of the *guest history record* that will become part of the *guest history file.* Since a hotel can gain a valuable competitive edge in the hospitality marketplace through the proper analysis of guest history data, guest history files can provide a powerful database for strategic marketing.

Front office management can better understand its clientele and determine guest trends when it develops and maintains a **guest history file.** This automated file is a collection of personal and financial data about guests who have stayed at the hotel or another property in a chain hotel company. An individual **guest history record** within the file normally contains personal and transactional information relevant to the guest's previous stays.

Many front offices use a computer-based system that automatically re-formats guest information into a guest history database. Automated front office systems can apply a pre-formatted template to automatically generate a guest history record.

Departure Procedures

Check-out and account settlement can be an efficient process when the front office is well-prepared and organized. The departure stage of the guest cycle involves serveral procedures designed to simplify check-out and account settlement. These procedures include:

- Inquiring about additional recent charges
- Posting outstanding charges

- Verifying account information
- Presenting the guest folio
- Verifying the method of payment
- Processing the account payment
- Checking for mail, messages, and faxes
- Checking for safe deposit box or in-room safe keys
- Securing the room key
- Updating the room's status
- Asking about the guest's stay and experience
- Asking the guest to complete a guest satisfaction survey

The procedures used will vary among front office operations. The amount of personal contact between the guest and front desk staff also varies as guests elect self-check-out.

A guest approaching the front desk should be greeted promptly and courteously. The front desk agent should check for any messages, faxes, or mail awaiting guest pickup. The front desk agent should also verify that the guest has cleared his or her safe deposit box or in-room safe and returned the guestroom key.

To ensure that the guest's folio is accurate and complete, the front desk agent should process any outstanding charges that need posting. In addition, the front desk agent should ask the guest if he or she incurred any recent charges and update the necessary postings to the guest's folio. Guests expect folios to be accurate and ready when they approach the front desk to check out. The guest may leave with a poor impression of the property if the bill is not up-to-date and accurate at check out.

Traditionally, at check-out the guest is presented a final copy of his or her account folio for review and settlement. During this time, the front desk agent should confirm how the guest intends to settle the account, regardless of which method of settlement the guest specified during the registration process. VIP guests or special guests of a group or corporate account should not be asked for settlement if their account is marked as a direct billing account.

After determining how the guest will pay, the front desk agent should then bring the guest's account balance to zero. This is typically called **zeroing out** the account. A guest's account balance must be settled in full for an account to be considered zeroed out.

Apply Your Learning 8.1

Please write all answers on a separate sheet of paper.

1. How could room status updates affect the property?

2. What is the purpose of a guest history file?

3. When is a guest account balance considered zeroed out?

4. Name four front office check-out procedures.

5. It is most effective to settle a guest's account:

    a. during pre-settlement verification activities.
    b. while the guest is still in the hotel.
    c. after each charge is posted to the guest folio.
    d. after the room status is updated.

6. In order for the housekeeping department to know a room is ready to be cleaned, the guestroom status should be changed to:

    a. non-occupied.
    b. on-change.
    c. ready.
    d. vacated.

8.2 *Settling Accounts*

AFTER STUDYING SECTION 8.2, YOU SHOULD KNOW HOW TO:

♦ Accept cash payment for a bill

♦ Transfer credit card payments

♦ Settle a direct-bill account

♦ Combine settlement methods to serve guests

A guest account can be brought to a zero balance in several ways. Methods of settlement include:

- Cash payment
- Credit or debit card
- Direct billing
- Combined settlement method

Cash Payment

A cash payment in full at check-out will bring a guest account balance to zero and be marked paid. If a guest had a credit card imprinted at registration, even though he or she intended to settle the account by cash, the front desk agent should then destroy the guest's credit card voucher.

Debit card settlements are considered cash payments because the funds are drawn directly from the guest's checking or savings account. Banks issuing debit cards will nto process a withdrawal transaction unless there is enough money in the account at the time of the transaction. Therefore, the hotel is assured of payment by the bank. Even though the guest's folio is brought to a zero balance, the amount due the hotel is normally transferred from the guest ledger to the city ledger until final payment is received.

Guests paying in foreign currency should first convert their money. Hotels often charge a fee to convert currencies, since banks charge hotels fees for currency conversion. Most front desks of major hotels display currency conversion rates for major countries, or have the rates readily available through the business section of newspapers or online resources.

Credit or Debit Card

Even though credit card settlement brings a guest account to zero, the amount of the charge must be tracked until payment is actually received from the credit card company. Therefore, credit card settlement creates a transfer credit on the guest's folio and moves the account balance from the guest ledger to a credit card account in the **city** (or non-guest) **ledger.**

After the front desk agent swipes the card through a credit card reader, a payment slip is printed showing the transaction amount. The credit card slip is then presented to the guest for signatures. In many hotels, the guest may be asked to sign a copy of the folio acknowledging and agreeing to the credit card balance instead of receiving a payment slip to sign. In many locations, imprinting vouchers is no longer necessary because the hotel front office system sends the settlement transaction directly to the credit card company. Hotels do not have to worry about currency exchange rates or fees when foreign guests present credit cards for payment because the credit card company always provides payment in local currency.

Direct Billing

Direct billing transfers a guest's account balance from the guest ledger to the city ledger. Responsibility for billing and collecting a direct billing lies with the hotel. Direct billings are not normally an acceptable method of settlement unless the billing has been pre-arranged and approved by the hotel's credit department before or during guest registration. To complete a direct billing settlement, the front desk agent should have the guest sign the folio to verify that its contents are correct and that the guest accepts responsibility for all charges contained on the folio (in case the direct billing account refuses payment).

Combined Settlement Methods

A guest may elect to use more than one settlement method to bring the folio balance to zero. For example, the guest may make a partial cash payment and charge the remainder of the account balance to an acceptable credit card. Front desk agents must accurately record the combined settlement methods and take care that all required paperwork is properly completed. Properly completed paperwork will help facilitate an effective front office audit. Once the guest has settled the account, the front desk agent should provide the guest with a copy of the folio.

Apply Your Learning 8.2

Please write all answers on a separate sheet of paper.

1. Name the four types of account settlement.

2. What is the difference between a credit card transfer and a direct billing transfer?

3. What is the process for guests who wish to pay in foreign currency?

4. A credit card settlement creates a _____ on the guest's folio.

   a. debit
   b. credit
   c. transfer debit
   d. transfer credit

5. Direct billings must be arranged and approved by the hotel's _____ before or during guest registration.

   a. front desk agent
   b. accounting department
   c. owner or general manager
   d. credit department

8.3 Check-Out Options

AFTER STUDYING SECTION 8.3, YOU SHOULD KNOW HOW TO:

♦ Explain why hotels may charge late check-out fees

♦ Describe express check-out options

♦ Describe self check-out procedures

Late Check-Out

Guests do not always check out by the hotel's posted check-out time. To minimize **late check-outs,** the front office should post check-out time notices in conspicuous places, such as on the back of all guestroom doors and in a prominent location at the front desk. A reminder of the check-out time can also be included in any pre-departure materials distributed to guests expected to depart on the current day. Late check-outs can be a problem for some resorts. Guests may wish to stay the full day and use the recreational facilities of the resort, including their room. It is important to properly communicate and tactfully enforce the check-out time in order to prepare the room for arriving guests.

Some hotels authorize the front desk to charge **late check-out fees.** A guest will probably be surprised to find such a fee on a folio, especially if he or she is not familiar with the hotel's check-out policy. Whenever a guest calls the front desk inquiring about a late check-out, the front desk agent should inform the guest about the hotel's policy regarding late check-out charges.

The hotel's check-out time is carefully selected and is not intended to inconvenience guests. Because guestrooms should be cleaned and readied for arriving guests before the housekeeping staff completes its workshift, management establishes a check-out time so sufficient time exists to prepare the rooms. For this reason, the hotel may feel justified in assessing a late check-out fee.

Express Check-Out

Guests may encounter long lines at the front desk when trying to check out between 7:30 A.M. and 9:30 A.M., a prime check-out period for many hotels. To ease front desk volume, some front offices initiate check-out activities before the guest is ready to leave. A common pre-departure activity involves producing and distributing guest folios to guests expected to check out. Front office staff, housekeeping staff, or even hotel security staff may quietly slip printed folios under the guestroom doors of expected check-outs before 6 A.M. Folios must be placed under guestroom doors so they cannot be seen or reached from outside the room.

Normally, the front office will distribute an **express check-out** form with each pre-departure folio. Express check-out

Exhibit 1
Self Check-Out Terminal

Courtesy of Hyatt Hotels Corporation

forms may include a note requesting that guests notify the front desk if departure plans change. Otherwise, the front office will assume the guest is leaving by the hotel's posted check-out time. This procedure usually reminds and encourages guests to notify the front desk of any changes in departure before the hotel's check-out time.

By completing such a form, the guest authorizes the front office to transfer his or her outstanding folio balance to the credit or debit card voucher that was created during registration. Once completed, the guest deposits the express check-out form at the front desk when departing. After the guest has left, the front office completes the guest's check-out by transferring the outstanding guest folio balance to a previously authorized method of settlement. Any ad-

ditional charges the guest makes before leaving the hotel (telephone calls, for example) will be added to his or her folio before the front desk agent brings the account to a zero balance via account transfer. When late charges are added to the account, a copy of the updated folio is mailed to the guest so that he or she has an accurate record of the stay.

Self Check-Out

In some hotels, guests can check themselves out of the hotel by accessing **self check-out terminals** (see Exhibit 1) in the lobby area or by using an in-room system (see Exhibit 2). Self check-out terminals and in-room systems are interfaced with the front office system and are intended to reduce both check-out time and front desk traffic.

To use a self check-out terminal, the guest accesses the proper folio and reviews its contents. Guests may be required to enter a credit or debit card number by using a keypad or by passing a card through a magnetic strip reader attached to the terminal. Settlement can be automatically assigned to an acceptable credit or debit card. Check-out is complete when the guest's balance is transferred to a credit or debit card account and an itemized account statement is printed and dispensed to the guest. A self check-out system should then automatically communicate updated room status information to the front office computer. The front office system, in turn, relays room status information to the housekeeping department and initiates action to create a guest history record.

In-room folio review and check-out usually relies on an in-room television set with a remote control device. The guest can confirm a previously approved method of

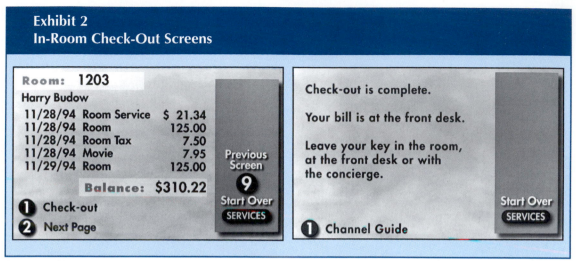

Exhibit 2
In-Room Check-Out Screens

Room: 1203

Harry Budow

11/28/94	Room Service	$ 21.34
11/28/94	Room	125.00
11/28/94	Room Tax	7.50
11/28/94	Movie	7.95
11/29/94	Room	125.00

Balance: $310.22

❶ Check-out

❷ Next Page

Previous Screen

9

Start Over

SERVICES

Check-out is complete.

Your bill is at the front desk.

Leave your key in the room, at the front desk or with the concierge.

❶ Channel Guide

Start Over

SERVICES

Courtesy of SpectraVision, Richardson, Texas

settlement for the account since the in-room television is connected via computer to the front office computer system. The front office computer directs the self check-out process. Generally, guests can pick up a copy of their printed folio copy at the front desk after completing self check-out. In-room self check-out technology usually automatically updates room status and creates guest history records.

Many guests carry mobile handheld devices or personal digital assistants (PDAs). Some hotel companies and front office system suppliers feature self check-out capabilities through these devices. Guests are able to access their account on their PDA through a secure Internet link. They can view their folio and approve payment, all online. The final billing is sent to the guest by e-mail or instant messenger.

Apply Your Learning 8.3

Please write all answers on a separate sheet of paper.

1. Why might hotels charge a late check-out fee?

2. What is the purpose of using express check-out?

3. What express check-out options are available?

4. What happens to additional guest charges that appear after the guest has checked out?

5. Explain the importance of a check-out time.

6. In order to use a self check-out terminal, you must settle your guest folio with:

   a. cash.
   b. a credit card.
   c. the front desk.
   d. self check-out forms.

7. Guests who choose to use express check-out procedures typically do so to avoid:

   a. paying late check-out fees.
   b. paying phone charges.
   c. last-minute charges.
   d. long lines during peak hours.

8.4 Internal Control

AFTER STUDYING SECTION 8.4, YOU SHOULD KNOW HOW TO:

♦ List the steps involved in internal control

♦ Describe procedures for cash banks

♦ Explain why hotels audit financial records

Internal control in the front office involves:

• Tracking transaction documentation

• Verifying account entries and balances

• Identifying vulnerabilities in the accounting system

Auditing is the process of verifying front office accounting records for accuracy and completeness. Each financial interaction produces paperwork which documents the nature and dollar amount of the transaction. For example, when a guest charges a meal to his or her individual folio. This transaction will likely be supported by the restaurant's guest check, cash register recording, and charge voucher. The charge voucher is prepared in the revenue center and sent to the front office as notification of the transaction.

Cash Banks

A primary set of front office accounting control procedures involves front office cashier banks. A **cash bank** is an amount of cash assigned to a cashier to handle the transactions that occur during a particular workshift. Good control procedures typically require that cashiers sign for their bank at the beginning of their workshift and that only the person who signed for the bank have access to it during the shift. At the end of a workshift, each front office cashier is solely responsible for depositing all cash, checks, and other negotiable instruments received during the workshift and ensuring that the bank is restored to the bank limit amount.

At the end of the shift, the cashier typically separates the amount of the initial bank, and then places the remaining cash, checks, and other negotiable items (such as paid-out vouchers) in a cash voucher or front office cash envelope. The cashier normally itemizes and records the contents of the front office cash envelope on the outside of the envelope before dropping it into the front office vault. From an internal control perspective, at least one other employee should witness this procedure and both employees should sign a log attesting the drop was actually done and stating the time of the drop.

Monetary differences between the money placed in the front office cash envelope and the cashier's net cash receipts should be noted on the envelope as overages or shortages. **Net cash receipts** are the amount of cash, checks, and other negotiable items in the cashier's drawer, minus the amount of the initial cash bank, plus the paid-outs.

For example, assume the front office cashier began the workshift with a $175 cash bank. During the shift, the cashier made paid-outs totaling $49. At the end of the workshift, the amount of cash, checks, and other negotiable items in the cash drawer totals $952. To determine the amount of net cash receipts, the front office cashier would first add together the value of the cash, checks, and other negotiable items in the cash drawer ($952). The cashier would next subtract the value of the initial cash bank ($175). By adding the amount of paid-outs ($49), the front office cashier will arrive at a net cash receipt position ($826):

$$\$952 - \$175 + \$49 = \$826$$

An **overage** occurs when, after the initial bank is removed, the total of the cash, checks, negotiables, and paid-outs in the cash drawer is greater than the net cash receipts. A **shortage** occurs when the total of the contents of the drawer is less than the net cash receipts. Neither an overage nor a shortage is typically considered "good" by front office management when evaluating the job performance of front office cashiers.

A **due back** occurs when a cashier pays out more than he or she receives; in other words, there is not enough cash in the drawer to restore the inital bank. Due backs do not reflect positively or negatively on the cashier's job performance, and may occur when net cash receipts are in or out of balance. Front office due backs are normally replaced with small bills and coins before the cashier's next workshift.

Audit Controls

A number of front office audit controls ensure that front office staff properly handle cash, guest accounts, and non-guest accounts. Publicly held lodging companies are required to have both their front and back office accounting records audited yearly by independent certified public accountants. In addition, companies with several lodging properties often employ internal auditors to make unannounced visits to individual properties for the purpose of auditing accounting records. In both instances, a report is completed for management and ownership review.

Apply Your Learning 8.4

Please write all answers on a separate sheet of paper.
Match the following words with their definitions:

cash bank	shortage
net cash receipts	due back
overage	

1. When the total of the cash, checks, negotiables, and paid-outs is greater than net cash receipts.

2. When the total of the cash, checks, negotiables, and paid-outs is less than net cash receipts.

3. The amount of cash assigned to a cashier during a particular workshift.

4. When a cashier pays out more than he or she receives.

5. The amount of cash, checks, and negotiables in the cashier's drawer, minus the initial cash bank, plus the paid-outs.

8.5 Evaluating Operations

AFTER STUDYING SECTION 8.5, YOU SHOULD KNOW HOW TO:

◆ Complete a daily operations report

◆ Calculate occupancy ratios

◆ Analyze room revenue

◆ Interpret rooms division budget reports

◆ Calculate operating ratios

Evaluating the results of front office operations is an important management function. Without thoroughly evaluating the results of operations, managers will not know whether the front office is attaining planned goals. Successful front office managers evaluate the results of department activities on a daily, monthly, quarterly, and yearly basis. This section examines important tools that front office managers can use to evaluate the success of front office operations. These tools include:

- Daily operations report

- Occupancy ratios

- Revenue management

- Rooms division budget reports

- Operating ratios and ratio standards

Daily Operations Report

The **daily operations report,** also known as the *manager's report,* the *daily report,* and the *daily revenue report,* contains a summary of the hotel's financial activities during a 24-hour period. The daily operations report provides a means of reconciling cash, bank accounts, revenue, and accounts receivable. The report also serves as a posting reference for various accounting journals and provides important data that must be input to link front and back office functions. Daily operations reports are uniquely structured to meet the needs of individual hotel properties.

Exhibit 1 presents a sample daily operations report for a hotel with food and beverage service. Rooms statistics and occupancy ratios form an entire section of a typical daily operations report. Enriched by comments and observations from the

Hitchcock's Dream Hotel

Kitsap County, Washington, was originally called Slaughter County, and the first hotel there was called the Slaughter House.

Exhibit 1
Sample Daily Operations Report

DAILY REVENUE REPORT

Day _____ Of _____   Day _____ Date _____ Year _____

Hotel _____

Completed By: _____

OCCUPANCY SUMMARY	ACTUAL TODAY	%	MONTH TO-DATE	%
SGL Rooms Occupied				
DBL Rooms Occupied				
COMP Rooms Occupied				
TOTAL Rooms Occupied				
O.O.O. Rooms				
Vacant				
TOTAL Available Rooms	100%		100%	
House Use				
TOTAL Hotel Rooms				
AVG House Rate (Inc. Comps & Perms)	$		$	
AVG Trans Rate (Excl. Comp & Perms)	$		$	
TOTAL # GUESTS				
Relocated				
Room Sales Efficiency				
TOTAL ROOMS OCCUPIED				
Forecast				
Budget				

REVENUE SUMMARY	TODAY	MTD	BUDGET MONTH END
Net Rooms			
Food			
Beverage			
Banquet Other			
Long Distance			
Local			
Laundry / Valet			
Garage			
Gift Shop			
Health Club			
Pro Shop (Merchandise)			
Golf Fees			
Tennis Fees			
TOTAL HOTEL			

ROOMS REVENUE ANALYSIS

Type	TODAY # Rooms	%	Ave. Rate	Revenue	MONTH-TO-DATE # Rooms	%	Ave. Rate	Revenue
Rack								
Corporate								
Guaranteed Corporate								
Preferred								
Weekend Rate								
Packages								
Government / Military								
Other								
Total Non Group								
Group								
Total Transient								
Permanents								
Complimentary								
Total		100%				100%		
Club Floor								
Club Express								
RSVP								
Breakations								

COMPLIMENTARY ROOMS

Guest Name	Room No	Company	Check In Date	Check Out Date	Authorized By

(continued)

Exhibit 1
(continued)

FOOD & BEVERAGE ANALYSIS

Outlet		Revenue (TODAY)	# Covers (TODAY)	Ave. Check (TODAY)	Revenue (MONTH-TO-DATE)	# Covers (MONTH-TO-DATE)	Ave. Check (MONTH-TO-DATE)
Room Service	Food						
	Food						
	Food						
	Food						
	Food						
	Food						
	Food						
Banquet	Food						
	Total Food						
Room Service	Bev.						
	Bev.						
	Bev.						
	Bev.						
	Bev.						
	Bev.						
	Bev.						
	Bev.						
	Bev.						
Banquet	Bev.						
	Total Bev.						
Total Food & Bev.							
Room Rental							
Customer Sev. Inc.							
Miscellaneous							
Total Food & Bev. Dept.							

GROUP ANALYSIS

Group	# Rooms	# Guests	Avg. Rate	Revenue
TOTAL				

MARKET SEGMENTS — MONTH-TO-DATE

Group	# Rooms	Avg. Rate	Revenue
National Assoc.			
Reg & State Assoc.			
Corporate			
Incentive			
SMERFE			
Tour & Travel			
Total Group			

ARRIVALS

	YESTERDAY	TODAY	ACTUAL MTD
6 PM Resv.			
Guaranteed Resv.			
Walk-ins			
Same Day Cancellations			
6 PM No Show			
Guaranteed No Show			
Relocated			
Total Actual Arrivals			

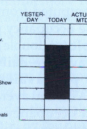

OUT OF ORDER ROOMS

Room No.	Reason	Number of Nights O.O.O.

DEPARTURES

	YESTERDAY	TODAY	ACTUAL MTD
Expected			
Unexpected			
Stayovers			
Total Actual Departures			

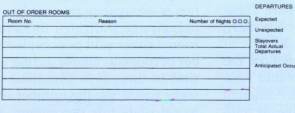

Anticipated Occupancy Tonight _____ %

The RevPAR for the Gregory Hotel is calculated as follows:

$$\text{RevPAR} = \frac{\text{Actual Room Revenue}}{\text{Number of Rooms Available}}$$

$$= \frac{\$6,960}{120}$$

$$= \underline{\$58}$$

Average Rate per Guest. Resort hotels, in particular, are often interested in knowing the average room rate per guest (ARG). This rate is normally based on every guest in the hotel, including children.

The average rate per guest for the Gregory Hotel is calculated as follows:

$$\text{Average Rate per Guest} = \frac{\text{Rooms Revenue}}{\text{Number of Guests}}$$

$$= \frac{\$6,960}{95}$$

$$= \underline{\$73.26}$$

Revenue Management

Front office staff are expected to sell rooms at the rack rate unless a guest qualifies for an authorized discounted room rate. A **room rate variance report** lists those rooms that have been sold at other than their rack rates. With this report, front office management can review the use of various special rates to determine whether staff have followed all appropriate front office policies and procedures. Automated front office systems can be programmed to routinely generate a room rate variance report.

Yield Statistic. One way for front office managers to evaluate the effectiveness of the front office staff in selling rooms is to look at the **yield statistic,** which is actual rooms revenue as a percentage of potential rooms revenue. Potential rooms revenue is the amount of revenue that can be generated if all the rooms in the hotel are sold at rack rates on a given day, week, month, or year. The potential revenue for the Gregory Hotel is $11,760 (if all 120 rooms sold at the rack rate of $98). Given actual rooms revenue of $6,960, the yield statistic for the Gregory Hotel can be calculated as follows:

$$\text{Yield Statistic} = \frac{\text{Actual Rooms Revenue}}{\text{Potential Rooms Revenue}}$$

$$= \frac{\$6,960}{\$11,760}$$

$$= .5918 \text{ or } \underline{59.18\%}$$

This result reveals that, for the day in question, actual rooms revenue was 59.18 percent of the amount that could have been generated if all 120 rooms had been sold at the full rack rate of $98.

Rooms Division Budget Reports

Generally, the hotel's accounting division also prepares monthly budget reports that compare actual revenue and expense figures with budgeted amounts. These reports can provide timely information for evaluating front office operations. Front office performance is often judged according to how favorably the rooms division's monthly income and expense figures compare with budgeted amounts.

A typical budget report format should include both monthly variances and year-to-date variances for all budget items. Front office managers are more likely to focus on the monthly variances since year-to-date variances merely represent the accumulation of monthly variances. Exhibit 2 presents a **rooms division budget report** for the Gregory Hotel for the month of January. This budget report does not yet contain year-to-date figures since January is the first month of the business year for this particular hotel. It is important to note that Exhibit 2 presents both dollar and percentage variances. The dollar variances indicate the difference between actual results and budgeted amounts. Dollar variances are generally considered either favorable or unfavorable as follows:

	Favorable Variance	Unfavorable Variance
Revenue	Actual exceeds budget	Budget exceeds actual
Expenses	Budget exceeds actual	Actual exceeds budget

For example, the actual amount of salaries and wages for rooms division personnel in the month of January was $20,826, while the budgeted amount for salaries and wages was $18,821, resulting in an unfavorable variance of $2,005. This dollar variance is bracketed to indicate that it is unfavorable. However, if the revenue variance is very favorable, an unfavorable variance in expenses (such as in payroll) is not necessarily negative. The comparative variance may merely indicate the greater expense associated with serving more guests than were anticipated when the budget was created. One way to verify whether a variance is really unfavorable or favorable is to divide the actual rooms occupied for the period into the actual cost and budgeted cost. If the actual cost is at or below the budgeted cost per room, the variance is actually positive, even though there was more expense.

Percentage variances are determined by dividing the dollar variance by the budgeted amount. For example, the 7.61 percent variance for net revenue shown in Exhibit 2 is the result of dividing the dollar variance figure of $11,023 by the budgeted net revenue amount of $144,780.

The budget report shows both dollar and percentage variances because dollar variances alone or percentage variances alone may not indicate the significance of the variances reported. For example, dollar variances fail to show the magnitude of change from the budgeted base. The monthly budget report for the front office of a large hotel may show that actual net revenue varied from the budgeted amount by $1,000. This may seem to be a significant variance, but if the $1,000 is based on a budgeted amount of $500,000, it represents a percentage difference of only 0.2 percent. Most front office managers would not consider this a significant variance. However, if the budget amount for the period was $10,000, a $1,000 dollar variance would represent a 10 percent variance, an amount most front office managers would consider significant.

Percentage variances alone can also be deceiving. For example, assume that the budgeted amount for an expense item is $10, and the actual expense was $12. The dollar variance of $2 represents a percentage variance of 20 percent. While this percentage difference appears significant, front office management's effort to investigate a $2 variance may not be productive.

The fact that actual results of front office operations differ from budgeted amounts on a budget report shouldn't be surprising. Any budgeting process, no matter how sophisticated, is unlikely to be perfect. Front office managers should not analyze every variance. Only significant variances require management analysis and action.

Exhibit 2
Sample Monthly Rooms Division Budget Report

Gregory Hotel
Budget Report—Rooms Division
For January 20XX

	Actual	Budget	Variances $	%
Revenue				
Room Sales	$156,240	$145,080	$11,160	7.69%
Allowances	437	300	(137)	(45.67)
Net Revenue	155,803	144,780	11,023	7.61
Expenses				
Salaries and Wages	20,826	18,821	(2,005)	(10.65)
Employee Benefits	4,015	5,791	1,776	30.67
Total Payroll and Related Expenses	24,841	24,612	(229)	(0.93)
Other Expenses				
Commissions	437	752	315	41.89
Contract Cleaning	921	873	(48)	(5.50)
Guest Transportation	1,750	1,200	(550)	(45.83)
Laundry and Dry Cleaning	1,218	975	(243)	(24.92)
Linen	1,906	1,875	(31)	(1.65)
Operating Supplies	1,937	1,348	(589)	(43.69)
Reservation Expenses	1,734	2,012	278	13.82
Uniforms	374	292	(82)	(28.08)
Other Operating Expenses	515	672	157	23.36
Total Other Expenses	10,792	9,999	(793)	(7.93)
Total Expenses	35,633	34,611	(1,022)	(2.95)
Departmental Income	$120,170	$110,169	$10,001	9.08%

Operating Ratios

Operating ratios assist managers in evaluating the success of front office operations, and should be compared against proper standards—budgeted percentages, for example. Because payroll and related expenses tend to be the largest single expense item for the rooms division (as well as the largest for the entire hotel), any significant differences between actual and budgeted labor cost percentages must be carefully investigated. Dividing the payroll and related expenses of the rooms division by the division's net room revenue yields one of the most frequently analyzed areas of front office operations—labor cost. For control purposes, labor costs are analyzed on a departmental basis.

Ratio Standards

Operating ratios are meaningful only when compared against useful criteria such as:

- Planned ratio goals
- Corresponding historical ratios
- Industry averages

Ratios are best compared against planned ratio goals. For example, a front office manager may more effectively control labor and related expenses by projecting a goal for the current month's labor cost percentage that is slightly lower than the previous month's. The expectation of a lower labor cost percentage may reflect the front office manager's efforts to improve scheduling procedures and other factors related to the cost of labor. By comparing the actual labor cost percentage with the planned goal, the manager can measure the success of his or her efforts to control labor costs.

Industry averages may also provide a useful standard against which to compare operating ratios. These industry averages can be found in publications prepared by the national accounting firms and trade associations serving the hospitality industry.

Experienced front office managers realize that operating ratios are only indicators; they do not solve problems or necessarily reveal the source of a problem. At best, when ratios vary significantly from planned goals, previous results, or industry averages, they indicate that problems may exist. Considerably more analysis and investigation are usually necessary to determine appropriate corrective actions.

Apply Your Learning 8.5

Please write all answers on a separate sheet of paper.

1. What is a daily operations report?

2. What information does a rooms division budget report provide?

Match the occupancy ratios listed below to their corresponding formula:

occupancy percentage
multiple (or double) occupancy ratio
average daily rate

revenue per available room
average rate per guest

3. $$\frac{\text{number of rooms occupied by more than one guest}}{\text{number of rooms occupied}}$$

4. $$\frac{\text{rooms revenue}}{\text{number of rooms sold}}$$

5. $\dfrac{\text{rooms revenue}}{\text{number of guests}}$

6. $\dfrac{\text{number of rooms occupied}}{\text{number of rooms available}}$

7. $\dfrac{\text{actual room revenue}}{\text{number of available rooms}}$

Quick Hits

SECTION 8.1—OVERVIEW OF CHECK-OUT

- Guest account settlement depends on an effective front office accounting system that maintains accurate guest folios, verifies and authorizes settlement methods, and resolves discrepancies in account balances.

- After the guest has checked out, room status update information should be exchanged quickly and accurately between the front office and housekeeping departments. The change in room status goes from occupied to on-change, which means the room is ready to be cleaned.

- After verifying and authorizing a payment settlement method, the front desk agent should bring the account balance to zero. This is known as **zeroing out** the account.

- **Guest history files,** a collection of personal and financial data about previous guests, are compiled from individual **guest history records.** This information can be used to provide better guest service as well as provide the hotel a powerful database for strategic marketing.

SECTION 8.2—SETTLING ACCOUNTS

- Cash payments, credit and debit card transfers, direct billing transfers, and combined settlement methods are all acceptable ways of bringing the guest account to a zero balance.

- Even though credit card settlement brings a guest account to zero, the charge amount must be tracked until payment is actually received from the credit card company.

- Direct billings are not normally an acceptable method of settlement unless the billing has been arranged by the hotel's credit department before or during guest registration. Responsibility for billing and collecting a direct billing lies with the hotel.

- When a guest elects to use one or more settlement methods to pay his bill, it is referred to as a combined settlement method.

SECTION 8.3—CHECK-OUT OPTIONS

- A variety of check-out options exist for guests including late check-out, express check-out, and self-check-out.

- **Late check-outs** occur when guests do not depart by the hotel's posted check-out time. Some hotels authorize the front desk to charge **late check-out fees** to justify the inconvenience of delaying the housekeeping staff.

- To avoid long lines at the front desk when checking out, guests can choose to use **express check-out.** This is accomplished by authorizing a credit card payment during registration.

- Self check-out allows guests to check themselves out of the hotel by accessing **self check-out terminals** in the lobby area or by using an in-room system. The terminals allow guests to input their credit card information and receive a printed account statement for their records.

SECTION 8.4—INTERNAL CONTROL

- Internal control involves tracking transaction documentation, verifying account entries and balances, and identifying vulnerabilities in the accounting system. Proper cash handling procedures and controls must be established, implemented, and enforced.

- **Cash banks** provide a cashier with an assigned amount of cash so that he or she can handle the various transactions that occur during a particular workshift. Good control procedures require that cashiers sign for their bank at the beginning of the shift, are the only employee to have access to it during the shift, and are responsible for all deposits at the end of the shift.

- Hotels audit financial controls to assure that front office staff properly handle cash, guest accounts, and non-guest accounts.

SECTION 8.5—EVALUATING OPERATIONS

- Evaluating the results of front office operations is an important management function to be sure the front office is attaining planned goals. The tools management uses to evaluate the success of front office operations include: daily operations reports, occupancy ratios, rooms revenue analysis, rooms division budget reports, and operating ratios and standards.

- **Daily operations reports** contain a summary of the hotel's financial activities during a 24-hour period. They provide a means of reconciling cash, bank accounts, revenue, and accounts receivable.

- **Occupancy ratios** measure the success of the front office in selling guestrooms. The ratios include **occupancy percentage, multiple** (or double) **occupancy ratio, average daily rate, revenue per available room (RevPAR),** and **average rate per guest.**

- A rooms revenue analysis utilizes a **room rate variance report** that lists rooms that have been sold at other than rack rates. Front office management uses this report to review the use of various special rates to determine whether staff followed all appropriate policies and procedures.

- The **rooms division budget reports** compare actual revenue and expense figures with budgeted amounts. Front office performance is often judged according to how favorable the rooms divisions' monthly income and expense figures compare with budgeted amounts.

- Operating ratios, consisting of payroll and related expenses, should be compared against budgeted percentages. Any significant differences between actual and budgeted percentages must be carefully investigated since payroll and related expenses represent the largest single expense category.

Profile

Bob Winston
CEO of Winston Hotels, Inc.

Most kids can't stand the thought of washing dishes. But for Bob Winston, getting his arms soaked in a sink of dirty plates is one of his fondest childhood memories.

Winston always loved to serve customers—no matter how down and dirty it got. So, it comes as no surprise that Winston, president/CEO of REIT Winston Hotels Inc., started a hospitality company.

He got his first taste of the business as a youngster growing up in Raleigh, North Carolina—the city where he still lives and works. His parents ran a popular North Carolina steak house called Angus Barn.

"I spent a lot of nights in the [restaurant] office watching TV while my mom and dad worked. When an employee didn't show up, my brother and I ended up in the kitchen filling in. I loved it."

Winston, who helped out with odd jobs from the time he was 9 or 10, really started working at the restaurant as a janitor as a teenager. "I always loved working. Through my parents, I learned how to take pride in serving customers and doing things right. That was ingrained in us as children."

Although he loved the restaurant business, the 36-year-old executive decided early on he was better suited to the hotel industry. Right out of college Winston took a job in equity sales. After a couple of years, he went to work for Promus Hotel Corp. in Memphis. He started out in the sales department at a new Hampton Inn in Raleigh. He moved up to night auditor and then assistant manager at a Hampton Inn in Greensboro.

Right from the start, he knew the Hampton Inn concept was a winner. Yet, he was itching to be his own boss. So, in 1991, he started his own Hampton Inn. A couple of years later, his new company, Winston Hospitality, started construction on a Homewood Suites.

Winston's father was growing a hotel company with nine hotels. Winston approached his father about merging the two companies. His father agreed and they went public in 1994.

The company now owns 47 hotels, under a variety of mid-market and high-end extended-stay flags.

Excerpted with permission from Lodging, *May 1998, the management magazine of the American Hotel & Motel Association.*

The Front Office Audit

Sections

9.2 *Discovery and Correction*

AFTER STUDYING SECTION 9.2, YOU SHOULD KNOW HOW TO:

♦ Complete outstanding postings

♦ Reconcile room status discrepancies

♦ Balance departmental revenue

♦ Verify room rates

♦ Verify no-show reservations

One of the primary functions of the front office audit is to ensure that all transactions affecting guest and non-guest accounts are posted to appropriate folios. Posting errors are problematic and can lead to discrepancies and delays at check-out. This can prove time-consuming since the debated charges will have to be researched for explanation.

Audit Posting Formula

 The steps in the audit routine are based on the following basic **account posting formula:**

Previous Balance + Debits − Credits = Net Outstanding Balance
    PB   + DR   − CR   =   NOB

Complete Outstanding Postings

While effective front office practice dictates that transactions be posted to the proper accounts as they occur, the front office auditor must confirm that all transactions received at the front desk have been posted before starting the audit routine. This may mean waiting until all food and beverage outlets are closed. Incomplete postings will result in errors in account balancing and complicate summary reporting.

The front office auditor also verifies that all vouchers for revenue center transactions are posted. If the hotel does not have an interfaced computerized telephone call accounting system, outstanding telephone charges may require manual posting. If the hotel supports point-of-sale or call accounting systems interfaces to the front office accounting system, then the previously posted totals should be verified to ensure that all outlet charges have been posted. This can be done by generating printed posting reports and comparing them with the totals reported by the front office accounting system. If the figures are identical, the systems are in balance. If they are not the same, the front office auditor begins to compare transactions between the two systems to identify the transactions that have been omitted or improperly posted.

Reconcile Room Status Discrepancies

Room status discrepancies must be resolved in a timely manner since imbalances can cause confusion in the front office which can lead to lost business, lost and uncollectible room revenues, and omissions in postings. The front office must maintain current and accurate room status information to effectively determine the number and types of rooms available for sale. For example, if the front desk agent fails to properly complete the check-out procedure, the guest's vacant room may actually appear occupied. This procedural error could prevent the room from being rented until the error is discovered and corrected.

The front office auditor compares the daily housekeeper's report with the system's room status report. If the housekeeping report indicates that a room is vacant, but the front office believes it is occupied, the auditor should search for an active electronic folio and registration card. If the folio exists and has a current outstanding balance, there are several possibilities:

- A guest may have departed but forgotten to check out.

- A guest may be a skipper who left with no intention of checking out.

- The folio may have been improperly closed at check-out.

After verifying that the guest has left the hotel, the night auditor should process the check-out and set the folio aside for front office management review and follow-up. If the folio has been settled, the front office room status system should be corrected to show that the room is vacant. The night auditor should verify the guest folio against the housekeeping and the room status reports to ensure that all three are consistent and in balance. The check-out process is normally linked to a rooms management function that automatically monitors and updates the room's status.

Few, if any, room status discrepancies should occur in a computerized front office system, but the night audit process is still necessary to ensure accuracy.

Verify Room Rates

This step is usually done at the same time as reconciling the room status because they are both part of the bucket check and it is more efficient to perform both simultaneously. The front office auditor will review a system-generated room report. This report provides a means for analyzing room revenue since it shows the rack rate (price) for each room and the actual rate at which the room was sold. If a room's rack and actual rates do not match, the front office auditor should consider several factors:

- If the room is occupied by a member of a group or by a corporate-rate customer, is the discounted rate correct?

- If the room is occupied by a guest

- If there is only one guest in a room and the actual rate is approximately half the rack rate, is the guest part of a shared reservation? If he or she is, did the second guest register?

- If the room is complimentary, is there appropriate supporting back-up for the rate (for example, a complimentary room authorization form)?

This verification is usually done by comparing the registration form to the front office system record. The registration form provides a snapshot of the guest's information, including room rate, at the time of check-in. Any changes made to the guest's record would come during or after check-in, resulting in changes from the original record. The proper use of room revenue and

---

Exhibit 1
Departmental Balancing Sequence

1. Sort vouchers by originating departments.
2. Consider each department's vouchers.
   a) Separate the correction vouchers according to the departments they are to be applied against.
   b) Total the corrections for each department.
3. After verifying each of the corrections with the departments affected, total the correction vouchers. The corrections total must coincide with the correction figures on the front office shift report.
4. Consider the vouchers again.
   a) Total the rest of the outstanding vouchers.
   b) Check individual transaction values on the bottom of the voucher against the figure appearing on the department detail report.
5. The vouchers should agree with the corrected figures of the departments. If the totals do not agree with either figure, the error should be resolved before proceeding.
   a) Verify that the date on the voucher is the current day's date.
   b) Check off each individual posting against its support document (voucher) until the error is found. This can be tedious if there are several errors. However, if the front office uses validating printers, a thorough check of the support document validations will help pinpoint errors.
   c) Post any additional corrections or adjustments.
6. In a computerized system, revised individual shift reports can be printed after the corrections and adjustments have been made. In any operations mode, all of the backup data should be packaged for the accounting office to review.

---

count information form the foundation for room revenue analysis. The front office auditor may be required to produce this report for review by front office management.

Balance All Departmental Accounts

The front office audit process can become quite complicated when errors are discovered. The front office auditor typically balances all revenue center departments using source documents that originated in the revenue center. The front office auditor seeks to balance all front office accounts against departmental transaction information. Vouchers received at the front desk and other docu-

ments are totaled and compared with revenue center summaries. Source documents help resolve discrepancies as they arrive.

When the front office accounting system is out of balance, the correctness and thoroughness of account postings must be investigated. A detailed department audit (by shift or by cashier) may be conducted and individual postings reviewed until the front office accounting error is corrected. It is generally considered more efficient to balance all departments first and then look for individual posting errors within an out-of-balance department.

The process used to balance the revenue center departments is often called the **trial balance.** The trial balance is a test of the front office accounts to see whether they are in balance before the final audit is completed. The front office system may generate the trial balance before initiating final audit reports. The trial balance usually uncovers any corrections or adjustments that need to be made during the audit process. Front office auditors often perform the trial balance before the system posts room and tax charges. Doing so can simplify the final audit procedure. If the trial balance was correct and the final balance is wrong, the auditor can deduce that the error must relate to the room and tax posting.

It is important to note that a mathematical balance in guest and non-guest accounts against departmental totals does not necessarily mean that the proper accounts were selected for posting. Posting the correct amount to an incorrect account would still present an in-balance total. This type of error usually goes unnoticed until a guest has a problem with an entry on his or her statement.

Verify No-Show Reservations

The front office auditor may also be responsible for clearing the reservation file and posting charges to no-show accounts. When initiating the electronic posting of no-show charges, the front office auditor must be careful to verify that the reservation was guaranteed and the guest never registered with the hotel. Sometimes duplicate reservations may be made for a guest or the guest's name may be misspelled and another record accidentally created by the front office staff. If these are not identified by front office or reservations staff, the guest may actually arrive but appear to be a no-show under the second reservation.

No-show billings must be handled with extreme care. A front desk agent who does not record cancellations properly may cause clients to be billed incorrectly. Incorrect billing may lead the credit card company to reevaluate its legal agreements and relationship with the hotel and may also cause the hotel to lose the guest's future business and (if applicable) the business of the travel agency that guaranteed the reservation. All front office staff must adhere to established no-show procedures when handling reservation cancellations or modifications.

Apply Your Learning 9.2

Please write all answers on a separate sheet of paper.

1. What is the basic account posting formula?
2. How are outstanding postings completed?
3. How can room status discrepancies lead to lost business?
4. What is a trial balance and what is it used for?
5. What happens when the front office accounting system is out of balance?

6. If a room's rack and actual rates don't match, what factors should the night auditor consider?

7. What may be the possible causes of a no-show reservation?

8. Why must no-show billings be handled with extreme care?

9.3 Preparation for Next Day

AFTER STUDYING SECTION 9.3, YOU SHOULD KNOW HOW TO

♦ Post room rates and taxes

♦ Prepare required reports

♦ Prepare a cash deposit

♦ Back up the system

♦ Distribute reports

Post Room Rates and Taxes

The automatic **posting** of room rates and taxes to guest folios typically takes place at the end of the day. Once posted, a room rate and tax report may be generated for front office management review.

Once the front office initiates room rate postings, the system is capable of auto-posting rates and taxes to the appro-priate electronic folios in a matter of minutes. System postings are highly reliabile since automatic charge postings are guaranteed to be accurate, with no chance for pickup, tax calculation, or posting errors. This feature is especially helpful to hotels in municipalities that have bed or occupancy taxes in addition to a sales tax. Some hotels pre-set their front office systems to post daily recurring charges, such as valt parking or gratuities. Auto-posting these charges can save front office audit time and improve accuracy.

Prepare Required Reports

The front office auditor typically prepares reports that indicate the status of front office activities and operations. Among those prepared for management review are the final department detail and summary reports, the daily operations report, the high balance report, and other reports specific to the property.

Final department detail and summary reports are produced and filed along with

Class of '42

In 1921, the National Cash Register Company (NCR) took the hotel industry's first step toward the automated front desk: The Class 2000 mechanical posting machine. It became the "sweetheart of front desk accounting." The NCR 42 followed in 1955 and eventually was used in more than 90 percent of all hotels. It simplified jobs for the posting clerk and night auditor who could now keep a running tab of accounts.

their source documents for accounting division review. These reports help prove that all transactions were properly posted and accounted for.

The daily operations report summarizes the day's business and provides insight into revenues, receivables, operating statistics, and cash transactions related to the front office. The high balance report identifies guests whose charges are approaching an account credit limit designated by the hotel (the house limit).

In a front office system, the software may be programmed to produce many reports on demand. For example, the high balance report may be produced at any time during th eday. Another important report is the daily summary, or flash report. The daily summary provides a snapshot of important operating statistics for the previous day, as well as month-to-date totals. The daily summary may also show an occupancy and rate forecast for the new business day, alerting management to any changes that may have happened overnight.

A group sales report shows each group in the hotel, the number of rooms occupied by each group, the number of guests for each group, and the revenue generated by each group. This report helps the hotel sales department with the group history. The same type of report may also be generated for guests staying in the hotel due to a special promotion or advertising program. Other reports may list frequent guests or VIPs. This type of marketing information can be automatically tracked, sorted, and reported.

Deposit Cash

The front office auditor frequently prepares a cash deposit voucher as part of the audit process. If front office cash receipts have not yet been deposited in a bank, the front office auditor compares the postings of cash payments and paid-outs (net cash receipts) with actual cash on hand. A copy of the front office cashier shift report may be included in the cash deposit envelope to support any overage, shortage, or due back balances. Since account and departmental balancing often involve cash transactions, accurate cash depositing may depend on an effective audit process.

Clear or Back Up the System

Front office accounting depends on the continuous functioning of the computer system. Back-up reports must be run and various media duplicated in a timely manner so that the front office can continue to run smoothly should the computer become inoperable.

Normally, at least two guest lists are printed for back-up and emergency use: one for the front desk and one for the switchboard. A printed **room status report** enables front desk agents to identify vacant and ready rooms should the front office system become inoperable. A guest ledger report, such as the report shown in Exhibit 1, contains the opening and closing account balances for all registered guests.

A front office activity report can also be generated that contains expected arrival, stayover, and departure information for several days. In some front office systems, the next day's registration cards are pre-printed as part of the front office activity report. Due to requirements of the

Exhibit 1
Guest Ledger Report

Lodgistix Resort & Conference Center (90003)

Preliminary Audit Report—July 12—Guest Ledger Balances

Status	Open Balance	Room/ Tax	Incdntl	Food	Beverage	Payment	Close Balance
Canceled-Keep	.00	.00	.00	.00	.00	220.00–	220.00–
Canceled-Return	.00	.00	.00	.00	.00	165.00–	165.00–
No Show	480.00–	.00	.00	.00	.00	.00	480.00–
Checked-out	312.31+	104.55+	.00	.00	.00	104.55–	312.31+
Registered	5485.36+	2441.23+	58.36+	311.31+	21.62+	1440.00–	6877.88+
House Accounts	.00	.00	8.40+	.00	.00	.00	8.40+
Group Master Accounts	.00	.00	15.00+	14.00+	21.00+	.00	50.00+
Total Guest Ledger	5317.67+	2545.78+	81.76+	325.31+	42.62+	1929.55–	6383.59+

Courtesy of Sulcus, Phoenix, Arizona

Americans with Disabilities Act, hotels must also keep track of guests with disabilities. One reason for this is to ensure that they are accounted for in case of an emergency.

System-generated front office information should be copied (backed up) onto magnetic, optical, or other media, depending on the system configuration. A system back-up should be conducted after each night audit and stored in a safe place.

Distribute Reports

The distribution of audit reports is the final step in the nigt audit routine and is important to efficient front office operations. Due to the sensitive and confidential nature of front office information, the front office auditor must promptly deliver appropriate reports to authorized individuals. Informed managerial decisions can be made if all audit reports are completed accurately and delivered on time.

Apply Your Learning 9.3

Please write all answers on a separate sheet of paper.

1. Why must hotels keep track of guests with disabilities?

2. Why is it important to conduct system back-ups after each night audit?

3. When are room rates and taxes typically posted to guest folios?

The night auditor prepares reports that indicate the status of front office activities and operations. For statements 4–10, match each management request with the necessary report.

Final department detail and
    summary reports
Daily operations report
High balance report

Group report
Rooms status report
Guest ledger report
Front office activity report

4. "Give me a summary of the day's business."

5. "Which of our guests are approaching the house limit?"

6. "Show me the opening and closing account balances for all registered guests."

7. "Prove to me that all transactions were properly posted and accounted for."

8. "Tell me how many arrivals and stayovers are expected in the next three days."

9. "Which rooms are ready for sale?"

10. "Which groups are staying in the hotel and how many rooms are they using?"

Quick Hits

SECTION 9.1—THE FRONT OFFICE AUDIT

- The front office audit is concerned with the following functions: verifying posted entries to guest and non-guest accounts, balancing all front office accounts, resolving room status and rate discrepancies, monitoring guest credit limits, and producing operational and managerial reports.

- The **front office auditor** prepares daily summaries of all front office financial transactions, tracks standard operating statistics, and reports results to front office management.

- The front office audit focuses on two areas: the discovery and correction of front office accounting errors and the creation of accounting and management reports.

- The following steps are common to the sequence of an audit: complete outstanding postings, reconcile room status discrepancies, verify room rates, balance departmental revenue, verify no-show reservations, prepare required reports, deposit cash, clear or back up the system, and distribute reports.

SECTION 9.2—DISCOVERY AND CORRECTION

- The basic account posting formula is previous balance + debits – credits = net outstanding balance.

- The first step of the audit is to complete all outstanding postings and verify that all vouchers for revenue center transactions are posted. The front office auditor must confirm that all transactions received at the front desk have been posted before starting the audit routine.

- The front office auditor compares the daily housekeeper's report with the room status report of the system. Any discrepancies must be resolved in a timely manner since imbalances can cause confusion in the front office which can lead to lost business.

- The process used to balance the revenue center departments is often called the **trial balance.** The front office auditor completes the trial balance before verifying the final system balance and creating final front office audit reports. The trial balance usually uncovers any corrections or adjustments that need to be made during the audit process.

- A room revenue and count report verifies room rates and provides a means for analyzing room revenues.

- In posting no-show charges, the front office auditor must be careful to verify that the reservation was guaranteed and the guest never registered.

SECTION 9.3—PREPARATION FOR NEXT DAY

- In order to prepare for the next day, the front office auditor typically posts room rates and taxes, prepares required reports, deposits cash, clears or backs up the system, and distributes reports.

- Reports are prepared which indicate the status of front office activities and operations. These reports include the final department detail and summary reports, the daily operations report, the high balance report, and other reports specific to the property.

- A **room status report** enables front desk agents to identify vacant and ready rooms should the system become inoperable.

- A system back-up, including back-up reports, must be run so that the front office can continue to run smoothly if the system becomes inoperable.

- The distribution of front office audit reports is the final step in the audit routine and is important to efficient front office operations.

Nothing sends a stronger message than cleanliness in a hospitality operation. No level of service, friendliness, or glamour can equal the sensation a guest has upon entering a spotless, organized, tidy, and conveniently arranged room.

To send this message of quality, housekeeping must have the same professionalism as other hospitality functions. Managers must systematically achieve the standards expected by guests in today's lodging and food service establishments.

This unit is an excellent resource for students who are either interested in becoming an executive housekeeper or professional who makes housekeeping decisions on a daily basis—which includes any rooms manager or general manager. It also provides important technical information for students seeking careers in this pivotal area.

The unit covers the day-to-day complexities of the housekeeping profession—from planning and organizing to inventorying, supervising, and performing the work itself.

In some of the chapters, there are reprints from the bimonthly newsletter *The Rooms Chronicle*. *The Rooms Chronicle* was created to provide an interesting, educational tool to help department managers be better at their jobs and thus improve the hotel's profits while giving consistent, higher quality service to the guest. The articles were written by managers in the industry about issues they have faced and problems they have solved. The articles were reprinted with permission from *The Rooms Chronicle*.

Unit

3

Housekeeping

Profile

Aleta Nitschke
Founder, The Rooms Chronicle

Aleta Nitschke began her career as a maid in a resort on Lake Erie. She eventually traded her dustmop and housekeeping cart for such positions as payroll clerk, front desk manager, executive housekeeper, and then corporate rooms director for Radisson Hotels.

"That's the good thing about the industry," Nitschke said. "You can kind of hop in and make your way around." Nitschke worked at 13 different hotels in 10 different cities, "You really do have to move to move up."

Now a recognized expert on rooms management, she is the founder of *The Rooms Chronicle,* a bimonthly newsletter focusing on the rooms division. In 2003, Nitschke handed the journal over to Niagra University and Dr. William Frye, CHE.

"The housekeeping department is about taking care of the asset," Nitschke said. She points out that the executive housekeeper manages people of many different backgrounds and interacts with all hotel departments.

"The lovely thing about working in housekeeping is that each day has a beginning and an end, which the front office does not have. A great housekeeping department has a feeling of 'family.' It's a wonderful environment. If I were going back to work in a hotel, I would choose housekeeping."

Because executive housekeepers must interact with all departments, they must learn to carry themselves as managers. Nitschke said that one of her first general managers helped her move away from the line employee mentality. "He really taught me how to be a manager: how to lead meetings, how to talk to employees, how to guide employees to achieve high standards. I think he loved the hotel industry and wanted to see all his managers learn the business and be successful."

Nitschke observed the changes that have taken place in the industry: "When I think about the business when I began, it's amazing how different it is. Today's technology has the potential to move us away from taking care of guests. We stare at the computer screen, worry about the printer working, or analyze every database we can create. We need to work extra hard to remember that the reason we're working in a hotel is to take care of the guest."

Housekeeping Management

Sections

10.1 The Housekeeping Department

AFTER STUDYING SECTION 10.1, YOU SHOULD KNOW HOW TO:

♦ Explain the importance of the housekeeping department

♦ Identify typical cleaning responsibilities for the housekeeping department

The cleanliness, maintenance, and aesthetic appeal of lodging properties depend on efficiently managed housekeeping departments. The housekeeping department not only prepares clean guestrooms for arriving guests, it cleans and maintains everything in the hotel so the property is as attractive and inviting as the day it opened for business.

To continually work that minor miracle, the housekeeping department employs more employees than any other hotel department—including room attendants; department managers; employees assigned to clean public spaces, back-of-the-house areas, meeting and banquet rooms; and employees working in the laundry and linen rooms. The tasks they perform are critical to the smooth daily operation of a hotel.

Housekeeping works most closely with the front office department, specifically the front desk. Front desk agents cannot assign guestrooms until those rooms have been cleaned, inspected, and released by the housekeeping department.

The executive housekeeper uses available resources to reach the goals set by top management executives. Resources include people, money, time, work methods, materials, energy, and equipment. These resources are in limited supply, and most executive housekeepers will readily admit that they rarely have all the resources they would like. An important part of the job, then, is planning how to make the best use of the limited resources available.

Housekeeping Responsibilities

Most housekeeping departments are responsible for cleaning:

• Guestrooms

• Corridors

• Public areas, including the lobby and public restrooms

• Pool and patio areas

• Management offices

• Storage areas

• Linen and sewing rooms

- Laundry room
- Back-of-the-house areas, such as employee locker rooms

Housekeeping departments at mid-range and world-class hotels are generally responsible for additional areas, including:

- Meeting rooms
- Dining rooms
- Banquet rooms
- Convention exhibit halls
- Hotel-operated shops
- Game rooms
- Exercise rooms

When it comes to the food and beverage areas, housekeeping's cleaning responsibilities vary from property to property. In most hotels, housekeeping has very limited responsibilities in relation to cleaning areas for food preparation, production, and storage; the special cleaning and sanitation tasks required for maintaining these areas are usually carried out by kitchen staff under the supervision of the chief steward. In some properties, the dining room staff cleans service areas after breakfast and lunch periods; housekeeping's night cleaning crew does the in-depth cleaning after dinner service or early in the morning before the dining room opens for business.

Similarly, the banquet or convention staff generally sets up banquet and meeting rooms and is responsible for some cleaning after the rooms are used; the in-depth cleaning is left to the housekeeping crew. The final responsibility for the cleanliness and overall appearance of these areas falls squarely on the shoulders of the housekeeping staff.

Balancing Responsibilities Between Departments

The general manager typically designates which areas housekeeping will clean. If areas of responsibility cross department lines, the managers of those departments must get together and develop a solution. Their decision is then reported to the general manager for approval. A good housekeeping manager can effectively

"So who are the Gideons and why'd they put this book in here?"

Gideons International, a nonprofit organization, distributes more than 45 million Bibles and New Testaments annually. The group began on July 1, 1899, when businessmen John Nicholson and Samuel Hill met with friend Will Knights to form a group that would bring Christian businesspeople together and evangelize. Among the suggestions that day: place Bibles in hotels so everyone seeking spiritual comfort could find it.

One hundred years later, a Fodor's survey of American travelers noted that 23 percent of those surveyed read the Gideon's Bible in their hotel room. "I've seen many with passages underlined and notes written in the margins," says Jack Vaughn, president of the Opryland Lodging Group in Nashville, Tennessee. "When they get too frayed, the Gideons replace them for free."

solve problems with other managers, thereby relieving the general manager of day-to-day, operational problems.

The executive housekeeper should obtain a floor plan of the hotel and highlight those areas for which housekeeping isresponsible. Different colors can be used to designate those areas for which other departments are responsible. To ensure that all areas of the property have been covered— and to avoid future misunderstandings about responsibilities—copies of this color-coded floor plan should be distributed to the general manager and to all department managers. Everyone will see at a glance who is responsible for cleaning each area in the hotel. The color-coded floor plan also presents a clear and impressive picture of the housekeeping department's significant role in cleaning and maintaining the hotel.

Apply Your Learning 10.1

Please write all answers on a separate sheet of paper.

1. What is the ultimate goal of the housekeeping department?

2. With which other department does the housekeeping department work most closely?

3. What major areas of a hotel is the housekeeping department typically responsible for cleaning?

4. Who is the ultimate decision maker when there are disputes regarding cleaning responsibilities?

10.2 *Planning*

AFTER STUDYING SECTION 10.2, YOU SHOULD KNOW HOW TO:

♦ Create an inventory list of work to be performed

♦ Create a frequency schedule

♦ Develop performance standards

♦ Implement productivity standards

Planning focuses on analyzing the work required for cleaning and maintaining each area. It is probably the executive housekeeper's most important management function. Without competent planning, every day may present one crisis after another.

Since the housekeeping department is responsible for cleaning and maintaining so many different areas of the hotel, a systematic, step-by-step approach to planning is essential to keep the executive housekeeper from becoming overwhelmed. It also helps to ensure that the work is done correctly, efficiently, on time, and with the least cost to the department.

Exhibit 1 shows how the executive housekeeper can plan the work of the department.

Area Inventory Lists

Planning the work of the housekeeping department begins with creating **inventory lists** of all items within each area that need housekeeping's attention. The lists are bound to be long and extremely detailed. Since most properties offer several different types of guestrooms, separate inventory lists may be needed for each room type.

When preparing a guestroom area inventory list, follow the sequence in which room attendants will clean items and in which supervisors will inspect items. This enables the executive housekeeper to use the inventory lists as the basis for developing cleaning procedures, training plans, and inspection checklists. For example, items within a guestroom may appear on an inventory list as they are found from right to left and from top to bottom around the room. Other systematic techniques may be used, but the point is that *some* system should be followed—and this system should be the same one used by room attendants and inspectors in the daily course of their duties.

Frequency Schedules

Frequency schedules indicate how often items on inventory lists are to be cleaned or maintained. Items that must be cleaned daily or weekly become part of a routine cleaning cycle and are incorporated into standard work procedures. Other items are inspected daily or weekly, but they become

---

Exhibit 1
Basic Planning Activities

INITIAL PLANNING QUESTIONS	RESULTING DOCUMENTS
1. What items within this area must be cleaned or maintained?	Area Inventory List
2. How often must the items within this area be cleaned or maintained?	Frequency Schedules
3. What must be done in order to clean or maintain the major items within this area?	Performance Standards
4. How long should it take an employee to perform an assigned task according to the department's performance standards?	Productivity Standards
5. What amounts of equipment and supplies will be needed in order for the housekeeping staff to meet performance and productivity standards?	Inventory Levels

---

part of a **deep cleaning** program and are scheduled as special cleaning projects. Exhibit 2 presents a sample frequency schedule for light fixtures found in a public area of a large convention hotel.

Tasks that become part of housekeeping's deep cleaning program should be transferred to a calendar plan and scheduled as special cleaning projects. The calendar plan guides the executive housekeeper in scheduling the appropriate staff to perform the necessary work. Whenever possible, days marked for guestroom deep cleaning should coincide with low occupancy periods. Also, the deep cleaning program must be flexible in relation to the activities of other departments. If maintenance schedules extensive repair work for several guestrooms, the executive housekeeper should make every effort to coordinate a deep cleaning of these rooms with maintenance's timetable.

Performance Standards

Standards are required quality levels of performance. **Performance standards** state not only *what* must be done; they also describe in detail *how* the job must be done.

One of the main objectives of planning the work of the housekeeping department is to ensure that all employees do their jobs consistently. The keys to consistency are the performance standards that the executive housekeeper develops, communicates, and manages. When performance standards are not properly developed, effectively communicated, and consistently managed, the department's productivity suffers.

The most important aspect of developing standards—which may well vary from one property to another—is gaining

Exhibit 2
Sample Frequency Schedule

PUBLIC AREA #2—LIGHT FIXTURES

LOCATION	TYPE	NO.	FREQ.
Entrance #1	Sconce	2	1/W
Lobby	Chandelier	3	1/M
Entrance #2	Crown Sconce	2	1/M
Behind Fountain	Sconce	3	1/W
Catwalk	Pole Light	32	1/M
Lower Level	Pole Light	16	1/M
Fountain Area	Pole Light	5	1/M
Restaurant Courtyard	Pole Light	10	1/M
Restaurant Courtyard	Wall Light	5	1/M
Restaurant Patio	Half-Pole Light	16	1/W
Restaurant Entrance	White Globe Pole Light	6	1/W
Crystal Gazebo	White Globe Pole Light	8	1/W
2nd Stairs to Catwalk	White Globe Pole Light	2	1/W
Fountain	White Globe Pole Light	4	1/W
Lounge Patio	Wall Light	4	1/W
Restaurant Entrance	Chandelier	1	1/W

consensus on how tasks are to be carried out. One important consensus-building action is to seek input from the people who actually perform the tasks. Workers are much more likely to accept and implement standards which they helped to develop.

Well-written standards are useless unless they are applied. Performance standards must be communicated through ongoing training programs.

The executive housekeeper must also manage those standards. Managing standards means ensuring conformity to standards by inspection. Experienced housekeepers know the truth of the adage "You can't expect what you don't inspect." Daily inspections and periodic performance evaluations should be followed by specific on-the-job coaching and retraining. The executive housekeeper should review the department's performance standards at least once a year and make appropriate revisions as new work methods are implemented.

Productivity Standards

While performance standards establish the expected quality of the work to be done, **productivity standards** determine the acceptable quantity of work to be done. An executive housekeeper begins to establish productivity standards by answering the question, "How long should it take a housekeeping

the ROOMS CHRONICLE

The Housekeeping Dilemma: Are We Measuring the Right Stuff?
by Janet Jungclaus

How does hospitality fit in an industrial–age framework? Such a complex question, but the answer is simple: IT DOESN'T. Let's take a look at why.

During the greater part of this century, our companies were run by numbers. Everything revolved around the amount of time it took to do a task, the number of things produced per hour, the numerical ratings of employees' performance, the number of hours worked per day, and so on. As a result, companies lost sight of how to honestly measure productivity and quality.

I'd like to suggest that the most effective approach is to decide what we want to achieve and what it will look like when it's done right. Our greatest opportunity in the hospitality world, where success is measured by guest satisfaction, is housekeeping, where the typical measure of achievement is rooms cleaned per hour.

As a teenager, I worked in a factory where the greatest emphasis was on the number of cans produced. I know that more often than not, quality suffered because we looked only at quantity. Let's not make the same mistake in hospitality. Let's prove through the use of meaningful measurements that we want to make the room perfect for the guest.

In these days, when our success depends upon the return guest, let's find ways to challenge our room attendants to produce quality. Look at your property; look at your room layouts; and, with the help of the housekeeping staff, decide on the most efficient system for cleaning rooms that ensures a standard of quality and guest satisfaction. Avoid arbitrarily accepting the traditional measure of 28 minutes per room, and focus instead on standards of cleanliness. Determine what you want, what it will look like when it's done right, and what methods will be used to get successful results.

Source: *The Rooms Chronicle*, Volume 1, Number 3.
For subscription information, visit www.roomschronicle.com.

employee to perform an assigned task according to the department's performance standard?" Productivity standards must be determined to properly staff the department within the limitations of the budget.

Since performance standards vary at each hotel, it is impossible to identify productivity standards that would apply to every housekeeping department. Room attendant duties vary widely among economy, mid-market, and luxury hotels.

When determining realistic productivity standards, an executive housekeeper does not have to carry a tape measure, stopwatch, and clipboard and scientifically evaluate every step necessary to clean each item on an inventory list. However, house-

keeping managers must know how long it should take an employee to perform the major tasks identified on the cleaning frequency schedules—such as guestroom cleaning. Once this information is known, productivity standards can be developed.

Let's assume that, at a mid-market hotel, the executive housekeeper determines that a room attendant can meet performance standards and clean a typical guestroom in approximately 27 minutes. Exhibit 3 presents a sample productivity standards worksheet and shows how a productivity standard can be calculated for room attendants working 8-hour shifts. (Calculations within the exhibit assume that room attendants take a half-hour, unpaid

Exhibit 3
Sample Productivity Standard Worksheet

Step 1

Determine how long it should take to clean one guestroom according to the department's performance standards.

Approximately 27 minutes*

Step 2

Determine the total shift time in minutes.

8 hours × 60 minutes = 480 minutes

Step 3

Determine the time available for guestroom cleaning.

Total Shift Time	480	minutes
Less:		
Beginning-of-Shift Duties	20	minutes
Morning Break	15	minutes
Afternoon Break	15	minutes
End-of-Shift Duties	20	minutes
Time Available for Guestroom Cleaning	410	minutes

Step 4

Determine the productivity standard by dividing the result of Step 3 by the result of Step 1.

$$\frac{410 \text{ minutes}}{27 \text{ minutes}} = 15.2 \text{ guestrooms per 8-hour shift}$$

*Since performance standards vary from property to property, this figure is used for illustrative purposes only. It is not a suggested time figure for cleaning guestrooms.

lunch period.) The exhibit shows that the productivity standard for room attendants should be to clean 15 guestrooms per 8-hour shift.

Quality and quantity can be like two sides of a coin. On one side, if the quality expectations (performance standards) are set too high, workers won't be able to produce a sufficient quantity of work. This forces the executive housekeeper to add more and more staff to ensure that all the work gets done. Sooner or later—and probably sooner than expected—the general manager will be forced to cut the high labor expense of the housekeeping department. And this will force the executive

housekeeper to reduce the staff size and realign quality and quantity by redefining performance standards in light of more realistic productivity standards.

On the other side of the coin, if performance standards are set too low, the quantity of work that can be done accordingly will be unexpectedly high. At first, the general manager may be delighted. However, as complaints from guests and staff increase and the property begins to reflect neglect, the general manager may choose to replace the executive housekeeper with a person who will establish higher performance standards and monitor department expenses more closely.

The challenge is to effectively balance performance standards and productivity standards. Attention to productivity need not necessarily lower performance standards—it can sharpen and refine current work methods and procedures. If room attendants are constantly returning to the housekeeping area for cleaning and guestroom supplies, there is something wrong with the way they set up and stock their carts. Wasted motion is wasted time, and wasted time depletes the most important and most expensive resource of the housekeeping department: labor.

An executive housekeeper will rarely have all the resources necessary to do everything she or he may want to accomplish. Therefore, labor must be carefully allocated to achieve acceptable performance standards and realistic productivity standards.

Apply Your Learning 10.2

Please write all answers on a separate sheet of paper.

1. Planning the work of the housekeeping department begins with creating _____
    _____ .

2. Frequency schedules indicate:
    a. whether a room is empty or occupied, cleaned or yet to be cleaned.
    b. how often inventory list items are to be cleaned or maintained.
    c. how often housekeeping staff report room status information to the front desk.
    d. the number of minutes it typically takes to clean a guestroom.

3. Items that are only cleaned or maintained biweekly, monthly, bimonthly, and so on become part of the _____ _____ program.

4. Describe the difference between performance standards and productivity standards.

5. Under what circumstances are workers more likely to implement performance standards?

Answer whether statements 6–9 are true or false.

6. Housekeeping managers should determine what they want, what it will look like when it's done right, and what methods will achieve successful results.

7. Wise managers recognize that it should always take .5 hours to clean a guestroom and adjust their performance and productivity standards accordingly.

8. Room attendant duties are fairly standard among economy, mid-market, and luxury hotels.

9. Housekeeping departments that are well-managed do not require regular inspections.

10.3 Staffing and Scheduling

AFTER STUDYING SECTION 10.3, YOU SHOULD KNOW HOW TO:

♦ Distinguish between fixed and variable staff positions

♦ Develop a staffing guide for room attendants

♦ Develop a staffing guide for other housekeeping positions

♦ Develop employee work schedules

♦ Identify alternative scheduling techniques

Labor is the greatest single housekeeping expense. Managing labor is one of the most important managerial functions of the executive housekeeper.

When too many employees are scheduled to work, the department is overstaffed, resulting in excessive labor costs. If too few employees are scheduled to work, the department is understaffed. Understaffing lowers labor costs, but it may also lower hotel profits because performance standards will not be met, leading to dissatisfied guests and lost business.

Fixed and Variable Positions

The first step toward efficient scheduling is to determine which positions within the housekeeping department are fixed and which are variable depending upon occupancy levels at the hotel.

Fixed staff positions are those that must be filled regardless of the volume of business. They are generally managerial and administrative and may include:

• Executive housekeeper

• Assistant executive housekeeper

• Supervisor (day shift)

• Department clerk (day shift)

• Department clerk (afternoon shift)

Employees in these positions are usually scheduled to work at least 40 hours a week, regardless of the occupancy level of the hotel.

Variable staff positions include:

• Room attendants (day and afternoon shifts)

• Housepersons (day and afternoon shifts)

• Inspectors

• Lobby attendants

The number of employees scheduled to work in these positions is determined primarily by the number of rooms occupied during the previous night (or expected to be occupied, based on past history and existing reservations). Generally, the higher the previous night's occupancy, the more employees must be scheduled to work the next day. The number of housepersons and lobby attendants needed for any given shift may also vary in relation to meeting room and banquet functions, and convention and restaurant business.

A Room Attendant Staffing Guide

In order to schedule the right number of employees occupying variable staff positions within the department, the executive housekeeper should develop a staffing guide. A **staffing guide** is a scheduling and control tool that enables the executive housekeeper to determine the total labor hours, number of employees, and estimated labor expense required.

The following sections present a step-by-step procedure for developing a staffing guide for day-shift room attendants at the fictional King James Hotel, a 250-room property providing mid-range services.

Step 1. The first step is to determine the total labor hours for positions that must be scheduled when the hotel is at specific occupancy levels. This can be calculated by using productivity standards. Let's assume that the productivity standard for day-shift room attendants at the King James Hotel is approximately 30 minutes (.5 hours) to clean one guestroom. Given this information, we can calculate the total number of labor hours required for day-shift room attendants at various hotel occupancy levels.

If the hotel is experiencing 90 percent occupancy, there will be 225 rooms to clean the next day (250 rooms × .9 = 225). It will take a total of 113 labor hours to clean them (225 rooms × .5 hours = 112.5 labor hours,

rounded to 113). At 80 percent occupancy, there will be 200 rooms to clean (250 rooms × .8 = 200), and it will take 100 labor hours to clean them (200 rooms × .5 hours = 100).

Step 2. Determine the number of employees that must be scheduled to work when the hotel is at specific occupancy levels. The staffing guide expresses this number only in relation to full-time employees.

Since the productivity standard is .5 hours to clean one guestroom, a day-shift room attendant at the King James Hotel is expected to clean 16 guestrooms during an 8-hour shift. Divide the number of occupied rooms by 16 to get the number of full-time day-shift room attendants that must be scheduled at various occupancy levels.

For example, when there will be 225 rooms to clean the next day, dividing 225 rooms by 16 indicates that 14 full-time, day-shift room attendants will be needed. When the hotel is at 80 percent occupancy, there will be 200 rooms to clean. It will take 13 room attendants to clean them (200 rooms ÷ 16 = 12.5 room attendants, rounded to 13).

The actual number of room attendants scheduled to work on any given day will vary depending on the number of full-time and part-time employees the executive housekeeper schedules to work.

Step 3. The third step in developing a staffing guide is to calculate the estimated labor expense required to operate the housekeeping department when the hotel is at specific occupancy levels. This can be done for day-shift room attendants at the King James Hotel simply by multiplying the total labor hours by the average hourly rate for room attendants. Assume the average hourly rate is $10.00. When the King James Hotel is at 90 percent occupancy, the next day's estimated labor expense for day-shift room attendants is $1,130 (113 total labor hours × $10.00 per hour = $1,130). Regardless of the combination of full-time and part-time employees that is eventually scheduled to work, the total labor expense for day-shift room attendants should not exceed $1,130 when the hotel is at 90 percent occupancy.

A Staffing Guide for Other Positions

Similar calculations must be made for other variable staff positions in the housekeeping department. Suppose that the executive housekeeper at the King James Hotel has reviewed the productivity standards for other full-time positions and has determined that during one 8-hour shift:

- One inspector is needed for every 80 occupied rooms, yielding a productivity standard of .1 (8 hours ÷ 80 occupied rooms = .1).

- One day-shift lobby attendant is needed to service public areas when 100 rooms are occupied, yielding a productivity standard of .08 (8 hours ÷ 100 occupied rooms = .08).

- One day-shift houseperson is needed for every 85 occupied rooms, yielding a productivity standard of .094 (8 hours ÷ 85 occupied rooms = .094).

- One afternoon-shift room attendant is needed for every 50 occupied rooms, yielding a productivity standard of .16 (8 hours ÷ 50 occupied rooms = .16).

- One afternoon-shift houseperson is needed for every 100 occupied rooms, yielding a productivity standard of .08 (8 hours ÷ 100 occupied rooms = .08).

These productivity standards are multiplied by the number of occupied rooms to determine the total labor hours required for each position when the hotel is at specific occupancy levels. Dividing the total labor hours for each position by 8 determines the number of full-time employees that must be scheduled to clean the hotel the next day. Multiplying the required labor hours by an average hourly rate determines the estimated labor expense for each position. Exhibit 1 presents the complete staffing guide for variable staff positions at the King James Hotel.

Developing Employee Work Schedules

Occupancy forecasts are used with the staffing guide to determine the right number of employees to schedule each day for every position in the housekeeping department. Executive housekeepers have found the following tips helpful when developing employee work schedules:

- A schedule should cover a full work week, which is typically defined as Sunday through Saturday.

- Schedules should be posted at least three days before the beginning of the next work week.

- Days off, vacation time, and requested days off should all be indicated on the posted work schedule.

- The work schedule for the current week should be reviewed daily in relation to occupancy data. If necessary, changes to the schedule should be made.

- Any scheduling changes should be noted directly on the posted work schedule.

Exhibit 1
Sample Variable Staffing Guide

King James Hotel

Occupancy %	100%	95%	90%	85%	80%	75%	70%	65%	60%	55%	50%
Rooms Occupied	250	238	225	213	200	188	175	163	150	138	125
Room Attendants (A.M.) (Productivity STD + .5)											
Labor Hours	125	119	113	107	100	94	88	82	75	69	63
Employees	18	17	16	15	14	13	12	12	11	10	9
Expense	$750	$714	$678	$642	$600	$564	$528	$492	$450	$414	$378
Housepersons (A.M.) (Productivity STD + .08)											
Labor Hours	20	19	18	17	16	15	14	13	12	11	10
Employees	3	3	3	2	2	2	2	2	2	2	1
Expense	$120	$114	$108	$102	$96	$90	$84	$78	$72	$66	$60
Lobby Attendants (Productivity STD + .07)											
Labor Hours	18	17	16	15	14	13	12	11	11	10	9
Employees	3	2	2	2	2	2	2	2	2	1	1
Expense	$108	$102	$96	$90	$84	$78	$72	$66	$66	$60	$54
Inspectors (Productivity STD + .09)											
Labor Hours	23	21	20	19	18	17	16	15	14	12	11
Employees	3	3	3	3	3	2	2	2	2	2	2
Expense	$138	$126	$120	$114	$108	$102	$96	$90	$84	$72	$66
Room Attendants (P.M.) (Productivity STD + .14)											
Labor Hours	35	33	32	30	28	26	25	23	21	19	18
Employees	5	5	5	4	4	4	4	3	3	3	3
Expense	$210	$198	$192	$180	$168	$156	$150	$138	$126	$114	$108
Housepersons (P.M.) (Productivity STD + .07)											
Labor Hours	18	17	16	15	14	13	12	11	11	10	9
Employees	3	2	2	2	2	2	2	2	2	1	1
Expense	$108	$102	$96	$90	$84	$78	$72	$66	$66	$60	$54
Total Labor Hours	239	226	215	203	190	178	167	155	144	131	120
Total Expense	$1,434	$1,356	$1,290	$1,218	$1,140	$1,068	$1,002	$930	$864	$786	$720

- A copy of the posted work schedule can be used to monitor attendance. This copy should be retained as part of the department's records.

Alternative Scheduling Techniques

Alternative scheduling varies from the typical 9:00 A.M. to 5:00 P.M. workday. Variations include part-time and flexible hours, compressed work schedules, and job sharing.

Part-Time Employees. Students, young parents, retirees and others may prefer to work part-time hours. Employing part-time workers can allow extra scheduling flexibility. It can also reduce labor costs, because benefits and overtime costs usually decrease.

Flexible Work Hours. Flexible work hours, or **flextime,** allow employees to vary the times at which they begin and end workshifts. Certain hours of each shift necessitate the presence of all employees. The rest of the shift can be flexible, allowing employees to determine for themselves when their shifts begin and end. The benefits of flextime include heightened staff morale, productivity, and job satisfaction. Moreover, the property will be more attractive to quality employees.

Compressed Work Schedules. Compressed work schedules offer housekeeping employees the opportunity to work the equivalent of a standard work week in fewer than the usual five days. One popular arrangement compresses a 40-hour week into four 10-hour days. Primary benefits from the employer's viewpoint include enhanced recruiting appeal and employee morale, and reduced absenteeism.

Job Sharing. In job sharing, the efforts of two or more part-time employees together fulfill the duties and responsibilities of one full-time job. Job sharing may alleviate department turnover and absenteeism and increase employee morale. In addition, the department profits: even if one job-sharing partner leaves, the other usually stays and can train the incoming partner.

Apply Your Learning 10.3

Please write all answers on a separate sheet of paper.

1. What is the greatest single housekeeping expense?

2. What are the drawbacks of overstaffing and understaffing?

3. Positions that must be filled regardless of business volume are _____ _____ positions.

4. Put the following staffing guide steps in the correct order:

   - Calculate the estimated labor expense required to operate the housekeeping department, based on hotel occupancy.
   - Determine the total labor hours for positions that must be scheduled, based on hotel occupancy.
   - Determine the number of employees that must be scheduled to work, based on hotel occupancy.

5. What are the advantages of compressed work schedules and job sharing?

Quick Hits

SECTION 10.1—THE HOUSEKEEPING DEPARTMENT

- Most housekeeping departments are responsible for cleaning guestrooms, corridors, public areas, pool and patio areas, offices, storage areas, laundry rooms, and back-of-the-house areas.

- Housekeeping responsibilities at larger properties may also include meeting rooms, dining/banquet rooms, exhibit halls, hotel-operated shops, and game and exercise rooms.

- The general manager has ultimate responsibility for designating housekeeping's areas of oversight.

- Effective housekeeping managers must know how to solve problems in cooperation with other department managers.

SECTION 10.2—PLANNING

- Planning is probably the executive housekeeper's most important management function.

- **Inventory lists** note all items within each area that need housekeeping's attention. They form the basis for developing cleaning procedures, training plans, and inspection checklists.

- **Frequency schedules** note how often inventory list items are to be cleaned or maintained.

- Items that are cleaned or maintained less than daily or weekly become part of a **deep cleaning** program and are transferred to a calendar and scheduled as special cleaning projects. The calendar plan guides staff scheduling decisions.

- It is important to balance performance and productivity standards, so employees perform their jobs as consistently and efficiently as possible, while continuing to provide the expected level of guest satisfaction.

SECTION 10.3—STAFFING AND SCHEDULING

- **Fixed staff positions** must be filled regardless of the volume of business and include the executive housekeeper, assistant executive housekeeper, day-shift supervisor, and department clerks.

- **Variable staff positions** vary depending upon occupancy levels and include room attendants, housepersons, inspectors, and lobby attendants.

- Developing a **staffing guide** is a three-step process:

  1. Determine the total labor hours for positions that must be scheduled, depending on the hotel's occupancy.

  2. Determine the number of employees that must be scheduled to work to fulfill the required labor hours.

3. Calculate the estimated labor expense involved.

- Occupancy forecasts from the rooms division are used with the staffing guide to determine the right number of employees to schedule each day.

- Alternative scheduling varies from the typical 9-to-5 workday and includes variations such as part-time workers, flexible work hours (known as **flextime**), compressed work schedules, and job sharing.

Don Landry

Owner, Top Ten Marketing and Hospitality Consulting

Like many of today's hospitality industry leaders, Sunburst Hospitality's Don Landry discovered his career interest as a teenager. He started on the ground floor when he was 15, working as a dish-room steward, a waiter, and a lifeguard. He also worked the night telephone switchboard at a Catholic parish rectory.

"As a perk, we were given dinner and it was always first-class fare," recalled Landry. "I was not interested in the priesthood, but I was interested in gourmet food, so I decided to explore the hospitality business."

The catering department of a country club further piqued Landry's interest in a hospitality career. From country clubs, he moved to hotels "to expand the volume and variety of people I could meet on the job," he said. His first management job was as breakfast manager of the 346-room Royal Orleans Hotel. He then moved through many positions with Sonesta Hotels.

Landry became a general manager of the 380-room LeBaron Hotel in Dallas, Texas, when he was 26 years old. By the time he was 30, he was vice president of MHM, the largest independent management company at that time. Ten years later, he was president of the company. From there, he became chief operating officer of Richfield, president of Manor Care Hotels, president of Choice Hotels International, and then CEO of Sunburst Hospitality Corporation. Landry stepped down as CEO and created his own consulting firm in 2000.

"What I love about the industry is simply the tremendous volume and variety of people you meet and the opportunity you get to learn from them while developing leadership skills at a relatively young age," Landry said. "Few industries offer the variety and therefore the opportunity to practice so many disciplines while in the job of general manager or corporate operations executive—for instance, marketing, human resources, finances, communications, public relations, asset management, and maintenance—and all this at a pace that never allows boredom!"

Carpet Construction and Maintenance

Sections

11.1 Carpet Construction

AFTER STUDYING SECTION 11.1, YOU SHOULD KNOW HOW TO:

♦ Describe how the carpet's face affects its durability

♦ Identify the types of primary backings

♦ Explain how secondary backings are applied to carpets

Until human beings learn to defy the laws of gravity, carpets will be walked on, spilled on, tracked in on, crushed, and eventually worn down.

In a lodging operation, thousands of feet travel the carpets every day. They become worn and dirty very quickly. A hotel with a soiled, stained, or faded carpet makes a poor impression on guests. It's why lodging properties care deeply about their carpets' durability, appearance, and ease of maintenance.

Carpeting reduces noise in halls and guestrooms, prevents slipping, and keeps floors and rooms warmer. Carpeting is also easier to maintain than many other floor coverings.

In general, carpets have three components: the face, the primary backing, and the secondary backing. Exhibit 1 shows a cross section of these components.

Carpet Face

The **face** or **pile** of the carpet is the part you see and walk on. The face may be made of synthetic fibers or yarns such as polyester, acrylic, polypropylene (olefin), or nylon. The face may also be made of such natural fibers as wool or cotton, though cotton is seldom used as a face fiber today. Some carpets are made of blends of synthetics and natural fibers, or blends of different kinds of synthetics.

The carpet's **face fibers**, as well as their density, height, twist, and weave, will affect the carpet's durability, texture retention, and serviceability.

A carpet's durability can be measured by the density of face fibers. In general, the

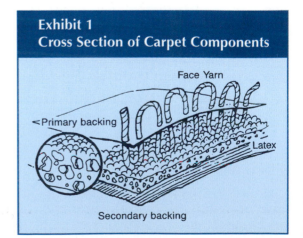

Exhibit 1
Cross Section of Carpet Components

Face Yarn

Primary backing

Latex

Secondary backing

greater the density, the better the grade of carpet. Dense carpets keep their shape longer and resist matting and crushing. They also keep stains and dirt at the top of the fibers. To determine how dense a carpet is, bend a corner of the carpet and see how much backing shows underneath the pile. The less backing that shows, the denser the carpet.

In carpets of equal density, the one with the higher pile and tighter twist will generally be the better product. Carpet that is more tightly twisted is more resilient and will retain its appearance better. When examining a carpet, you should be able to see the twist. The tips of the fibers should not be flared or open. Good quality cut-pile carpets have a heat-set twist.

Pile weight, while not as important as density, also can affect the carpet's durability. Pile weight is measured in **face weight**—the weight of the face fibers in one square yard of carpet. The greater the weight, the more durable the carpet.

Primary Backing

Face fibers are attached to a **primary backing** that holds the fibers in place. This backing may be made of natural material (typically jute) or synthetic material such as polypropylene.

Jute backings are durable and resilient but may mildew under damp conditions. Polypropylene has most of the advantages of jute and is mildew-resistant.

Secondary Backing

In the past, all carpeting was installed over a separate pad. Today, carpeting may be glued directly to the floor or installed over a **secondary backing,** one of a variety of pads. Sometimes, particularly with carpet tiles, a pad may be bonded directly to the backing when it is made.

A cheap pad will reduce the life of the carpet as well as its insulating, sound-absorbing, and cushioning abilities. A thick pad will prevent the carpet from shifting—*unless the carpet is installed in an area where heavy equipment will be rolled over it frequently;* in this case, a thinner pad is preferred.

Piece by Piece

The Hilton Palacio del Rio Hotel in San Antonio was the first modular construction hotel. The first four floors were built on sight; the rest of the hotel was built one room at a time eight miles south of town by the H.B. Zachary Company. The rooms were completely furnished and carpeted. They even came with a Bible in the dresser. They were brought into town on flatbed trucks and hoisted into place by a giant crane and plugged into the hotel's main utility line.

Apply Your Learning 11.1

Please write all answers on a separate sheet of paper.

1. What are the three components of carpeting?

2. What is the purpose of the primary backing?

3. The best measure of carpet durability is:

    a. cost.
    b. face fiber density.
    c. the quality of the pad.
    d. pile weight.

4. In which instance would a thinner pad be the best choice for the secondary backing?

    a. in the hotel's dining room
    b. in the majority of guestrooms
    c. between loading docks and the exhibit hall
    d. behind the front desk

11.2 Carpet Problems

AFTER STUDYING SECTION 11.2, YOU SHOULD KNOW HOW TO:

◆ Explain how to correct pile distortion

◆ Identify shading in carpeting

◆ Describe how to prevent faded carpet

◆ Explain how to prevent wicking

◆ Describe the effects of mildew on carpet

◆ Identify solutions to carpet shedding or pilling

There are common carpet problems that housekeeping can remedy:

• Pile distortion

• Shading

• Fading

• Wicking

• Mildew

• Shedding/pilling

Pile Distortion

Pile distortion describes a number of problems with the carpet's face fibers. Fibers can become twisted, pilled, crushed, or flared and matted. Pile distortion occurs when the carpet receives heavy foot or equipment traffic. Improper cleaning methods can also cause pile distortion.

It may be impossible to remedy pile distortion in high-traffic areas. Mats, runners, and furniture glides can help prevent crushing. Regularly vacuuming or using a pile lifter or pile brush on high-traffic areas will help to remove dry soil, which can wear on fibers and cause pile distortion. A pile lifter will help pick up crushed pile while removing gritty soils, which can damage the carpet. Pile distortion can also be prevented by grooming high-traffic areas with a carpet rake.

Shading

Shading occurs when the pile in a carpet is brushed in two different directions so that dark and light areas appear. Shading is a normal feature of almost all carpets. Vacuuming or pile lifting the carpet in one direction can help to reduce a shading problem, but not eliminate it. Some properties instruct room attendants to leave shading marks while vacuuming. Guests will see the vacuuming pattern and may feel that the room has been properly cleaned.

Fading

Every carpet will fade with time. Sunlight, wear, cleaning, and natural aging can combine to accelerate color loss. Premature fading may occur if the carpet is improperly cleaned. Improper cleaning or spot removal can actually do more damage than some permanent stains. Spot-removal and cleaning solutions should always be tested on small, hidden areas of carpets before being used aggressively.

Some professional carpet service companies can dye carpets that have faded.

Wicking

Wicking (also called browning) occurs when the backing of the carpet becomes wet and the face yarns draw or wick the moisture and color of the backing to the surface of the carpet. Wicking can often be prevented by promptly attending to spills and by following proper cleaning procedures that avoid overwetting the carpet. Wicking occurs most frequently in jute-backed carpet with a light-color face fiber.

Vinegar or synthetic citric acid solutions used in postcleaning treatments or added to certain cleaning chemicals can help prevent or cure browning problems. As always, check with the manufacturer and/or pretest the application before proceeding with an antibrowning treatment.

Mildew

Mildew forms when moisture allows molds in the carpet to grow. Mildew can cause staining, odor, and rotting. Natural fibers are especially prone to mildew, but all carpets should be kept dry and/or treated with an antibacterial agent to prevent the problem. Proper cleaning procedures that avoid overwetting the carpet can help prevent mildew from forming.

Shedding/Pilling

Loose pieces of face fibers are often trapped in the carpet when it is manufactured. As the new carpet is walked upon, these pieces shed, working themselves to the surface of the carpet and making a new carpet look littered and unkempt. Shedding will eventually stop. In the meantime, frequent vacuuming will prevent the carpet from looking littered. Pilling, small balls of loose fabric that often appear as a result of cleaning, can be removed by heavy vacuuming or by gently cutting loose fibers from the carpet with scissors.

Apply Your Learning 11.2

Please write all answers on a separate sheet of paper.

1. Carpet fibers that have become twisted or crushed are experiencing:

   a. pilling.
   b. shedding.
   c. wicking.
   d. pile distortion.

Label the following statements either True or False.

2. Shading is a normal feature of most carpets.

3. Furniture glides cannot help prevent pile distortion.

4. "Browning" is another term for the effects of mildew on a carpet.

5. Some guests actually like to see shading in a carpet.

11.3 Carpet Maintenance

AFTER STUDYING SECTION 11.3, YOU SHOULD KNOW HOW TO:

♦ Explain how to use floor plans and calendars to schedule maintenance

♦ Describe how routine inspections are part of a carpet and floor care program

♦ Explain how preventive maintenance can prolong the life of carpets

♦ Describe how routine maintenance of carpets is performed at a property

The aim of any carpet maintenance program is to keep the carpet clean and "like new" for as long as possible. The carpet's fiber, backing, and construction are factors in the maintenance needed to keep it looking good. Efficient cleaning schedules are based on the amount of traffic in the various areas of the property.

Scheduling Carpet Maintenance

Heavy soiling typically occurs in high-traffic public areas, track-off areas, and funnel areas. Track-off areas are those directly in front of doors leading to the outside. Funnel areas are those in which traffic converges into a narrow space. Funnel areas typically occur around elevators and stairways and in front of vending machines.

When establishing a carpet cleaning schedule, start with a color-coded property floor plan. For example, one color or shade could indicate high-traffic areas, which need to be cleaned at least once daily. Areas with less traffic that soil more slowly can be depicted with other colors or shades to indicate weekly, monthly, or quarterly cleaning. Exhibit 1 shows such a floor plan.

Once the floor plan is completed, it is time to develop a calendar plan. The calendar plan should list the cleaning tasks—vacuuming, spot cleaning, deep cleaning—to be performed on specific days and the time required for each task. Implementing a regular cleaning schedule has a number of advantages:

• Housekeepers can accurately forecast monthly and yearly cleaning costs.

• Regular maintenance will prevent major problems and will extend the life of the carpet.

• Regularly scheduled carpet and floor cleaning allows the executive housekeeper to budget time for other major department projects.

Routine Inspection

Inspection is an important part of all carpet and floor care programs. Housekeeping staff generally inspect carpets and floors in all areas of the property each day.

Exhibit 1
Sample Floor Plan of Carpet Traffic Areas

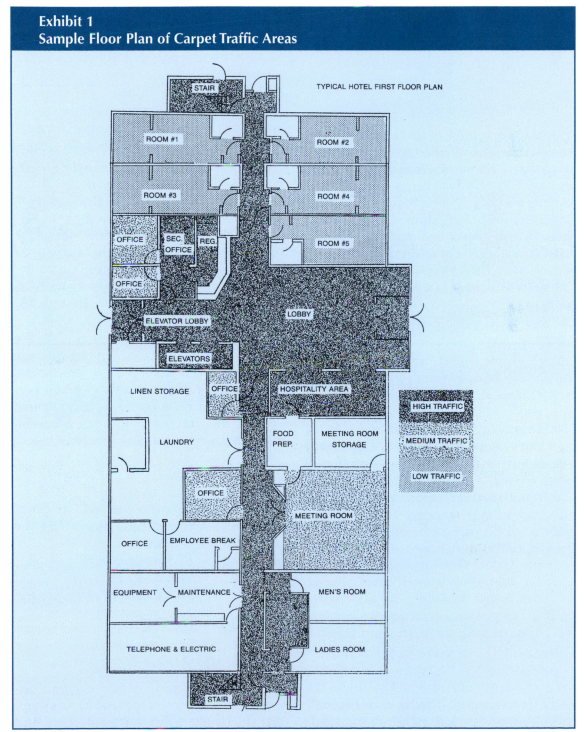

Courtesy of Flagship Cleaning Services, Newtown Square, Pennsylvania

All hotel employees need to promptly reporting spots and spills to the housekeeping department. Good maintenance depends on immediately removing spots and spills.

Preventive Maintenance

Lodging properties can prevent carpet soiling and damage by frequently changing mats and runners. Furniture glides on the bottoms of chairs and tables can help reduce pile distortion or tearing. Waterproof plastic carpet protectors or regularly cleaned mats can help reduce damage from food and beverage spills around self-serve bars in dining rooms or near vending machines. Carpet tiles, which can be easily replaced or rotated in high-use areas, can be used to reduce pile distortion.

Routine Maintenance

Most housekeeping departments vacuum all carpets at least once a day as part of **routine maintenance.** Routine maintenance also includes periodic deep cleaning (using shampoos and hot or cold water extraction) and stain removal, when necessary. Spots should be removed quickly before they set into the fabric.

The executive housekeeper compiles the manual for spot and stain removal, stating the proper procedures and cleaning fluids to use on the carpets throughout the property. Carpet suppliers often provide care and maintenance instructions and spot removal techniques.

Apply Your Learning 11.3

Please write all answers on a separate sheet of paper.

1. Heavy soiling typically occurs in what three kinds of areas?

2. The space around elevators and stairways is known as a(n) _____ area.

3. What are the benefits of implementing a regular cleaning program for carpets?

4. Which of the following is not typically useful for preventive carpet maintenance?

    a.   furniture glides
    b.   carpet tiles
    c.   mats and runners
    d.   carpet dyes

11.4 Carpet Cleaning Methods

AFTER STUDYING SECTION 14.5, YOU SHOULD KNOW HOW TO:

♦ Explain proper vacuuming procedures

♦ Identify when to use dry powder cleaning methods

♦ Explain the use of bonnet spin pad cleaning equipment

♦ Describe the use of rotary shampoo equipment

♦ Describe water extraction techniques

There are a number of carpet cleaning methods, from simple vacuuming to **hot- or cold-water extraction.** Carpet experts frequently disagree over which cleaning methods are most effective and which methods produce less wear on the carpet itself. For example, some say that shampooing can wear down the carpet and leave soap residue that will actually attract dirt.

Many types of carpets and floors have very different care and maintenance requirements. Simple ammonia solutions that work on most synthetic carpets will cause immediate and irreversible damage to natural fibers. Similarly, olefin carpets can be cleaned with bleaching solutions that would damage nylon carpets. Executive housekeepers should carefully follow manufacturers' recommendations regarding cleaning methods.

Vacuuming

Carpet experts do agree on one thing: you can't vacuum too much. Daily vacuuming prevents abrasives (gritty materials such as sand and gravel) from working into the carpet and causing stains and wear over time. It also helps restore the carpet's pile.

The most effective vacuuming equipment agitates the carpet to loosen the dirt and removes it with suction.

• Beater-bar vacuums use a bar to agitate the carpet to loosen dirt. These vacuums are best for carpets installed over pads.

• Brush vacuums agitate the carpet with a brush and are best for carpets glued to the floor.

• Pile-lifter machines have a strong suction capacity and a separate brush motor that help restore crushed carpet pile.

An upright sweeper has a large agitator/suction head that pulls dirt up into a bag attached along the handle of the machine. Canister models collect dirt in a tank that moves on casters for easy maneuvering.

Dry Powder Cleaning

With the dry powder carpet cleaning method, dry powder or crystals are

the Rooms CHRONICLE

Carpet Cleaning: When, How, and Why

By Gail Edwards

Begin Outside. Installing good walk-off mats for a measured distance into the hotel will ensure that minimal amounts of dirt are tracked onto the hallway or lobby carpet.

Vacuum Regularly. An upright vacuum cleaner with a rotating brush or beater bar will remove dry soil from the carpet very quickly and efficiently. A carpet's life is extended by regular (daily) vacuuming and the removal of soil that otherwise might be ground into the fibers.

Limited Fluid Methods of Cleaning.

Dry Powder Method. A powder cleaning compound is spread on the surface of the carpet, agitated, allowed to dry, then removed by vacuuming. This compound is a surface cleaner. The advantage of this method is that spills and spots can be quickly treated. The disadvantage is that absorbent powders fail to emulsify and remove dirt below the surface of the carpet.

Bonnet Method. The bonnet method requires that a liquid cleaning agent be applied to the carpet, allowed to soak into the carpet for a short time, and then buffed with an absorbent bonnet pad. This system resembles the dry powder method and is also a surface cleaner. The advantage of the bonnet method is speed and fast drying time. The disadvantage is that this method fails to reach and remove the soils that fall into the fibers and backing.

"Dry" Foam or Shampoo Cleaning Methods. These methods use a limited amount of liquid (a high-foaming detergent or shampoo), which is applied to the carpet nap with a reel- or rotary-type brush to suspend soils and emulsify oils. The carpet can then be vacuumed with a wet vacuum.

The advantage of these limited-fluid methods is speed and a short drying time. Also, the top surface looks clean. But the disadvantage is the insufficient amount of fluids introduced into the fibers to penetrate, emulsify, and remove dirt below the surface of the carpet. Surface soils are driven deeper into the carpet's pile. And if the shampoo is not thoroughly vacuumed out of the carpet, it could leave a residue that attracts dirt.

Continual use of these limited fluid methods can result in a dull, matted, flat carpet appearance caused by buildup of dirt and chemicals.

Free Fluid Method: Extraction Method. This is the deepest cleaning method available—it forces water and chemicals into the carpet fibers under pressure. Considered a wet or restoration method, it involves the application of a soil-releasing detergent (preconditioner) to the carpet followed by soaking time and subsequent removal with a hot- or cold-water or chemical treatment.

The advantage is that a good extractor can deliver adequate pressure to loosen the soil in the carpet's pile and enough extraction power to remove as much as 90 percent of the water or solution. The disadvantage is that drying time can range from one hour to one day, depending on the equipment selected. Some extractors recover only a portion of the dirty solution that soaks through fiber and backing, thus extending drying time, providing a breeding ground for bacteria, and promoting resoiling.

(Thanks to Andy Holt of CFR Corporation in New Brighton, MN, and Tom Messmer of Clean Sweep Carpet Care in St. Louis, MO, for contributing information for this article.)

Source: *The Rooms Chronicle*, Volume 3, Number 2.
For subscription information, visit www.roomschronicle.com.

sprinkled onto the carpet and worked into the pile with a hand brush or a special machine that dispenses the powder. The powder absorbs oily soils, which are then removed by vacuuming. Since no drying time is required, carpets in high-traffic areas need not be closed off. Properties may schedule dry powder cleaning between deeper cleaning activities.

Dry powder cleaning may be a good way to clean carpets that should not be cleaned with water. Dry powder cleaning also does not leave a soap residue on the carpet or excess water that could give rise to mold or mildew. The brushes in the dry powder machine, however, may cause cut-pile fibers to flare. Periodic extraction or wet cleaning is suggested to remove residue from carpets. Some experts also caution that there are some types of dirt that dry powder cleaning will not remove very well.

Dry Foam Cleaning

With this method, dry foam is sprayed on the carpet and a rotary floor machine brushes the foam into the carpet. The foam is then removed with a wet vacuum. Machines are available that will accomplish both tasks. Dry foam can also be sprayed and brushed into carpets by hand. Since this method requires little drying time, housekeepers often use dry foam cleaning in high-traffic areas as frequently as once a day.

Dry foam cleaning can cause flaring in some cut-pile carpets. If proper cleaning procedures are not followed, overwetting can occur, which could lead to shrinking, mildew, fading, and other conditions. A manufacturer's sample carpet maintenance program using extraction is shown in Exhibit 1.

Bonnet Spin Pad Cleaning

Bonnet spin pad cleaning is similar to the dry foam method in that it can be used daily for surface cleaning, even though it is a wet process. A rotary floor machine with a special holder and pad agitates the tips of the carpet fibers and lifts and absorbs soil as it moves across the carpet. Pads are made of synthetic or natural fibers and can be laundered and reused as often as necessary. After the carpets have dried, they are vacuumed.

Rotary Shampoos

Rotary or brush shampoo offers more effective cleaning than dry powder or dry foam cleaning. With this method, a rotary bristle brush is used instead of a pad or bonnet. The brush design allows the shampoo to drain down through the bristles directly onto the carpet. The shampoo is agitated by the machine into a foam that can then be left to dry or be vacuumed by a wet vacuum or extractor. When the carpet is vacuumed, it is necessary to use a defoamer in the wet vacuum or extractor tank.

Water Extraction

Water extraction is the deepest cleaning method available for most carpets. Hot water extractors should never be filled with water that is hotter than 150°F/66°C. Since wool carpets can shrink, they are only cleaned with warm or cool water.

Hot water extractors spray a detergent and water solution onto the carpet under low pressure and, in the same pass, vacuum out the solution and soil. A good extractor can pull 70 percent to 90 percent

Exhibit 1
Sample Carpet Extraction Maintenance Program

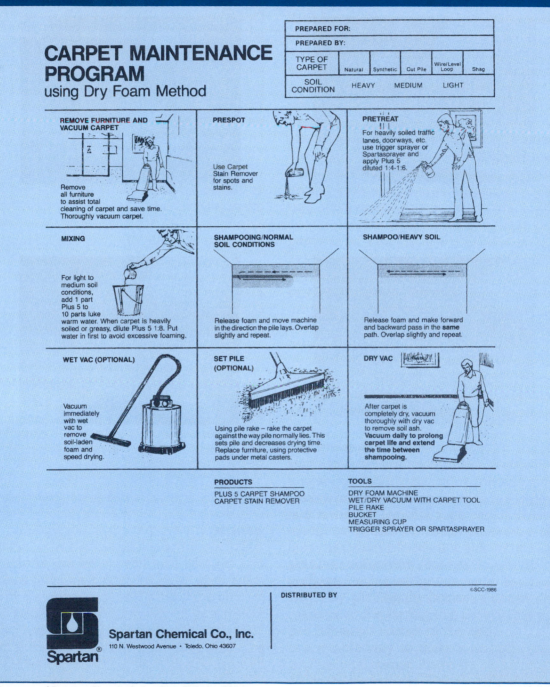

CARPET MAINTENANCE PROGRAM
using Dry Foam Method

PREPARED FOR:					
PREPARED BY:					
TYPE OF CARPET	Natural	Synthetic	Cut Pile	Wire/Level Loop	Shag
SOIL CONDITION	HEAVY		MEDIUM	LIGHT	

REMOVE FURNITURE AND VACUUM CARPET
Remove all furniture to assist total cleaning of carpet and save time. Thoroughly vacuum carpet.

PRESPOT
Use Carpet Stain Remover for spots and stains.

PRETREAT
For heavily soiled traffic lanes, doorways, etc. use trigger sprayer or Spartasprayer and apply Plus 5 diluted 1:4-1:6.

MIXING
For light to medium soil conditions, add 1 part Plus 5 to 10 parts luke warm water. When carpet is heavily soiled or greasy, dilute Plus 5 1:8. Put water in first to avoid excessive foaming.

SHAMPOOING/NORMAL SOIL CONDITIONS
Release foam and move machine in the direction the pile lays. Overlap slightly and repeat.

SHAMPOO/HEAVY SOIL
Release foam and make forward and backward pass in the **same** path. Overlap slightly and repeat.

WET VAC (OPTIONAL)
Vacuum immediately with wet vac to remove soil-laden foam and speed drying.

SET PILE (OPTIONAL)
Using pile rake – rake the carpet against the way pile normally lies. This sets pile and decreases drying time. Replace furniture, using protective pads under metal casters.

DRY VAC
After carpet is completely dry, vacuum thoroughly with dry vac to remove soil ash. **Vacuum daily to prolong carpet life and extend the time between shampooing.**

PRODUCTS
PLUS 5 CARPET SHAMPOO
CARPET STAIN REMOVER

TOOLS
DRY FOAM MACHINE
WET/DRY VACUUM WITH CARPET TOOL
PILE RAKE
BUCKET
MEASURING CUP
TRIGGER SPRAYER OR SPARTASPRAYER

DISTRIBUTED BY

©SCC-1986

Spartan Chemical Co., Inc.
110 N. Westwood Avenue • Toledo, Ohio 43607

Spartan®

Courtesy of Spartan Chemical Co., Inc., Toledo, Ohio

of the water out of the carpet. Some extraction machines have a special tool called a power head that agitates the carpet before the solution is extracted. Other tools, such as upholstery and stair tools, can be attached to the extractor, making the unit useful for a variety of cleaning functions.

With proper extraction, a carpet will dry in an hour or two. Housekeeping staff using hot water extraction are careful to control the amount of water that goes into the carpet. Overwetting can be a problem if the equipment is underpowered or if the operator does not take care to thoroughly vacuum the cleaned area.

Hot water extraction requires a great deal of hot water. This can be hard on some carpets. Properties trying to cut their hot water consumption may want to consider models that use cold water in this process. In some cases, cold water extraction works as well as hot water extraction and helps reduce color fading, running, and shrinking.

Excessively soiled carpets are most effectively cleaned with a combination of rotary shampoo and water extraction methods.

Apply Your Learning 11.4

Please write all answers on a separate sheet of paper.

1. What are the benefits of regular, daily vacuuming?

2. What cleaning method might be best for a lightly soiled carpet in a high-traffic area that cannot easily be closed off?

3. For most carpets, the deepest cleaning method is:

    a.   dry foam.
    b.   water extraction.
    c.   dry powder.
    d.   brush shampoo.

Quick Hits

Chapter 11

SECTION 11.1—CARPET CONSTRUCTION

- Density of **face fibers** is the best indicator of carpet durability. In general, the greater the density, the better the grade of carpet.

- Face fibers are attached to a **primary backing** that holds the fibers in place. This backing may be made of natural material (typically jute) or synthetic material such as polypropylene.

- When choosing a **secondary backing,** a thick pad will prevent the carpet from shifting. In areas where heavy equipment will be rolled over it frequently, a thinner pad is preferred.

SECTION 11.2—CARPET PROBLEMS

- Carpet problems include pile distortion, shading, fading, wicking, mildew, and shedding/pilling.

- **Pile distortion** refers to problems with a carpet's face fibers, largely as a result of heavy foot or equipment traffic.

- **Shading** occurs when the pile in a carpet is brushed in two different directions so that dark and light areas appear. It is a normal feature of almost all carpets, and it leads some guests to feel that the area has been properly cleaned.

- Fading is caused by sunlight, wear, cleaning, and natural aging. Improper cleaning can lead to premature fading.

- **Wicking** (also called browning) occurs when the backing of the carpet becomes wet and the face yarns draw the moisture and color of the backing to the surface of the carpet. It occurs most frequently in jute-backed carpet with a light-color face fiber.

- Mildew forms when moisture allows molds in the carpet to grow. It can cause staining, odor, and rotting.

- Shedding is caused by loose pieces of face fibers that are trapped in the carpet when it is manufactured and then rise to the top after a period of use.

- Pilling refers to small balls of loose fabric that often appear as a result of cleaning. They can be removed by heavy vacuuming or by gently cutting loose fibers from the carpet with scissors.

SECTION 11.3—CARPET MAINTENANCE

- Heavy soiling typically occurs in high-traffic areas, which includes track-off and funnel areas.

- A track-off area is an area directly in front of doors leading to the outside.

- Funnel areas are those in which foot traffic converges into a narrow space—for example, around elevators and stairways.

- Developing a carpet cleaning schedule begins with creating a color-coded property floor plan that indicates the areas to be cleaned daily, weekly, monthly, etc.

- The floor plan is used to develop a calendar plan that lists the cleaning tasks to be performed on specific days and the time required for each task.

- Regular inspection is an important part of all carpet and floor care programs.

- **Preventive maintenance** might involve the use of mats and runners, furniture glides, plastic carpet protectors, and carpet tiles that can be easily replaced or rotated.

- **Routine maintenance** includes vacuuming all carpets at least once a day, periodic deep cleaning, and stain removal when necessary.

SECTION 11.4—CARPET CLEANING METHODS

- Because different carpets and floors require different care and maintenance, executive housekeepers should carefully follow manufacturer's recommendations regarding cleaning methods.

- Daily vacuuming prevents dirt and other abrasives from working into the carpet and causing stains and wear over time.

- The most effective vacuuming equipment agitates the carpet to loosen the dirt and removes it with suction.

- Beater-bar vacuums use a bar to agitate the carpet to loosen dirt and are effective for carpets installed over pads.

- Brush vacuums agitate the carpet with a brush and are best for carpets glued to the floor.

- Pile-lifter machines have a strong suction capacity and a separate brush motor that help restore crushed carpet pile.

- Dry powder cleaning: Powder sprinkled onto the carpet absorbs oily soils and is then removed by vacuuming. There are some types of dirt that dry powder cleaning will not remove very well.

- Dry foam cleaning: Dry foam is sprayed on the carpet and a rotary floor machine brushes the foam into the carpet. The foam is then removed with a wet vacuum.

- Bonnet spin pad cleaning: A rotary floor machine fitted with a special holder and pad agitates the tips of the carpet fibers and lifts and absorbs soil as it moves across the carpet.

- Rotary shampoo: A bristle brush on a rotary floor machine is used to agitate shampoo into a foam that can be left to dry or vacuumed by a wet vacuum or extractor. When the carpet is vacuumed, it is necessary to use a defoamer in the wet vacuum or extractor tank.

- Water extraction is the deepest cleaning method available for most carpets.

- Hot water extractors spray a detergent and water solution onto the carpet under low pressure and, in the same pass, vacuum out the solution and soil.

- Excessively soiled carpets are most effectively cleaned with a combination of rotary shampoo and water extraction methods.

Gail Edwards

Director of Housekeeping
Adams Mark Hotel

It's not the money, Gail Edwards will tell you. When she first started out 28 years ago, it was as a waitress at a job that paid 82 cents an hour. She had to attend classes, and upgrade her attitudes and people skills. She was told that women were not predominant in the hospitality field.

From that job, she worked her way up to food and beverage manager and held that job for seven years. "Don't go into any job for the money," Edwards says. "You have to believe that what you're doing is what you need to do and want to do as a career. Hospitality is a very demanding profession."

Edwards later moved to housekeeping and was surprised at the job's demands. "I failed miserably," Edwards says about her first management job in housekeeping. "I was a young person and I did not know the importance of people skills. In the front of the hotel, you're pleasant and cordial. You see the guest for ten minutes. The person behind the scenes, you see them every day for an hour or two a day. You communicate on a daily basis. You become a part of their life. If you stereotype all departments in hospitality, you become territorial and not a team player."

She eventually started her own business refurbishing properties. When she returned to hospitality, she entered the front office area as a rooms executive in charge of front office and rooms division. It was there that she met the woman who would be her mentor for the rest of her career.

"If it wasn't for her, I would have left the business a long time ago," Edwards says. "She's the type of a leader who will tell you what you did wrong and not fix it for you. Managers need to solve their own problems, that's why they're managers. They need to think how they could have done it better and been proactive. They don't need to be beat up because they didn't do it right. Managing people is a magic trick. No two people are alike."

Edwards also points out that people entering the industry now must have more training and education than when she entered. "I was very fortunate because when I started out, you didn't need the credentials. The credentials now are very stringent. Getting the knowledge, ability, and education is an important step in your career."

Housekeeping Inventory

Sections

12.1 Types of Inventory

AFTER STUDYING SECTION 12.1, YOU SHOULD KNOW HOW TO:

♦ Identify recycled inventories and how they are maintained

♦ Explain how the housekeeping department maintains non-recycled inventory

♦ Calculate expected inventories

The executive housekeeper ensures that employees have the necessary equipment and supplies to get their jobs done. Maintaining appropriate inventory levels ensures smooth daily housekeeping activities and forms the basis for planning an effective purchasing system.

Essentially, the executive housekeeper is responsible for two types of inventories. One type stores items that are recycled during the course of hotel operations; the other type stores non-recyclable items.

Recycled Inventories

Recycled inventories include linens, most equipment items, and some guest supplies. Recycled equipment includes room attendant carts, vacuum cleaners, carpet shampooers, floor buffers, and many other items. Recycled guest supplies include such items as irons, ironing boards, cribs, and refrigerators, which guests may need during the course of their stay.

The number of recycled items that must be on hand to ensure smooth operations is expressed as a par number. Par refers to the number of items that must be on hand to support daily, routine housekeeping operations.

Non-Recycled Inventories

Non-recycled inventories include cleaning supplies, most guestroom supplies (such as bath soap), and guest amenities (which may range from toothbrushes and shampoos and conditioners to scented bath powders and colognes). Since non-recyclable items are used up, inventory levels are closely tied to the purchase ordering system. A purchase ordering system for non-recyclable inventory items establishes a par number that is based on two figures—a minimum quantity and a maximum quantity.

The **minimum quantity** is the fewest number of purchase units that should be in stock at any time. Purchase units are normal-size shipping containers, such as cases or drums. The inventory level should never fall below the minimum quantity. When the inventory level of a non-recyclable item reaches the minimum quantity, additional supplies must be ordered.

The actual number of additional supplies that must be ordered is determined by the maximum quantity. The **maximum**

Exhibit 1
Sample Form for Calculating Expected Inventories

Month _____

HOUSEKEEPING DEPARTMENT
SUPPLIES AND EQUIPMENT
INVENTORY CALCULATION SHEET

Item	Beginning Inventory	+	Purchases	–	Issues	=	Ending Inventory
CLEANING SUPPLIES							
All-purpose cleaner							
Dusting solution							
Glass cleaner							
Wastebasket liners							
Carpet shampoo							
Stain remover							
Cleaning cloths							
Sponges							
Work gloves							
Eye covering							

quantity is the greatest number of purchase units that should be in stock at any time. This maximum quantity must be consistent with available storage space and must not be so high that large amounts of the hotel's cash resources are tied up in an overstocked inventory. The shelf life of an item also affects the maximum quantity of purchase units that can be stored.

Calculating Inventory

The executive housekeeper can monitor the actual use rates for each product kept in inventory by recording both purchases and issues of cleaning supplies. Exhibit 1

shows a form the executive housekeeper can use to determine the expected inventory for each cleaning supply and equipment item.

The results of a physical inventory—an actual count of everything that is on the shelves—are listed in the beginning inventory column for the next month. Monthly purchases are added to these initial quantities, while the amounts of supplies issued are deducted. The total—or ending inventory column—estimates the quantity of each item that should be in stock at the end of the month.

The results of the physical count can be compared to the expected ending inventory. The difference between the actual quantities on hand and the amounts expected to be on hand represent the loss of cleaning supplies and equipment during the month. If this variance is unacceptably high, the executive housekeeper should investigate whether proper storage, issuing, and recordkeeping controls are being followed.

Apply Your Learning 12.1

Please write all answers on a separate sheet of paper.

1. What are some examples of recycled equipment?
2. What are some examples of recycled guest supplies?
3. What are some examples of non-recycled inventories?

For questions 4–9, calculate the estimated ending inventory.

Item	Beginning inventory	Purchases	Issues
4. Glass cleaner	40 gallons	8 gallons	24 gallons
5. Sponges	400	150	328
6. Work gloves	500 pairs	250 pairs	105 pairs
7. Mops	40	3	12
8. Buckets	452	230	500
9. Vacuums	85	2	18

12.2 Cleaning Supplies

AFTER STUDYING SECTION 12.2, YOU SHOULD KNOW HOW TO:

♦ Identify the types of cleaning supplies

♦ Establish inventory levels for cleaning supplies

♦ Control cleaning supply inventories

Controlling inventories of all cleaning supplies and ensuring their effective use is an important responsibility of the executive housekeeper. The executive housekeeper must work with all members of the housekeeping department to ensure the correct use of cleaning materials and that cost-control procedures are followed.

Types of Cleaning Supplies

A variety of cleaning supplies is needed for the housekeeping department. Basic cleaning supplies include all-purpose cleaners, disinfectants, germicides, bowl cleaners, window cleaners, metal polishes, furniture polishes, and scrubbing pads.

Establishing Inventory Levels for Cleaning Supplies

Since cleaning supplies are part of non-recycled inventories, par levels are closely tied to the rates at which these items are consumed.

The minimum quantity for any given cleaning supply item is determined by adding the lead-time quantity to the safety stock level for that particular item. The **lead-time quantity** refers to the number of purchase units that are used up between the time that a supply order is placed and the time that the order is received.

The **safety stock level** for a given cleaning supply item refers to the number of purchase units that must always be on hand for the housekeeping department to operate smoothly during emergencies, spoilage, unexpected delays in delivery, or other situations. By adding the number of purchase units needed for a safety stock to the number of purchase units used during the lead-time, the executive housekeeper can determine the minimum number of purchase units that always needs to be stocked.

Inventory Control of Cleaning Supplies

Controlling the inventory of cleaning supplies involves establishing strict issuing procedures to regulate the flow of products from the main storeroom to the floor cleaning closets. It also involves maintaining accurate counts of the products in the main storeroom.

Exhibit 1
Sample Inventory Record

<table>
<tr>
<td colspan="3">HOTEL: _____
LOC. NO. _____
DEPT.: _____</td>
<td colspan="3" align="center">✳ *Holiday Inn*
INVENTORY RECORD
DATE _____</td>
<td colspan="3">CALLED BY _____
RECORDED BY _____
APPROVED BY _____
PAGE _____ OF _____</td>
</tr>
</table>

ITEM DESCRIPTION	STD. UNIT	MIN./ MAX	INVENTORY				TOTAL INV.	UNIT COST	TOTAL COST
			STORE ROOM	1	2	3			

Courtesy of Holiday Inn Worldwide

The executive housekeeper can establish a system of par levels for floor cleaning closets from which room attendants supply their carts. By tracking the amounts of cleaning supplies issued from the main storeroom to the floor stations, the executive housekeeper can monitor usage rates and spot instances of under- or overuse. Shortages of cleaning supplies in floor cleaning closets can result in inspection deficiencies, inconvenience to guests, and lost labor hours as room attendants search for supplies they need to do their job.

A **perpetual inventory** of all cleaning supplies is often used with the par stock system. The perpetual inventory provides a record of all materials requisitioned for supply closets. As new purchases are received by the main storeroom and as quantities are issued to floor cleaning stations, the amounts of cleaning supplies are adjusted on the perpetual record.

The executive housekeeper needs to make regular physical inventories of each property storeroom. More frequent physical inventories need to be made for those items that are depleted more quickly. An inventory record, such as the one shown in Exhibit 1, can be used as a worksheet. Physical inventories are quicker and easier if the items listed on the inventory record are in the same order as they are arranged on storeroom shelves.

Apply Your Learning 12.2

Please write all answers on a separate sheet of paper.

1. What is a perpetual inventory?

2. List several types of cleaning supplies.

3. What factors affect the lead-time quantity of supplies?

4. The hotel places two bars of soap in each guestroom. There are 150 guestrooms in the property. The executive housekeeper wants to keep one par of soap in the guestrooms, two par in floor closets, three par replacement stock, and one par for emergencies. How many bars of soap does the property need?

5. The hotel uses 12 gallons of shampoo each day. The vendor takes four days to deliver shampoo from the date that the order is placed. The safety stock level is 60 gallons. What is the minimum quantity needed for shampoo?

6. The hotel uses 340 pairs of disposable gloves each day. The vendor takes two weeks to deliver gloves once the order is placed. The safety stock is 1,000 pairs of gloves. What is the minimum quantity needed for disposable gloves?

12.3 Linen Inventory and Control

AFTER STUDYING SECTION 12.3, YOU SHOULD KNOW HOW TO:

♦ Identify the types of linens

♦ Establish par levels for linens

♦ Describe procedures for effective inventory control of linens

♦ Take a physical inventory of linens

Linen is the most important recycled inventory item under the executive housekeeper's responsibility. Next to personnel, linen costs are the highest expense in the housekeeping department. Careful policies and procedures are needed to control the hotel's inventory of linen supplies. The executive housekeeper is responsible for developing and maintaining control procedures for the storage, issuing, use, and replacement of linen inventories.

Types of Linen

The executive housekeeper is generally responsible for three main types of linen: bed, bath, and table.

Bed linens include sheets (of various sizes and colors), matching pillowcases, and mattress pads or covers. Bath linens include bath towels, hand towels, specialty towels, washcloths, and fabric bath mats. The housekeeping department may also be responsible for storing and issuing table linens for the hotel's food and beverage outlets. Table linens include tablecloths and napkins. Banquet linens are a special type of table linen. Due to the variety of sizes, shapes, and colors, banquet linens may need to be kept separate from other restaurant linens.

Establishing Par Levels for Linens

The first task in effectively managing linens is to determine the appropriate inventory level for *all* types of linen used. Shortages occur when the inventory level for linens is set too low. Shortages disrupt the work of the housekeeping department, irritate guests who have to wait for clean rooms, reduce the number of readied rooms, and shorten the useful life of linens as a result of intensified laundering. Although housekeeping operations run smoothly when inventory levels are set too high, management will object to the excessive amount of cash tied up in an overstock of supplies.

The **par number** for linen inventories is the standard stock level needed for efficient housekeeping operations. One **par** of linens equals the total number of each type of linen that is needed to outfit all guestrooms one time.

Exhibit 1
Sample Par Calculation

This is a sample calculation of how to establish a par stock level for king-size sheets for a hotel that uses an in-house laundry operation and supplies two sheets for each of the property's 300 king-size beds.

300 king-size beds × 2 sheets per bed = 600 per par number

One par in guestrooms	1	× 600	=	600
One par in floor linen closets	1	× 600	=	600
One par soiled in the laundry	1	× 600	=	600
One par replacement stock	1	× 600	=	600
One par for emergencies	1	× 600	=	600
Total number				3,000

3,000 sheets ÷ 600 sheets/par = 5 par

One par of linen is not enough for an efficient operation. Linen supplies should be several times above what is needed to outfit all guestrooms just once. If you are establishing a par number for linens, you must consider three things: the laundry cycle, replacement linens, and emergency situations.

The hotel's laundry cycle is the most important factor in determining linen pars. Quality hotels change and launder linens daily. At any given time, large amounts of linen are moving between guestrooms and the laundry. If housekeeping manages an efficient on-premises laundry operation, the laundry cycle indicates that housekeeping should maintain three par of linens:

1. One par—linens laundered, stored, and ready for use today

2. A second par—yesterday's linens which are being laundered today

3. A third par—linens to be stripped from the rooms today and laundered tomorrow

The frequency of collection and delivery services from outside commercial laundry will affect the quantities of linen the property needs to stock.

The second factor to consider when establishing linen par levels is the replacement of worn, damaged, lost, or stolen linen. Since linen losses vary from property to property, executive housekeepers will need to determine a reasonable par level for linen replacement based on the property's history.

Finally, the executive housekeeper must be prepared for emergencies. A power failure or equipment damage may shut down a hotel's laundry operation and interrupt the continuous movement of linens through the laundry cycle. The executive housekeeper may decide to hold one full par of linens in reserve so that housekeeping operations can continue to run smoothly during an emergency.

Exhibit 1 illustrates a sample par calculation for the number of king-size sheets required for a hotel with 300 king-size beds. In this example, 3,000 king-size sheets should be in the hotel linen inventory at all times. Similar calculations are needed for every type of linen used.

Inventory Control of Linens

The executive housekeeper needs to cooperate with the laundry manager to maintain an accurate daily count of all linens sent to and received from the laundry. Effective communication with the laundry manager can help the executive housekeeper spot shortages or excessive amounts of linen.

Storage. Much of a hotel's linen supply is in constant movement between guestrooms and laundry facilities. Laundered linens rest in storage for at least 24 hours. This helps increase the useful life of linens and provides an opportunity for wrinkles to smooth out in permanent press fabrics.

Linen storage rooms need to be relatively humidity-free and have adequate ventilation. Shelves are smooth and free of any things that could damage fabric and be organized by linen type. Linen storage rooms are kept locked.

Issuing. An effective method for controlling linen is to maintain floor pars for all floor linen closets. A **floor par** equals the quantity of each type of linen that is required to outfit all rooms serviced from a particular floor linen closet. Executive housekeepers establish and post linen pars in each floor linen closet.

The executive housekeeper can use the occupancy report to create a linen distribution list that indicates how much linen is needed to bring each floor linen closet back up to par for the next day.

At the end of the day shift, a member of the housekeeping evening crew restocks the floor linen closets with the linen set aside by the laundry manager. Linens are issued daily only in the amounts needed to bring each floor linen closet up to its par level.

Special procedures are also required for linen that needs replacement. Any clean linen item that is judged unsuitable due to holes, tears, stains, or excessive wear should not be used in guestrooms. A special linen replacement request form should be filled out. The laundry manager will increase the floor distribution count the next day to accommodate the need for replacement.

Clean but damaged linen should be held separately and delivered to the laundry manager (or other appropriate personnel) who determines whether it is unusable or whether it can be repaired.

Inventory control procedures for table linens should be designed in the same way. A par stock level of all table linens used in each food and beverage outlet should be established. Soiled linens should be counted nightly, and a list of items sent to the laundry should be prepared. Both the laundry manager and the executive housekeeper can use the list as a control and as an issue order for the next day. Linen needs for special events can be noted on the nightly count sheet and included on the next day's delivery.

Taking a Physical Inventory of Linens

A **physical inventory** of all linen items is the most important part of managing linen inventories. A complete count is conducted as often as once a month. At the very least, physical inventories are taken quarterly.

The regular physical inventories provide accurate figures on the number of all items in use, as well as those discarded, lost, or in need of replacement. The inventory helps the housekeeping department maintain a careful budget and ensure that adequate supplies are on hand to meet the hotel's linen needs. It also determines the need to replenish the hotel's linen supply.

Typically, two people work together to take inventory. One person calls out the count for each type of linen while the other records the quantity on an inventory count sheet. It is not unusual for the hotel's controller or an accounting department employee to spot check counts and verify the accuracy of the final inventory report. When the inventory is complete, a final report is sent to the controller or general manager for final verification and entry.

All linens in *all* locations must be included in the count. The executive housekeeper will take the inventory at a time when the movement of linen between guestrooms and the laundry can be halted.

The next step is to determine all the locations in the hotel where linens may be found. This may include:

- Main linen room
- Guestrooms
- Floor linen closets
- Room attendant carts
- Soiled-linen bins or chutes
- Soiled linen in laundry
- Laundry storage shelves
- Mobile linen trucks or carts
- Made-up rollaway beds, cots, sofa beds, cribs, etc.

The executive housekeeper prepares a linen count sheet, which records the counts for every type of linen in each location.

When the counting is done, the executive housekeeper collects the sheets and transfers the totals to a master inventory control chart. The results of the inventory is compared to the previous inventory count to determine actual usage and the need for replacement purchases. The executive housekeeper now can determine which linens and what amounts of each type are needed to replace lost stock and maintain established par levels.

The same gereneral rules and procedures are followed for physical inventories of table linen used in the food department— and the same general forms used. Inventory lists that itemize all types, sizes, and colors of table linens the hotel uses are prepared for each food and beverage outlet— including banquet facilities. By following the same procedures used for room linens, the total inventory of table linens is calculated, and the executive housekeeper determines the need for replacement stock.

Apply Your Learning 12.3

Please write all answers on a separate sheet of paper.

1. List examples of bed linens, bath linens, and table linens.

2. What is the definition of one par of linens?

3. What is the minimum par of linen that a hotel should maintain on an annual basis?

4. What factors should be considered when storing linen?

5. **Pillowcases.** The hotel uses three pillowcases in each guestroom. There are 200 guestrooms in the property. The executive housekeeper wants to keep one par in guestrooms, one par in floor linen closets, one par soiled in the laundry, one par replacement stock, and one par for emergencies. How many pillowcases does the property need?

6. **Queen size sheets.** A hotel with an in-house laundry supplies two sheets for each of the property's 230 queen-size beds. How many sheets does it need to maintain five par of sheets?

7. **Bath mats.** A hotel provides one terry bath mat for each regular guestroom and two for each suite. They contract with an outside service for laundry. It has 200 regular guestrooms and 50 suites. How many bath mats are needed for six par of linen?

12.4   Linen Purchases

AFTER STUDYING SECTION 12.4, YOU SHOULD KNOW HOW TO:

♦ Describe the purchasing responsibilities of the executive housekeeper

♦ Identify factors to consider when determining the size of an annual linen purchase

♦ Evaluate the quality of linens and their long-term costs

♦ Control linen purchases as they are received

Efficient purchasing practices can help control housekeeping expenses. Inventory control procedures show when to buy and how much to buy for each inventoried item. The executive housekeeper must also decide what to buy, whom to buy it from, and exactly how to purchase it.

Role of the Executive Housekeeper

The executive housekeeper submits quantities and specifications of items to the purchasing department. The executive housekeeper will need to fill out and sign a purchase order such as that shown in Exhibit 1.

The housekeeper recommends the content, quantities, and source of all items purchased for the housekeeping department. The executive housekeeper needs to know how to obtain the best value when purchasing the items needed by the housekeeping department.

Size of Purchase

Next to salaries and wages, linens are the highest expense item in the housekeeping budget. The initial purchase of linens for the hotel will greatly influence the costs of replacing lost or damaged linens. The fabric type, size, and color will influence both initial purchases and replacement costs. Colored items are usually more expensive and have shorter life spans than white ones since the colors fade through repeated washings.

The physical inventory records show the executive housekeeper how long the existing stock of linens will last and how much of each type of linen needs to be reordered to maintain par levels. Typically, linen purchases are made annually with deliveries scheduled to be drop-shipped on a quarterly basis. This arrangement helps the executive housekeeper save storage space.

The executive housekeeper determines the quantity of linen to purchase by assessing the hotel's quarterly requirements to maintain linen at the proper par level. The executive housekeeper can use physical inventories of linens to calculate

Exhibit 1
Sample Purchase Order

Purchase Order

Purchase Order
Number: _____

Order Date: _____

Payment Terms: _____

To: _____
           (supplier)

From/
Ship to: _____
              (name of food service operation)

_____

_____

_____
           (address)

_____
              (address)

Please Ship:

Delivery Date: _____

Quantity Ordered	Description	✔	Units Shipped	Unit Cost	Total Cost

Total Cost _____

Important: This purchase order expressly limits acceptance to the terms and conditions stated above, noted on the reverse side hereof, and any additional terms and conditions affixed hereto or otherwise referenced. Any additional terms and conditions proposed by seller are objected to and rejected.

_____
Authorized Signature

an annual consumption rate that shows how much linen is "used up" either by normal wear and tear, damage, loss, or theft. With this information, the executive housekeeper can use the following formula to determine the size of annual linen purchases:

Annual Order = Par Stock Level – Linen on Hand

Selecting Suppliers

The executive housekeeper is expected to carefully select suppliers and linen products to ensure that the hotel receives good value for money spent. The most important considerations are the suitability of the products for their intended uses and whether the products are economical.

Regarding linen, the expected useful life of the linen is often more important than purchase price. The cost of laundering linens over their useful life is usually much greater and more important than their initial price. The life span of linen is measured in terms of how many times it can be laundered before becoming too worn to be suitable for guestroom use.

Durability, laundry considerations, and purchase price are the main criteria to use in selecting linen. A cost per use can be calculated to evaluate alternative linen purchases using the following formula:

$$\text{Cost per use} = \frac{\text{Purchase Cost} + \text{Life Span Laundering Cost}}{\text{Number of Life Span Launderings}}$$

The laundering costs over the life span of a linen product can be determined by multiplying the item's weight by the hotel's laundering cost per pound—and then multiplying again by the number of launderings the item can withstand before showing excessive wear.

Receiving Linens

When orders of new linens are received, shipments are checked against purchase orders and inspected to ensure that the linens meet all quality and quantity specifications. Newly received linen orders must be immediately moved to the main linen room for storage.

Hotels keep perpetual inventories for all new linen received and issued. This means that a running count is kept for on-hand quantities of every type of new linen stored in the main linen room. The inventory record shows the linen type, specific item, price, storage location, and dates of ordering and receiving. As linen items are put into service to replace worn, damaged, lost, or stolen linen, the quantity recorded on the perpetual inventory record is adjusted accordingly.

Apply Your Learning 12.4

Please write all answers on a separate sheet of paper.

1. What role does the executive housekeeper play in making linen purchases?

2. What is the formula for determining annual linen purchases?

3. What is the formula for determining the cost per use of linen?

4. What information should be contained in the inventory record?

Quick Hits

SECTION 12.1—TYPES OF INVENTORY

- There are two main types of inventory: recycled inventories and non-recycled inventories.

- **Recycled inventories** include linens, most equipment items, and some guest supplies. They are those items which do not get consumed during use and can be reused.

- **Non-recycled inventories** include cleaning supplies, most guestroom amenities, and guestroom supplies. They are consumed during use.

- Inventory procedures for non-recycled inventories involve determining the **minimum quantity,** the **maximum quantity,** and the **par number.**

- **Minimum quantity** refers to the fewest number of purchase units that should be in stock at any one time.

- **Maximum quantity** refers to the greatest number of purchase units that should be stock at any one time.

- The estimated ending inventory can be calculated by taking the beginning inventory, adding purchases, and subtracting issues. Any difference between the estimated ending inventory and the actual ending inventory is due to loss, damage, or theft.

SECTION 12.2—CLEANING SUPPLIES

- Basic cleaning supplies for the housekeeping department include all-purpose cleaners, disinfectants, germicides, bowl cleaners, window cleaners, metal polishes, furniture polishes, and scrubbing pads.

- **Minimum quantity** for cleaning supplies is determined by adding the lead-time quantity to the safety stock level.

- **Lead-time quantity** is the number of purchase items that are used up between the time a supply order is placed and the time that the order is received.

- **Safety stock level** refers to the number of purchase units that must always be on hand in case of spoilage, emergencies, unexpected delays in delivery, or other situations.

- An executive housekeeper maintains accurate counts of products in the main storeroom and on floor cleaning closets.

- A **perpetual inventory** provides a record of items issued from the supply closet.

- Regular physical inventories are an important part of controlling the inventory of cleaning supplies.

SECTION 12.3—LINEN INVENTORY AND CONTROL

- Linen costs are the second highest expense in the housekeeping department.

- There are three major types of linen: bed, bath, and table.

- The **par number** of linens is the standard stock level needed to accommodate typical housekeeping operations.

- One **par** of linen is the total number of each type of linen that is needed to outfit all guestrooms one time.

- Three things affect the par number of linens: laundry cycle, replacement linens, and emergency situations.

- Most hotels with in-house laundry operations keep at least five par of linen—one washed, stored, and ready for use; one being laundered; one in use in the guestrooms; one to replace damaged, lost, or stolen items; and one par for emergency situations.

- Linens should rest in storage for at least 24 hours to extend their useful life.

- Hotels often maintain a floor par of linen in floor linen closets.

- The occupancy report helps the executive housekeeper determine how much linen is needed each day.

- Each hotel establishes special procedures for handling the disposal or re-use of damaged linen.

- **Physical inventories** are conducted at least quarterly, if not monthly. They involve two people counting all of the linen and recording the amounts on an inventory count sheet.

- Linen is stored in various locations around the hotel, including main linen room, guestrooms, floor linen closets, room attendant carts, soiled-linen bins or chutes, laundry room, mobile linen trucks or carts, and made-up rollaway beds, cots, sofa beds, cribs, etc.

SECTION 12.4—LINEN PURCHASES

- The executive housekeeper helps the purchasing department make housekeeping purchases by identifying quantities, suppliers, and the specifications of items to be purchased.

- The physical inventory identifies how much linen must be purchased.

- The annual order can be determined by subtracting the linen on hand from the par stock level.

- When selecting suppliers, the executive housekeeper must determine purchase price, laundry considerations, durability and expected useful life span.

- Cost per use can be calculated by adding purchase cost and life span laundering costs and dividing the sum by the number of life span launderings.

- The person receiving linens must check the shipment against the purchase order.

Profile

Jonathan Tisch
Chairman and CEO, Loews Hotels

Innovative. Synergistic. Passionate. These are just three words that can be used to describe Jonathan Tisch. However, one word you will never find associated with him is "typical." As chairman and chief executive officer of Loews Hotels, as well as chairman of NYC & Company, Tisch certainly breaks the proverbial mold of the traditional hotelier or typical businessman.

Growing up in a family with a hospitality background, was Tisch destined to enter the industry? "[It] most definitely provided me an advantage with respects to knowing the hotel industry. I remember when I was a child, I would spend my summers with my family at one of our hotel properties. When I was tired of swimming or playing around with friends, I would go and assist behind the front desk. I would help with the check-in or shuttle bags back and forth from the guestrooms. I think that over the years, I worked almost every possible position in a hotel," said Tisch.

In 2004, Tisch participated in the TLC television program, "Now Who's Boss?" where he spent a week working line-level jobs at a Loews property. "Returning back to fulfill the duties and responsibilities of some of those positions [I held early in my career], now as chairman and CEO of Loews, most definitely provided me with valuable perspective on the commitment and dedication of our employees," said Tisch. "This experience clearly demonstrated for me that our employees strive for the highest level of professionalism when performing their duties. Also, I painfully learned that I could never survive in housekeeping."

Tisch's advice to hospitality students: "When [you] graduate, just take a job in the industry, any job, even if it is not the perfect job. All of the good business people I know express time and time again that each has grown and benefited from all of their past experiences. Thus, these individuals were able to apply the lessons learned from their previous positions to a plan that has led to their current success."

Tisch also shared his profile of a successful hospitality leader: "If you are an individual who is creative, willing to take some chances, effectively networks, has a strong sense of self, and possesses discipline, you can and will go far in the hospitality and tourism industries."

Excerpted with permission from Hospitality and Tourism Graduate Student Society, *Preston Robert Tisch Center, New York University.*

Guestroom Cleaning

Sections

13.1 Preparation

While the housekeeping manager is not usually responsible for cleaning rooms on a regular basis, the overall success of the department will be much improved if management understands the procedures and concerns involved in guestroom cleaning. When problems arise, knowledgeable managers will be better equipped to resolve them. When performance exceeds expectations, informed managers will be better equipped to recognize and reward noteworthy accomplishments.

Stocking the Cart

A room attendant requires a special set of tools to do his or her job. For the professional room attendant, these tools include cleaning supplies and equipment, linens, room accessories, and **amenities** that are necessary for preparing a guest's room. All such items are stocked on the **room attendant's cart**.

A well-organized and well-stocked cart is key to efficiency.

Carts are generally large enough to carry the supplies needed for a half-day's room assignments. Most carts have three shelves—the lower two for linen and the top for supplies. Housekeepers should understand the importance of not overstocking or understocking a cart. Overstocking increases the likelihood that some items will be damaged, soiled, or stolen in the course of cleaning. Understocking means that room attendants may waste time making trips back to the linen room for more supplies.

Items typically found on a room attendant's cart include:

Keeping It Colonial

The Williamsburg Inn recreates colonialism to create a true trip back in time for its guests. Room attendants don't use carts in an effort to make a stay at the inn seem more like a night at home. The cleaning team goes back and forth to the rooms from the hallway closets to keep it quieter for the guests. All bedspreads, curtains, and bed canopies are made by hand and the modern conveniences—telephones, air conditioning, and electric lamps—are usually well-hidden.

- Sheets, pillowcases, and mattress pads
- Towels and washcloths
- Bath mats
- Toilet and facial tissue
- Drinking glasses
- Soap bars
- Ashtrays and matches

In most cases, cleaning supplies are kept in a **hand caddy** that can be carried into the guestroom and bathroom. This way, the room attendant does not have to bring the entire cart into the room in order to have easy access to supplies. Items stocked in the caddy include:

- All-purpose cleaner

- Glass cleaner in a spray bottle
- Toilet bowl brush
- Dusting solution
- Cloths and sponges
- Rubber gloves

A laundry bag for dirty linens is usually placed at one end of the cart and a trash bag at the other. A broom and vacuum are also positioned on either end of the cart for easy access. Exhibit 1 illustrates one efficient stocking arrangement for a room attendant's cart.

To guard against theft and possible security breaches, room attendants' personal items and room keys should not be stored on the cart. It is also important that

the Rooms CHRONICLE

Ask Gail—Start of Day

Dear Gail:

Any tips to help avoid mass confusion in housekeeping in the morning when everyone is trying to sign in? What a mess with room attendants waiting for keys, grabbing rags, and fighting over spray bottles.

D.B., Boston, MA

Dear D.B.:

It's easy to start the day if you are prepared before the rush. Fill the bottles and restock carts or caddies in the evening so that a room attendant does not have to search for supplies.

Have assignment papers written and laid out on the desk with the necessary keys on top of each paper. Room attendants should form a line to be handled one at a time. The room attendant signs in (or punches in), signs the key control log, receives the keys and assignment, and moves on to another window or counter to pick up the supply caddy.

Smaller properties put the assignment sheet and keys in the caddy to simplify handing out equipment. Larger properties stagger the start times so that labor hours are not wasted by employees waiting to begin. For example, at an 800-room property, three groups can be started 15 minutes apart.

Source: *The Rooms Chronicle*, Volume 2, Number 4.
For subscription information, visit www.roomschronicle.com.

**Exhibit 1
Sample Stocking Arrangement for
Room Attendant's Cart**

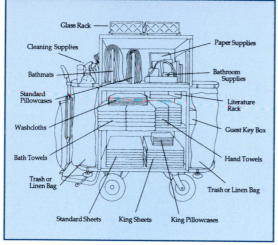

Courtesy of Holiday Inn Worldwide

room attendants stock the proper eye, hand, and face protection and be thoroughly trained in their correct use.

Alternative Carts

Some hotels now use an integrated transporting and storing system as an alternative to the traditional room attendant cart. The equipment is modular, consisting of containers, caddies, and shelves that can be easily removed and arranged within a larger service cart. These components are loaded to convenient levels to allow for the efficient movement of linens and supplies when servicing guestrooms. A separate, detachable component accompanies the main unit and is used to catch trash and soiled linen.

Applying Your Learning 13.1

Please write all answers on a separate sheet of paper.

1. Why should a room attendant avoid overstocking or understocking his or her cart?

2. Which of the following items are likely to be included in a hand caddy?

   | towels and washcloths | glass cleaner | rubber gloves | bars of soap |
   | matches | ashtrays | sponges | |

3. Where should room attendants avoid storing guestroom keys?

13.2 Room Assignments

AFTER STUDYING SECTION 13.2, YOU SHOULD KNOW HOW TO:

♦ Interpret a room status report

♦ Complete a room assignment sheet

♦ Identify the order in which guestrooms should be cleaned

After assembling supplies, the room attendant is ready to begin cleaning guestrooms.

Room Status Report

The order in which a room attendant cleans rooms will be determined by the **room status report.** This daily report, sometimes called the house-keeping report, provides information on the occupancy or condition of the property's rooms. It is generated through communication between the front office and the housekeeping department.

The room status report should be easy to read and understand. Most use simple codes to indicate room status. For the most part, a room attendant's cleaning schedule will be determined by these three categories:

• Check-out—A room from which the guest has already checked out

• Stayover—A room in which the guest is scheduled to stay again

• Due out—A room from which a guest is due to check out that day

Another designation commonly used is "early makeup." This refers to rooms for which a guest has reserved an early check-in time or requested a cleaning as soon as possible.

Room Assignment Sheet

A floor or shift supervisor will use information from the room status report to draw up room assignments for housekeeping personnel. Room assignments are generally listed according to room number and room status on a standardized form. The number of rooms assigned to a room attendant is based upon the property's work standards for specific types of rooms and cleaning tasks. The room attendant uses the assignment sheet to set priorities for the workday and to report the condition of each assigned room at the end of the shift. In the sample form shown in Exhibit 1, room attendants are provided space to make written comments on each room and to indicate room items needing repair.

Cleaning Order

The order in which rooms are cleaned should be the order that best serves guests. Early-makeup rooms are cleaned first.

Exhibit 1
Sample Room Assignment Sheet

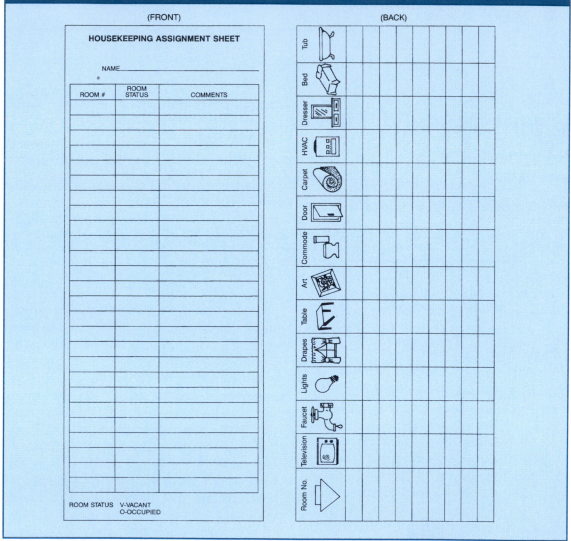

Courtesy of Holiday Inn Worldwide

Check-outs are next, so the front office can sell the rooms as guests arrive. After early makeups and check-outs, a room attendant will generally clean stayovers. Due outs are usually the last rooms cleaned. Sometimes, room attendants may be able to wait until the guest has actually checked out.

Room attendants should avoid disturbing guests. A "Do Not Disturb" sign clearly indicates that the room attendant should check back on the room later in the shift. Other rooms that room attendants must delay servicing include rooms that the guest has double-locked from the inside.

When a guest refuses service, a floor supervisor or other manager should call to arrange a convenient time for cleaning. Such calls are also made to check that the guest is not experiencing a situation that requires intervention, such as a serious illness or accident.

Apply Your Learning 13.2

Please write all answers on a separate sheet of paper.

1. The _____ _____ report determines the order in which specific rooms are cleaned.

2. The three primary categories of rooms are:
   a. due out, due in, and to do.
   b. check-out, due out, and stayover.
   c. early makeup, check-out, and "do not disturb."
   d. early makeup, late makeup, and check-out.

3. Room attendants set cleaning priorities for the workday using the _____ _____ sheet.

4. What fundamentally determines the order in which rooms are cleaned?

5. What is the typical order for cleaning the three primary categories of rooms?

6. What actions should be taken when a guest refuses service?

13.3 Cleaning Procedures

AFTER STUDYING SECTION 13.3, YOU SHOULD KNOW HOW TO:

♦ Enter the guestroom properly

♦ Perform beginning cleaning tasks

♦ Demonstrate the most efficient way to make a bed

♦ Clean a bathroom following safe procedures

♦ Dust

♦ Operate a vacuum cleaner in a safe and efficient manner

♦ Check a guestroom for cleanliness

No other feature or service provided by a property will impress a guest more than a spotlessly clean and comfortable guestroom. The condition of the guestroom conveys a critical message. It shows the care that the property puts into creating a clean, safe, and pleasant environment for its guests. Of course, this places a big responsibility on the housekeeping department. After all, the guestroom is the main product that a property sells. Housekeeping plays a greater role than any other department in ensuring that this product meets the standards guests need and expect.

To maintain the standards that keep guests coming back, room attendants must follow a series of detailed procedures for guestroom cleaning. A systematic approach can save time and energy—and reduce frustration.

The sequence of room cleaning consists of preparatory steps, actual cleaning tasks, and a final check. (Room inspections are also an integral part of the overall process of guestroom cleaning.) There is value and logic behind the organization of cleaning activities. Adhering to a careful routine can save time and ensure a professional job.

The best way to explain the following guestroom cleaning tasks is from the perspective of the room attendant.

Entering the Guestroom

Guestroom cleaning begins the moment the room attendant approaches the guestroom door. It is important to follow certain

Pardon me, please

The British word "loo" comes from the fact that the English did not like other guests to know when they were going to use the restroom in hotels, so, instead of writing the word "toilet" on the toilet door, they wrote the number 100, which looks like the word "loo."

procedures when entering the guestroom that show respect for the guest's privacy.

Knock on the door and announce, "Housekeeping." Never use a key to knock since it can damage the door's surface. If a guest answers, introduce yourself and ask what time would be convenient to clean the room. Note that time on your status sheet or schedule. If no answer is heard, wait a moment, knock again, and repeat, "Housekeeping." If there is still no answer, open the door slightly and repeat, "Housekeeping." If the guest does not respond after this third announcement, you may begin to enter the guestroom.

Sometimes the guest may be sleeping or in the bathroom. If this is the case, leave quietly and close the door. If the guest is awake, excuse yourself, explain that you can come back later, close the door, and proceed to the next room.

Position your cart in front of the open door with the open section facing the room. Doing so serves a triple purpose: it gives you easy access to your supplies, blocks the entrance to intruders, and alerts returning guests of your presence.

To help guard employees' safety and the guests' belongings, many properties now instruct room attendants to clean a guestroom with the door closed and locked. A sign on the door informs the guest that the attendant would be happy to return later if the guest wishes to enter the room using a key. This helps properties avoid the problem of requiring the room attendant to serve as a security guard.

Beginning Tasks

After entering the room, turn on all the lights. This helps you see what you are doing and

allows you to check for light bulbs that need to be replaced. Draw back the draperies and check the cords and hooks for any damage. Open the windows so the room can air out while you are cleaning. Check the air conditioning and heater to make sure they are working properly and are set according to property standards. Some properties require that the temperature be left where the guests set it in a stayover room. Turn the television on briefly to make certain it works; test the TV remote control.

Next, take a good look at the condition of the room. Make note of any damaged or missing items such as linens or wastebaskets. If anything of value is gone or if something needs repair, notify your supervisor.

Remove or replace dirty ashtrays and glasses. Always make sure that smoking materials are fully extinguished before dumping them in the trash. As you replace the ashtrays, be sure to replenish matches. Collect any service trays, dishes, bottles, or cans that might be scattered around the room. Empty the trash and replace any wastebasket liners. In stayover rooms, straighten any newspapers and magazines. Never throw out anything in a stayover room unless it is in the wastebasket.

Making the Bed

It is important to make the bed first—especially in stayover rooms. If the guest returns while you are elsewhere in the room, the freshly made bed will give the room a neat appearance—even if other areas have not been touched. In check-out rooms, some properties recommend that you strip the bed shortly after entering and remake it near the end of your cleaning. This way the bed has a chance to air out.

Exhibit 1
Step-by-Step Approach to Mitering

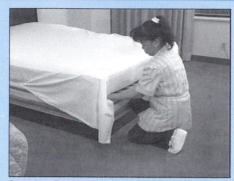

Step 1 Begin with the sheet hanging loosely over the corner. Tuck in the sheet along the foot of the bed, right up to the corner.

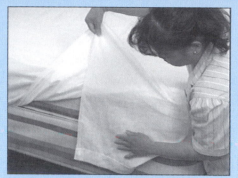

Step 2 Take the loose end of the sheet, about one foot from the corner, and pull it straight out, forming a flap.

Step 3 Pull up the flap so it is flat and wrinkle-free.

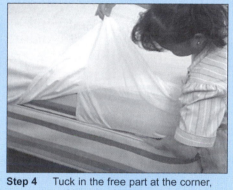

Step 4 Tuck in the free part at the corner, making sure it is snug.

Step 5 Pull the flap out toward you and down over the side of the bed.

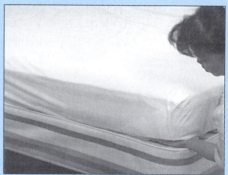

Step 6 Tuck in the flap and make sure the corner is smooth and snug.

Before you begin, remove any personal items from the bed and place them aside. Remove the bedspread and blanket and place them on a chair to keep them clean and free from dust and dirt. If the blanket or bedspread is dirty—or if you notice any holes or tears—be sure to replace it. Strip the bed of dirty linen and place the pillows on the chair with the bedspread and blanket.

The most efficient way of making a bed is to completely finish one side before beginning on the next. This system saves time walking back and forth around the bed. Begin by placing the bottom sheet on the mattress and mitering that sheet in the upper left-hand corner of the bed. **Mitering** is a simple way to make a smooth, neat, professional corner. A step-by-step method for mitering a corner is shown in Exhibit 1.

Next, move to the foot of the bed—still on the left side—and miter that corner of the sheet.

Place a fresh top sheet on the bed, wrong-side up. Then, place the blanket on top of the sheet. At the head of the bed, turn the top sheet over the blanket about six inches. Smooth your hand over the bed so the surface appears even and without wrinkles. Miter the top sheet and blanket in the bottom left-hand corner of the bed and tuck them in along the side of the bed. On the other side of the bed, miter the bottom sheet at the right foot of the bed, followed by the top sheet and blanket. Move down the right-hand side of the bed and miter the bottom sheet in the top right corner. Fold the top sheet over the blanket so it is even with the left side. Finally, make sure the blanket and top sheet are neatly tucked in along the sides and at the foot of the bed.

Center the bedspread evenly over the bed. Fold the bedspread down from the head of the bed, leaving enough room to cover the pillows. Fluff the pillows and put on the pillowcases. For sanitation reasons, never hold the pillow under your chin or with your teeth. Position the pillows at the head of the bed. Pull the bedspread over the pillows and tuck in the bedspread.

Cleaning the Bathroom

A clean bathroom is important for more than simply appearance. Health and safety considerations on the local, state, and federal levels necessitate that the room attendant take extra care when scrubbing, rinsing, and drying bathroom surfaces.

Bathrooms are usually cleaned in the following sequence: shower area, vanity and sink, toilet, walls and fixtures, and floor. Like most cleaning tasks, it is important to work from top to bottom to avoid spotting or dirtying areas already cleaned. The necessary cleaning equipment should be stocked in the hand caddy: an approved all-purpose cleaner for bathroom surfaces, cloths and sponges, glass and mirror cleaner, rubber gloves, and protective eye covering. Some properties also use an odorless disinfectant.

For personal safety, never stand on the edge of the tub when cleaning. As you wash and wipe the tub or shower walls, continually check their condition so you can report any needed repairs to your supervisor. If the tub has a drain trap, be sure to check it for hair. After cleaning the tub itself, clean the shower head and tub fixtures. Leave the shower head aimed in the correct position. To prevent spotting and add sparkle, immediately wipe and polish the fixtures with a dry cloth. Also, clean the shower curtain or door. Pay special attention to the bottom, where mildew may accumulate. Always

She's No Lady

First Lady Eleanor Roosevelt, a frequent guest at the St. Francis Hotel in San Francisco, arrived one evening and was shown to a suite. Due to a citywide room shortage, she asked to be moved to a standard room and that the suite be given to a serviceman. A late-arriving sailor got the room and invited a host of friends to experience the splendor of his surroundings. By morning, the room was littered with empty bottles, broken furniture, and discarded clothing. The housekeeper, upon arriving at the room, reportedly phoned the front desk and said, "I don't know about this Mrs. Roosevelt. She's no lady."

the Rooms CHRONICLE

Preparing a Room for Nonsmokers
By Mary Friedman

To change a room where smoking has occurred into a fresh, clean room for use as a nonsmoking room, the following procedures may be helpful:

- Wash down the walls.
- Change the filters in HVAC units.
- Clean the bathroom vents.
- Remove the drapes, wash sheers, dry-clean black-outs.
- Remove the furniture and deep-clean the entire carpet.
- Deep-clean the upholstered furniture.
- Wash wooden furniture with oil soap.
- Wash laminate furniture with all-purpose soap.
- Remove all lampshades. Vacuum or wash them if possible; replace them if necessary.
- Check the condition of the mattress and bedspring. If they smell of smoke, either replace them or cover them with zip-on plastic covers.
- Wash all pillows, mattress pads, and blankets.
- Wash or dry-clean the bedspreads.
- Wash the shower curtains and bath rugs.

This process can be very costly and labor intensive. Since one guest smoking in the room for just one evening can destroy all these special preparations, extra care should be taken to keep the rooms smoke-free.

Source: *The Rooms Chronicle*, Volume 3, Number 2.
For subscription information, visit www.roomschronicle.com.

---

reposition the door or curtain when you are finished cleaning.

When cleaning the vanity countertop and washbasin, wipe up any spillage or spots from toothpaste or soap. Rinse and polish chrome fixtures. Use a damp sponge followed by a clean cloth to clean mirrors. Remove any hair from the sink stopper and drain.

Next, clean the toilet bowl and exterior surfaces. Some cleaning procedures recommend applying an all-purpose cleaner before any other cleaning task. This way, the cleaner has time to stand while you clean other bathroom areas. All-purpose cleaners are preferable to acid bowl cleaners for use on a daily basis. Flush the toilet to remove any residue, and apply the cleaner around and under the lip of the bowl. Clean the exterior of the bowl, working down the sides to the base. Scrub the inside of the toilet with the brush around the insides and under the lip—then flush it again. Use a cloth damp with cleaning solution to clean the top of the seat, the lid, and the sides of the tank.

Towels, washcloths, bath mats, toilet and facial tissue, and guest amenities should be replenished according to property standards. Spot-clean for fingerprints and other obvious smudges on the walls, especially around light fixtures and electrical outlets.

Wipe down the walls and clean both sides of the bathroom door. Starting with the far corner of the bathroom and working back toward the door, mop or wipe down the floor—including the baseboards.

Dusting

Like bed making, the task of dusting requires a systematic approach. Some room attendants start dusting items at the door and work clockwise around the room. This reduces the chance of overlooking an area. In all cases, begin with the highest surfaces so dust doesn't fall on the items you have already cleaned. If your property uses a dusting solution, spray a small amount into the dust cloth. Never spray dusting solution directly onto an object since it can stain, cause stickiness, or actually blow dust into the air.

Clean all glass surfaces in the room using glass cleaner or water—including the front of the television set. Use a damp sponge followed by a clean cloth to clean mirrors. Some properties also use a special cleaner or disinfectant for telephone surfaces. As you dust your way around the room, note any bedroom supplies and amenities that may be needed; replenish them per the property's specifications. Finally, check the walls for spots and marks, and remove any smudges with a damp cloth and all-purpose cleaning solution.

Vacuuming

Before vacuuming, loosen dirt around baseboards with a broom or rag so it is easier to pick up. Run the vacuum over all exposed areas of the carpet that you can reach, including under tables and chairs and in the closet. Don't worry about inaccessible areas such as under the bed or dresser. Since cleaning these areas requires moving or lifting heavy furniture, most properties vacuum these areas only on a special-project basis. However, it is your responsibility to check under beds and furniture for guest belongings or for any debris that must be removed.

Start vacuuming at the farthest end of the room and work your way back. As you vacuum, be careful not to bump and mar the furniture. Some properties recommend closing windows and draperies and turning off lights as you work your way back to the door. Working in this fashion saves steps. It also eliminates the need to walk back across the floor after it has been vacuumed, thus preventing the footprints and tracks that can appear in certain types of carpet.

Final Check

The final check is a critical step in guestroom cleaning. It makes the difference between just cleaning the room and doing a professional job.

Take a few minutes to give the room a careful look from the guest's perspective. Scan from one corner to the next until you have visually inspected each item in the room. By doing so, you may discover something you overlooked or that was difficult to spot on the first cleaning.

Before you leave, make sure all furnishings are in their proper places. Look for little things like crooked lampshades or lampshades with their seams showing. Smell the air for any unpleasant odors; spray air freshener if needed. Report any unexpected odors—animals, smoke, drugs, sewer gases—to your supervisor. When you are satisfied that the guestroom is neat and thoroughly cleaned, turn off the lights, close the door, and make certain it is locked. Note the condition and status of the room on your assignment sheet, and proceed to the next room on your schedule.

Apply Your Learning 13.3

Please write all answers on a separate sheet of paper.

1. What three purposes are served by positioning the housekeeping cart in front of the open guestroom door when cleaning a room?

2. How might cleaning procedures vary when cleaning a stayover room, as opposed to a check-out?

3. The most efficient way of making a bed is to:

    a. completely finish one side before beginning on the next.
    b. start at the bottom and work up toward the pillows.
    c. work in groups of two.
    d. miter the bottom sheet.

4. What sequence is usually used for cleaning bathrooms?

5. When dusting, housekeepers can reduce the chance of overlooking a spot by dusting _____.

6. What kinds of procedures can help transform a room previously used by a smoking guest into a nonsmoking room?

7. Which areas of the guestroom are not typically the housekeeper's responsibility when it comes to vacuuming?

8. What steps are involved in the final check?

13.4 Inspection

AFTER STUDYING SECTION 13.4, YOU SHOULD KNOW HOW TO:

♦ Explain why guestrooms are inspected

♦ Inspect a guestroom that has been cleaned

♦ Identify technology affecting room inspections

Inspection programs can take many forms. In some properties, rooms are spot-checked randomly; in others, every room is checked daily. Supervisory personnel—such as a floor or shift supervisor, section supervisor, executive housekeeper, or other manager—conduct inspections.

Goals of Inspection

A **guestroom inspection** is meant to catch any problems that may have been overlooked during cleaning before the guest does. It ensures that the desired results of an established cleaning system are consistently achieved.

A well-conducted and diplomatic inspection program can also motivate employees. Most room attendants take pride in their work and enjoy having the opportunity to show it off to others. Quality cleaning jobs should be noted during inspections, and the appropriate personnel should be recognized.

Room inspections not only help identify ordinary problems with cleaning but also help identify areas in the room needing deep cleaning or maintenance.

Room Inspection Procedures

A room inspection report should note such items as the condition of furniture, fixtures, and equipment; the appearance of the ceiling and walls; the condition of the carpet and other floor coverings; and the cleanliness of window interiors and exteriors. Exhibit 1 shows a sample inspection form. Depending on the property's policies and procedures, the inspector may also be responsible for filling out any work orders or maintenance requests that are needed.

An inspection program is never any better than the follow-up that is given to an identified problem. Each situation noted on the inspection report or maintenance request should be initialed by the manager directly responsible for that area. As a rule, this should occur no later than 24 hours after the inspection.

Inspection Program Technology

Bar code technology saves time and ensures accuracy in a hospitality inspection program.

In a property using a bar code inspection system, each guestroom is identified with a small, permanently mounted bar code tag. The tag is placed in a discreet spot, such as

**Exhibit 1
Sample Room Inspection Report**

Room No. _____

Type _____   Date Inspected _____

Condition: ☐ Excellent   ☐ Acceptable   ☐ Unacceptable

	Bedroom	Condition			Bathroom	Condition
1	Doors, locks, chains, stops			21	Doors	
2	Lights, switches, plates			22	Lights, switches, plates	
3	Ceiling			23	Walls	
4	Walls			24	Tile	
5	Woodwork			25	Ceiling	
6	Drapes and hardware			26	Mirror	
7	Windows			27	Tub, caulking, grab bars	
8	Heating/air conditioning setting			28	Shower head and curtain	
9	Phone			29	Bath mat	
10	TV and radio			30	Vanity	
11	Headboards			31	Fixtures/faucets/drains	
12	Spreads, bedding, mattress			32	Toilet: flush/seat	
13	Dressers, nightstand			33	Towels: facial/hand/bath	
14	Promotional material			34	Tissue: toilet/facial	
15	Lamps, shades, bulbs			35	Soap	
16	Chairs, sofa			36	Amenities	
17	Carpet			37	Exhaust vent	
18	Pictures and mirrors					
19	Dusting					
20	Closet					

Other _____

_____

_____

_____

_____

Inspected By: _____
(Signature)

on the door frame. The inspector or maintenance person carries a bar code reader and a set of cards that list items or conditions that need to be inspected, attended to, or repaired. Like the guestroom itself, each of these items has a corresponding bar code. Exhibit 2 shows sample discrepancy and condition lists that can be customized to fit the needs of individual properties.

Upon entering the room, the inspector scans the room's bar code tag. This automatically records the room number, time, and date in the bar code scanner. The condition of each inspected item is noted by scanning the appropriate bar code or combination of bar codes on the inspection cards. At the end of the visit, the inspector "scans out" by scanning the room bar code a second time.

The information stored on the scanner can be retrieved by linking it with a special reader attached to a desktop computer system. Depending on the program and property needs, the information can be presented in a summary or report format that gives management an overview of the condition of each inspected room.

Hand-held technology is also making in-roads into the housekeeping department. Many hotels in the past several years have

Exhibit 2
Sample Inspection Forms Using Bar Code Technology

HOUSEKEEPING DISCREPANCY LIST   REGENCY TOWERS

DISCREPANCY	CALL BACK	FIXED
BED MADE IMPROPERLY		
BEDROOM DUST		
CARPET NEEDS VAC		
DIRTY LINEN		
MIRROR STREAKED		
SUPPLIES MISSING		
NAME OF DISCREPANCY		
NAME OF DISCREPANCY		
DAY, DATE & TIME		

CONDITION LIST   REGENCY TOWERS

MISSING   POOR   FAIR

GOOD   VERY GOOD   EXCELLENT

ENTRANCE DOOR		BATHROOM TILE	
ENTRANCE PAINT		BATHROOM FIXTURES	
ENTRANCE CARPET		SHOWER CURTAIN	
DESCRIPTION		DESCRIPTION	
DESCRIPTION		DESCRIPTION	

TUES, 5/22/88 2:45 PM   PAGE 1

Courtesy of Bar Code Technology, Eastham, Massachusetts

adopted software technology designed to speed up room inspections and maintenance checklists.

Hotel inspectors carry hand-held devices into which they record their inspection data. That data is transmitted to the main front office system and managers are able to use it for reports and efficiency evaluations. It also speeds room status updates.

The data is sent through either wireless technology or cradles. Wireless systems provide real-time, nearly instant communication but they require the hotel to be wired. If the hotel is not wired for wireless, small cradles can be placed throughout the hotel and the hand-held devices placed into them. The data are then transmitted to the property management system.

Apply Your Learning 13.4

Please write all answers on a separate sheet of paper.

1. What are the goals of guestroom inspection?

2. How can inspections be a useful tool for motivating employees?

3. As a rule, what should the time frame be for responding to and correcting problems that appear on a room inspection report?

4. How can properties improve guestroom inspection efficiency and accuracy using bar code or hand-held technology?

Quick Hits

Chapter 13

SECTION 13.1—PREPARATION

- The success of the housekeeping department is improved if management understands the procedures and concerns involved in guestroom cleaning.

- All cleaning supplies and equipment, linens, room accessories, and **amenities** that are necessary for preparing a guest's room are stocked on the **room attendant's cart.**

- Cleaning supplies are typically kept in a **hand caddy** that can be carried into the guestroom and bathroom.

- Some hotels use a variation on the traditional room attendant cart that consists of containers, caddies, and shelves that can be easily removed and arranged within a larger service cart.

SECTION 13.2—ROOM ASSIGNMENTS

- The **room status report,** also called the housekeeping report, provides information on the occupancy or condition of the property's rooms and determines the order in which rooms should be cleaned.

- There are three main categories of rooms: check-out, stayover, and due out.

- "Early makeup" refers to rooms scheduled for early check-in or cleaning as soon as possible.

- Early-makeup rooms are cleaned first. Check-outs are next. After early makeups and check-outs, a room attendant will generally clean stayovers, followed by due outs.

- When a guest refuses service, a floor supervisor or other manager should call to arrange a convenient time for cleaning.

SECTION 13.3—CLEANING PROCEDURES

- To maintain the standards that keep guests coming back, room attendants must follow a series of detailed procedures for guestroom cleaning.

- When entering the guestroom, it is important to show respect for the guest's privacy.

- The housekeeping cart should be positioned in front of the open door. It gives easy access to supplies, blocks the entrance to intruders, and, in the case of stayovers, alerts returning guests of housekeeping's presence.

- When beginning to clean, housekeepers should air out the room and make certain lights, the heating/air conditioning unit, and television are in good working condition.

- Damaged or missing items should be noted and reported.

- Never throw out anything in a stayover room unless it is in the wastebasket. Otherwise, discard empty bottles, newspapers, and magazines, and remove and replace dirty ashtrays and glasses. Collect any service trays and dishes.

- Following a consistent, step-by-step method for making the bed can yield smooth, neat, and professional results. Mitering is an important part of a professionally made bed.

- Bathrooms are usually cleaned in the following sequence: shower area, vanity and sink, toilet, walls and fixtures, and floor.

- Towels, washcloths, bath mats, toilet and facial tissue, and guest amenities should be replenished according to property standards.

- When dusting, room attendants can avoid overlooking areas by dusting items at the door and working clockwise around the room.

- When vacuuming, room attendants should vacuum all exposed areas of the carpet that can be reached, including under tables and chairs and in the closet.

- When finished, room attendants should give the room a careful look from the guest's perspective. They may discover something they overlooked or that was difficult to spot on the first cleaning.

SECTION 13.4—INSPECTION

- Supervisory personnel—such as a floor or shift supervisor, section supervisor, executive housekeeper, or other manager—should conduct inspections of cleaned guestrooms.

- A **guestroom inspection** should catch any problems before the guest does.

- A room inspection report should note the condition of furniture, fixtures, and equipment; the appearance of the ceiling and walls; the condition of the carpet and other floor coverings; and the cleanliness of window interiors and exteriors.

- Managers should see that each problem noted on the inspection report or maintenance request is handled within 24 hours of the inspection.

- **Bar code** technology can be a useful tool for saving time and ensuring the accuracy of a hospitality inspection program.

- **Hand-held technology** is being used more frequently. Inspectors carry hand-held devices into which they input inspection data.

Tony Farris
President & CEO, Quorum Hotels

It was a 3x5 index card that lured Tony Farris, President and Chief Executive Officer of Quorum Hotels, into the lodging industry. The index card read "NIGHT AUDITOR NEEDED, 11 P.M. TO 7 A.M."

"I didn't know what a night auditor was, but I knew what 11 P.M. to 7 A.M. was," Farris says. He was a college student with classes all day, and the shift had immediate appeal because it wouldn't interfere with his classes or studying. He applied for and got the night auditor job at a Holiday Inn. After a few years as night auditor, Farris was asked if he would work his college class schedule around a new job—that of assistant innkeeper. Farris agreed.

Despite this early success, Farris left the industry for several years after college and pursued jobs in finance and accounting. He eventually joined a real estate company that placed him as a hotel accountant once they learned of his previous lodging experience. He ended up being a controller for several hotels before going back into real estate.

The lodging industry continued to draw Farris back. He specialized in hotel development and management, eventually, along with his long-time direct reports, buying out his European financial partners in Quorum Hotels in 1994.

"If you like dealing with people," Farris says, "lodging is a great business to be in." He emphasizes that hospitality businesses—no matter in what area of the industry—need people who like people. "There is a mindset of 'service to people' that is not particularly prevalent today. If a student tries it and enjoys giving service, there are rewards in hospitality that are unlike any others. The opportunities in hospitality business are very significant. The industry is still experiencing significant growth. People are becoming even more mobile."

There is also great value in having mentors, Farris says. "No one gets far in this business without having had many mentors. I have had mentors too numerous to count. People can always continue to grow throughout their career. Mentoring is very healthy at virtually all stages of a hospitality career."

On-Premises Laundry Management

Sections

14.1   General Fabric Care

AFTER STUDYING SECTION 14.1, YOU SHOULD KNOW HOW TO:

♦ Explain the characteristics of cotton fabrics

♦ Explain the characteristics of wool fabrics

♦ Explain the characteristics of acrylic fabrics

♦ Explain the characteristics of polyester fabrics

♦ Explain the characteristics of nylon fabrics

♦ Explain the characteristics of blended fabrics

Synthetic fabrics introduced in the 1960s led to the development of no-iron sheets. Because this eliminated or reduced the need for ironing, many properties were able to switch from an outside laundry service to an on-premises laundry (OPL). Today's marketplace offers more fabrics to choose from than ever before—from all-natural fibers (wool and cotton) to a variety of synthetics (polyester and nylon). The choice of fabric is also more important than ever before because it directly affects the costs of operating the OPL. No matter what linens the property decides to buy, it is important to make certain that all items needing laun-dering include thorough instructions for care from the vendor. The following sections discuss some of the most popular fabrics used in hospitality operations. Exhibit 1 contains a summary of general care instructions for the fabrics listed here.

Cotton

Cotton is strong and actually becomes stronger when wet. It is very absorbent and can be starched, which makes it especially good for napkins and tablecloths. Although cotton can be washed and ironed at high temperatures, some shrinkage (from 5–15 percent) does occur in its first washings. Cotton fabrics also have a lower color-retention capability than polyester fabrics.

Wool

Once the fabric of choice for blankets, wool has fallen out of favor in many commercial

Dirty Laundry

During the California Gold Rush of 1849 miners sent their laundry to Honolulu for washing and pressing. Due to the extremely high costs in California during these boom years it was deemed more cost-effective to send the shirts to Hawaii for servicing.

Exhibit 1
General Care of Linen Fabrics

Fiber Group	Cleaning Method	Water Temperature	Chlorine Bleach	Dryer Temperature	Iron Temperature	Special Storage
Acrylic	launder	warm	yes	warm	medium	none
Cotton	launder	hot	yes	hot	high	store dry
Polycotton	launder	hot	yes	warm	medium	none
Nylon	launder	hot	yes	warm	low	none
Polyester	launder	hot	yes	warm	low	none
Wool	dry-clean	warm	no	warm	medium with steam	protect from moths; do not store in plastic bags

Fabric combinations should always be cared for by following the manufacturer's recommendations.

operations because it is not as durable as some synthetic materials and can be irritating to the touch. Although wool does resist soiling better than some other common fabric materials and is very absorbent, it is one of the weakest fibers and becomes even weaker when wet. It also shrinks and mats relatively easily. For this reason, many heavy-duty cleanings will quickly break down the fibers of a wool blanket.

Acrylic

Acrylic is lightweight and does not shrink. Its strength is similar to cotton's, but it decreases when wet. Because it holds moisture on its surface, acrylic is fairly slow-drying.

Polyester

Polyester is one of the strongest common fibers and does not lose its strength when wet. It dries quickly, is wrinkle-resistant, and does not soil easily. Although polyesters and polyester blends are good choices for uniforms, aprons, and other garments, they are less effective as napery (table linens) because polyester tends to break down at higher drying and ironing temperatures.

Nylon

Nylon is very strong when wet or dry. It is also easy to wash and quick to dry. Nylon, however, is sensitive to heat.

Blends

For most properties, the fabric of choice is a polyester/cotton blend (sometimes called **polycotton**) because it requires less care than all-natural fabric yet offers most of its comfort. This fabric gains strength with initial washings but can be damaged by high wash or high dryer temperatures. Specific fabric characteristics depend on the actual amount and types of fibers blended.

Apply Your Learning 14.1

Please write all answers on a separate sheet of paper.

1. What caused the switch from outside laundry services to on-premises laundry (OPL) facilities?

2. What is one disadvantage of cotton?

3. Why has wool fallen out of favor in many commercial operations?

4. What are some of the advantages of polyester?

5. Why is polycotton the fabric of choice for most properties?

14.2 Laundry Cycle

AFTER STUDYING SECTION 14.2, YOU SHOULD KNOW HOW TO:

♦ List the steps in the laundry cycle

♦ Oversee the collection of soiled linens

♦ Transport soiled linens to the laundry

♦ Sort linens by degree of soiling or by linen type

♦ Ensure that washing machines are properly loaded

♦ Describe the extraction process

♦ Finish linens by drying or ironing

♦ Establish proper folding techniques

♦ Explain the proper procedures for storing laundry

♦ Direct employees in the transfer of laundry

Every laundry uses a basic cycle of operation. This cycle includes the following steps:

1. Collecting soiled linens
2. Transporting soiled linens to the laundry
3. Sorting
4. Loading
5. Washing
6. Extracting
7. Finishing
8. Drying
9. Folding
10. Storing
11. Transferring linens to use areas

Exhibit 1 diagrams an abbreviated version of this process. Executive housekeepers or laundry managers should develop

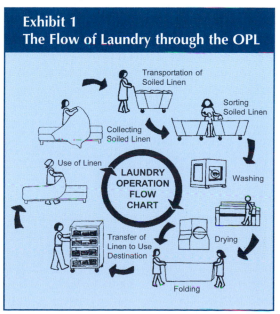

Exhibit 1
The Flow of Laundry through the OPL

Source: "On Premises Laundry Procedures in Hotels, Motels, Healthcare Facilitites, and Restaurants" (pamphlet) (St. Paul, Minn.: Ecolab, Institutional Products Division), undated.

procedures for each of these steps to prevent resoiling of clean linens, extend the life of the linens, and keep the OPL efficient and cost-effective.

Collecting Soiled Linens

Room attendants cleaning guestrooms should strip linens from beds and bath areas and put them directly into the soiled-linen bags attached to the housekeeping cart. In food and beverage outlets, buspersons gather soiled linens when tables are cleared. Items should never be piled on the floor where they can be walked on, soiled further, or damaged. Putting the linens directly into soiled-linen bags also prevents staff from using towels, sheets, napkins, or other items to blot spills or wipe smudges. *Staff should never use linens for any cleaning purposes.* Misuse of linens can permanently damage items—which can lead to higher replacement costs.

Room attendants may presort soiled linens as they are collected. This may simply mean tying a knot in one corner of a heavily soiled item to help laundry workers sort it more easily. Some hotels give attendants a bottle of stain-release agent to start treating a stain on-the-spot.

Transporting Soiled Linens

While some properties use linen chutes, soiled linens are generally hand-carried or carted to the OPL. Employees who are hand-carrying linens should be careful not to further soil the items by dragging them on the floor. Dragging linens can also create safety hazards for staff who could trip over trailing items. Linen carts should be free of protrusions that could snag or tear

items. Carts should move easily, and staff should be able to load and unload linens without undue bending and stretching. Workers should also be careful not to snag linens against the cart or the chute.

Sorting

The OPL should contain a sorting area large enough to store a day's worth of laundry without slowing down other activities in the OPL. Soiled linens should be sorted by the degree of soiling and by the type of fabric. Both types of sorting help prevent unnecessary wear and damage to linens. *Cleaning rags should always be separated and washed by themselves and never washed with linen that guests will use.*

Sorting by Degree of Soiling. When sorting by degree of soiling, laundry workers divide linens into three categories: lightly, moderately, and heavily soiled. Heavily soiled items require heavy-duty wash formulas and longer wash time. Moderately or lightly soiled linens are washed with gentler formulas and in fewer cycles. (Sheets are usually classified as lightly soiled, while pillowcases are considered moderately soiled.) Without sorting by soil, all linens would have to be washed in heavy-duty formula. Consequently, lightly soiled items would be overprocessed, leading to unnecessary wear. Sorting by soil also saves repeated washings of items to remove stubborn soils and stains.

Sorting, of course, can lead to partial loads of laundry. Doing too many partial loads wastes energy and water. However, if heavily soiled fabrics are not washed promptly, stains could set and ruin the item. Some OPLs solve this problem by providing several sizes of washers so that smaller loads can be washed promptly without wasting water and energy.

Sorting by Linen Type. Different fibers, weaves, and colors require different cleaning formulas and washing methods. Sorting by linen type includes sorting categories such as blankets, bedspreads, restaurant linen, and terry. Sorting linens by type ensures that the right temperature and formulas are used on similar fabrics. Wool and loosely woven fabrics, for example, require a mild formula and gentle agitation. All terry items can be kept in one group since they receive the same finishing process. Colors should not be washed with chlorine bleach. New colored linens should be washed separately the first few times to avoid dying other fabrics. Some special items such as aprons should be washed in nylon bags to prevent tangling.

Loading

Washing machines work best when optimally loaded. Washers are rated for poundage—that is, 50-pound washers, 35-pound washers, and so on. This weight refers to the clean, dry weight (CDW) of linen. Since bed linen is generally dry when dirty, a 50-pound washer should be loaded with 50 pounds of sheets. But terry cloth is generally wet when dirty and could weigh as much as 40 percent more. To get a full load of terry, for example, most manufacturers advise users to stuff the washer until there is room only to push in a hand's width on top of the load.

Improper loading can cost significant dollars. For instance, if there were 500 wet pounds of towels to process each day in a 50-pound washer, a user could load 7 loads of 71 pounds, or 10 loads of 50 pounds.

Assuming that each load costs $1.00 for chemicals, loading the machine to the maximum would save $3.00 per day or $1,095 per year just on chemicals. When the extra labor to handle loading and unloading three more loads is computed, and the time and energy costs of these wasteful loads is added, it becomes clear that loading properly can save a significant amount of money.

Washing

Today's modern washing equipment can overwhelm an inexperienced worker used to doing laundry on a wash-rinse-spin machine at home. OPL washing equipment requires workers to choose from as many as ten cycles and from a range of detergents, soaps, and fabric conditioners. Asking five basic questions makes these choices less confusing and helps determine the proper procedure for doing a particular batch of laundry.

- How much *time* will it take to wash any given item properly? Linens that are heavily soiled will take more time to wash; lightly soiled linens will take less time. Improperly regulating the time it takes to wash linens will result in a poor wash or unnecessary wear on fabric. It can also waste energy and water.

- At what *temperature* should the water be in order to get items clean? In general, laundry workers should "think low," choosing the lowest possible temperature to do the job in order to save energy. However, some detergents and chemicals work properly only in hot water, and some types of soils require higher temperatures.

- How much *agitation* (the scrubbing action of the machine) is needed to loosen soils? Too little agitation—which is frequently caused by overloaded washers—leads to inadequate washing. Too much agitation can cause fabric damage.

- What *chemicals*—detergents, bleaches, softeners, etc.—will do the best job on particular soils and fabric types?

- What *procedures* are used to facilitate washing? Different cycles should be chosen for different kinds of linen. For example, extraction time for terry cloth should be longer than extraction time for sheets.

The type of soil and fabric will dictate wash time, temperature, degree of agitation, which chemicals to use, and what procedures to follow. Each of these elements affects the others. For example, using too much detergent for the water level will create too many suds, and too many suds will impede the agitator. Exhibit 2 offers an overview of common washing problems, their causes, and some solutions.

Usually, time, temperature, and mechanical action are preset by supervisors in the laundry room. Equipment salespeople can also help with presetting.

Wash Cycles. The typical wash process consists of as many as nine steps.

1. Flush (1.5–3 minutes). Flushes dissolve and dilute water-soluble soils to reduce the soil load for the upcoming suds step. Items are generally flushed at medium temperatures at high water levels.

2. Break (4–10 minutes, optional). A high-alkaline **break** (soil-loosening) product is added, which may be followed by additional flushes. The break cycle is usually at medium temperature and a low water level.

3. Suds (5–8 minutes). This is the actual wash cycle to which detergent is added. Items are agitated in hot water at low water levels.

4. Carryover suds or intermediate rinse (2–5 minutes). This rinse cycle removes soil and alkalinity to help bleach work more effectively. This cycle rinses linens at the same temperature as the suds cycle.

5. Bleach (5–8 minutes). Bleach is added to this hot-water, low-water-level cycle. Bleach kills bacteria, whitens fabrics, and removes stains.

6. Rinse (1.5–3 minutes). Two or more rinses at medium temperatures and high water levels are used to remove detergent and soil from the linens.

7. Intermediate extract (1.5–2 minutes, optional). This high-speed spin removes detergent and soil from linens, usually after the first rinse step. This cycle should not be used after a suds step, because it could drive soils back into the fabric.

8. Sour/softener or starch/sizing (3–5 minutes). Softeners and sours are added to condition fabric. The cycle runs at medium temperature and at low water levels. Starches are added to stiffen cotton fabrics; **sizing** is added for polyester blends. Starching/sizing replaces the sour/softener step.

9. Extract (2–12 minutes). A high-speed spin removes most of the moisture from the linens. The length of the spin depends on fabric type, extractor capacity, and extractor speed.

Exhibit 2
Common Laundry Problems

Problem	Cause	Solution
Graying	Too little detergent	Increase amount of detergent; add bleach.
	Wash cycle temperature too low	Increase temperature.
	Poor sorting; transfer of soiling occurs	Rewash with increased detergent at hottest possible temperature. Use bleach suitable for fabric. Implement proper sorting procedures.
	Color "bleeding"	Do not dry. Rewash with detergent and bleach. Sort more carefully by color. Launder new colored fabrics separately the first few times.
Yellowing	Insufficient detergent	Increase the amount of detergent or use an *enzyme* product or bleach.
	Wash cycle temperature too low	Increase wash temperature.
	Use of chlorine bleach on wool, silk, or spandex items	Yellowed items cannot be restored. Avoid chlorine bleach on such items in the future.
Rust stains	Iron and/or manganese in water supply, pipes, or water heater	Rewash clothes with a commercial rust-removing product; *do not use chlorine bleach*. To prevent further staining, use a water softener to neutralize iron/manganese in water supply. Drain water heaters occasionally to remove rust buildup.
Greasy or oily stains	Too little detergent	Treat with prewash stain remover or liquid laundry detergent; increase amount of detergent.
	Wash temperature too low	Wash in higher temperature.
Holes, tears, or snags	Incorrect use of chlorine bleach	Always use a bleach dispenser and dilute bleach with 4 parts water; never pour directly on linens.
	Unfastened zippers, hooks, or belt buckles	Fasten zippers, hooks and eyes, and belt buckles before washing.
	Washer overload	Avoid overloading.
Poor soil removal	Too little detergent	Increase amount.
	Wash temperature too low	Inrease temperature.
	Overloading washer	Wash fewer items per load, sort properly, and use the proper amount of detergent and water temperature.

Source: Edwin B. Feldman, P.E., ed., *Programmed Cleaning Guide for the Environmental Sanitarian* (New York: The Soap and Detergent Association), pp. 163–168.

Exhibit 3
Common Finishing Problems

Problem	Cause	Solution
Wrinkling (synthetics)	Washing/drying temperatures too high, causing breakdown of no-iron characteristics	Reduce heat.
	Insufficient cool-down in dryer	Turn heat down during the last few minutes of drying time; remove linens before they are bone-dry.
Glazed or fused fibers (synthetics)	Dryer heat is too high	Reduce heat.
Loss of absorbency	Washing/drying temperatures too high	Reduce heat.
	Too much fabric softener	Use less softener.

Many OPLs are now choosing washers with cold-water options. Cold-water washes with synthetic bactericidal detergents can remove stains that hot water will set, preserve the wrinkle-free characteristics of no-iron fabric and absorbency of towels, and save energy costs.

Extracting

Extracting removes excess moisture from laundered items through a high-speed spin. This step is important because it reduces the weight of the laundry, making it easier for workers to lift the laundry and move it to dryers, and reduces drying time. Most washing machines now have extracting capabilities.

Finishing

Finishing, which may require drying and/or ironing, gives linens a crisp, wrinkle-free appearance. Linens should be sorted by fabric type before they are dried. Steam cabinets or tunnels (discussed later in the chapter) are often used to dry blends because they give these fabrics a finished, wrinkle-free look. Some common finishing problems and their solutions are outlined in Exhibit 3.

Drying

Drying times and temperatures vary considerably for various types of linens. In every case, however, drying should be followed by a cool-down tumbling period to prevent the hot linens from being damaged or wrinkled by rapid cooling and handling. After drying, linens should be removed immediately for folding. If folding is delayed, wrinkles will set in. Many times, employees keep turning the dryer control to continue the tumbling until they have time to fold the linen. But when dry linens tumble, the fibers are broken by hitting the sides of the dryer. Because this severely shortens the life of the linen and wastes energy, linens should be removed from the dryer immediately upon the cycle's end.

Always load dryers to capacity. Drying time is not a function of the percentage of linen loaded; a dryer may complete a full load in 45 minutes, but it may take 35 minutes for half a load. Energy costs can skyrocket with careless use of dryers.

Dryers should never be prewarmed or run when empty. Besides wasting energy, this can lead to "hot spots" which can damage fabric or cause fires. Dry all fabrics according to manufacturers' recommendations or until moisture is completely removed. Determining correct drying times depends on the following:

- Type of dryer
- Amount of water left in the goods after washing
- Time of year (temperature of the dryer-intake air)
- Temperature of the linen when it is removed from the washer

A 100-pound dryer will handle 100 pounds of clean, dry linen. Since linens are always wet when loaded into the dryer, allow for this difference. If the hotel has 100-pound washers and 100-pound dryers, the same load can be moved directly from a washer to a dryer. When the washer is rated for 100 pounds CDW and the dryer for 150 pounds CDW, the dryer will hold one and a half loads of wash.

Common dryer problems include clogged lint traps, gas flames out of adjustment, and broken thermostat controls. Slow drying times and smelly or scorched linens result from lack of attention to these items.

Ironing

Sheets, pillowcases, tablecloths, and slightly damp napkins go directly to flatwork irons. Ironers vary in size and degree of automation. Uniforms are generally pressed in special ironing equipment. Steam tunnels are being used more often than ironers for removing wrinkles from polyester blend uniforms.

Folding

Since some properties still do a lot of folding manually, folding usually sets the pace for the linen room. Washing and drying items faster than they can be folded leads to unnecessary wrinkling and resoiling.

Not all laundry rooms have an ironer to process linens. In this situation, the permanent-press linen should be removed from the dryer immediately after the cooldown phase has ended. If linens are folded immediately and stacked to a minimum of 12 inches for 12 hours, a very good result can be obtained. Linens will have a smooth appearance with proper creases.

Folding personnel must also inspect linens, storing those that are to be reused and rejecting stained, torn, or otherwise unsuitable items. This inspection may increase folding time. Folding and storing should be done well away from the soiled linen area to avoid resoiling clean laundry.

Storing

After folding, the items are postsorted and stacked. Postsorting separates any linen types and sizes that were missed in presorting. There should be enough storage room for at least one **par** (the standard quantity of a particular inventory item that must be on hand to support daily, routine housekeeping operations). Finished items should be allowed to "rest" on shelves for 24 hours after laundering, because many types of linens are more easily damaged right after washing. Once linens are on shelves, yellowing and fading can be spotted quickly.

Transferring Linens

Linens are usually transferred to their use areas via carts. Carts should be cleaned at least once daily and more often if necessary. Transferring linens just before use and covering carts can help prevent resoiling. It may be a good idea to have separate carts for soiled and clean linens to avoid accidental soiling.

Apply Your Learning 14.2

Please write all answers on a separate sheet of paper.

1. What is the process for collecting soiled linens?

2. What three ways are linens transported to the OPL?

3. What is the purpose of sorting by soil and linen type?

4. What does CDW stand for, and what does it refer to?

5. The OPL's sorting area should be large enough for how much laundry?

    a. One shift
    b. One day
    c. Two days
    d. One week

6. How much linen should be loaded in a 50-pound washer?

    a. 50 pounds of wet linen
    b. 50 pounds of dry linen
    c. 35 pounds of wet linen
    d. 35 pounds of dry linen

7. The *finishing* of linens refers to:

    a. washing and extracting.
    b. drying and ironing.
    c. storing and transferring.
    d. folding and delivering.

14.3 Chemical Use

AFTER STUDYING SECTION 14.3, YOU SHOULD KNOW HOW TO:

♦ Identify the importance of water as a chemical

♦ Explain the types of detergents and their composition

♦ Explain the purpose of brighteners

♦ Use bleach in an effective and safe manner

♦ Describe the function of alkalies

♦ Describe the function of antichlors

♦ Identify the proper use of mildewcides

♦ Make proper use of sours, fabric softeners, and starches

Hotel and other commercial OPLs use many more chemicals to wash linens than people use in their washers at home. The hotel laundry "fine-tunes" its chemicals to ensure an effective wash that leaves linens looking as close to new as possible. In general, a laundry's chemical needs depend mainly on the types of linens it uses and the soiling conditions encountered.

It is a good idea to deal with more than one chemical vendor. This ensures that you obtain good advice on chemical usage along with updates on new technology. However, juggling several vendors at the same time may not be the most effective use of the executive housekeeper's time. Some executive housekeepers accept bids from chemical vendors and select one vendor as the sole supplier for the upcoming year.

Water

Water is the major chemical used in the laundry process. Two to five gallons of water are used for every pound of dry laundry. Water that is safe to drink may not be suitable for washing linens. Certain minerals, for example, can stain or wear linens. Other substances can cause odors or "hard" water that hampers sudsing. Many of these substances can also clog pipes and machinery. Fortunately, other chemicals can be added to water to help it clean better. Many OPL operators recommend testing the laundry's water supply to identify potential problems.

Detergents

"Detergent" is actually a catchall word for a number of cleaning agents. **Synthetic detergents** are especially effective on oil and grease and often contain **surfactants** that aid in soil removal and act as antibacterial agents and fabric softeners. **Builders** or **alkalies** are often added to synthetic detergents to soften water and remove oils and grease. **Soaps** are another kind of detergent. Neutral or pure soaps contain no alkalies; built soaps do. Built soaps are generally used on heavily soiled fabrics; pure soaps are reserved for more lightly soiled items.

Fabric (Optical) Brighteners

Brighteners keep fabrics looking new. They are often premixed with detergents and soaps.

Bleaches

Used properly, bleaches help remove stains, kill bacteria, and whiten fabrics. **Chlorine bleach** can be used with any washable, natural, colorfast fiber. While safe for some synthetics, it destroys others. All synthetics should be tested before chlorine bleach is used. **Oxygen bleach** is milder than chlorine bleach and is generally safe for most washable fabrics. It works best in hot water and on organic stains. Oxygen bleach should never be used with chlorine bleaches as they will neutralize each other.

Alkalies

Alkalies or alkaline builders help detergents lather better and keep stains suspended in the wash water after they have been loosened and lifted from the fabric. Alkalies also help neutralize acidic stains (most stains are acidic), making the detergent more effective.

Antichlors

Antichlors are sometimes used in rinsing to ensure that all the chlorine in the bleach has been removed. Polyester fibers retain chlorine and for this reason are typically treated with antichlors when chlorine bleach is used.

Mildewcides

Mildewcides prevent the growth of bacteria and fungus on linens for up to 30 days. Both of these types of microorganisms can cause permanent stains that ruin linens. Because moisture makes a good breeding ground for mildew growth, soiled damp linen should be washed promptly and not allowed to sit in carts for long periods.

Sours

Sours are basically mild acids used to neutralize any residual alkalinity in fabrics after washing and rinsing. Detergents and bleaches contain alkali, and any residual alkali can damage fibers and cause yellowing and fading. In addition, residual alkalies can cause skin irritation and leave odors.

Fabric Softeners

Softeners make fabrics more supple and easier to finish. Softeners are added with sours in the final wash cycle. They can reduce flatwork ironing, speed up extraction, reduce drying time, and reduce static electricity in the fabric. Too much softener can decrease a fabric's absorbency.

Starches

Starches give linens a crisp appearance that stands up during the items' use. If they are used, starches should be added in the final step in the washing process.

Apply Your Learning 14.3

Please write all answers on a separate sheet of paper.

1. Explain why water is considered a chemical.

2. What is a detergent?

3. Name the two kinds of bleaches and explain how each is used.

4. What purpose does an alkaline builder serve in laundering?

5. What is an antichlor used for?

6. What prevents the growth of bacteria and fungus on linens?

   a. sours
   b. antichlors
   c. mildewcides
   d. detergents

7. _____ reduce ironing, speed up extraction, reduce drying time, and reduce static electricity.

   a. Fabric softeners
   b. Starches
   c. Sours
   d. Detergents

14.4 Equipment Use and Maintenance

AFTER STUDYING SECTION 14.4, YOU SHOULD KNOW HOW TO:

♦ Describe the washing machines used by hotels

♦ Identify the types of drying machines used at hotels

♦ Describe how steam cabinets and tunnels work

♦ Explain the function of flatwork ironers and pressing machines

♦ Explain how a folding machine works

♦ Describe how rolling and holding equipment is used for linen handling

♦ Outline the importance of a preventive maintenance program

OPL machinery is a major investment in itself and affects the life span of another major investment—linens. The choice of OPL machines and equipment could mean the difference between a financially successful and a disastrous OPL. Machines with insufficient capacity, for example, result in damaged linens, unsatisfactory clean-ing performance, excessive energy and water costs, or increased maintenance costs.

Washing Machines

Most washers are made of stainless steel and vary in size from 25- to 1,200-pound CDW capacities. A large-capacity washer may not resemble a conventional washer designed for home use. Some machines have separate "pockets" which hold several large loads at a time. Some, called **tunnel washers,** have several chambers, each of which is used for a particular wash cycle. As soon as the first cycle is finished on the first load, the wash moves into the second chamber and the laundry attendant can then load the first chamber with the next batch.

Most newer washers are electronically programmed for automatic detergent and solution dispensing in correct proportions. Other washers require an operator to add detergent and solutions manually. Since linens can be severely damaged by dumping chemicals directly onto them, machines that require manual dispensing usually have **ports** or **hoppers** (openings through which detergents can be poured).

While many automated machines are more economical to operate than washers requiring manual dispensing, they can also cause problems if improperly used. Allowing detergent salespeople to tinker with automated machines to "improve" the quality of the wash can, in fact, decrease the quality of the machine's performance.

Having the manufacturer's representative check the machine periodically is probably the surest way to get the most out of the machine.

Microprocessors—one of the latest innovations in washers—allow greater control over the washer's functions than more conventional automatic models. Operators have more flexibility and ease in programming combinations of detergents and solutions for specific fabric types and soil levels. Also, water temperature can be regulated more exactly.

Another new innovation is the reuse washer that can save energy, sewage, water, and chemical costs. A reuse washer is equipped with insulated storage tanks. Water that can be reused is siphoned into the tanks to maintain the proper temperature and then released into the proper cycle of the next batch of laundry. Control panels allow operators to make necessary adjustments to account for soil conditions, water hardness, and fabric type.

Although many hotels are beginning to use OPL wastewater to irrigate lawns and gardens, treatment is needed to neutralize the chemicals before the water can be used on plants. Special care also must be taken to ensure that recycled water is not accidentally used for drinking. Many properties color used water with a harmless vegetable dye to avoid mix-ups.

Most washers have extraction capabilities which remove most excess water after washing is completed. Many even offer high-speed extraction capabilities. Extractors are available in centrifugal, hydraulic, and pressure types.

Washing machines do break down; when one is out of operation, the hotel is faced with a series of expensive problems. For one, a broken machine may idle many of the hotel's housekeeping staff—which means wasted labor. Second, a broken machine may hamper the flow of linen and the makeup of guestrooms—which means lost sales. Finally, a breakdown means that the OPL will later be overworked—which translates into overtime expenses.

Three rules help reduce breakdown time. First, buy only strong, industrial equipment from a supplier you trust. Second, read, thoroughly understand, and follow the equipment's maintenance requirements—more than 90 percent of all machine failures can be prevented by following the manufacturer's maintenance recommendations. Finally, consider buying extended warranties on the equipment.

Drying Machines

Dryers remove moisture from articles by tumbling them in a rotating cylinder through which heated air passes. The airflow must be unrestricted to ensure the dryer's energy efficiency. Laundries are usually designed with greater drying capacity than washing capacity because it takes one and a half to two times longer to dry laundry than to wash it. As a result, work can continue relatively smoothly for a short time if a single dryer breaks down.

Like washers, dryers must be maintained properly. As dryers get older, they frequently receive less maintenance even though they require more—and this means they waste more energy. However, it is easier to keep dryers properly maintained in the first place than it is to work around broken machinery. Dirt or lint clogging the air supply to the dryer is the most frequent problem. Cleaning air vents twice daily can help eliminate this. The **Occupational Safety and Health**

Administration (OSHA) requires that lint levels in the air be controlled in institutional laundries. Most dryers are equipped with a system of ducts which eject lint into containers and minimize air contamination. Ducts should be checked regularly for leaks, and containers should be emptied regularly.

Steam Cabinets and Tunnels

Steam cabinets or **tunnels** effectively eliminate wrinkles from heavy linens such as blankets, bedspreads, and curtains. A steam cabinet is simply a box in which articles are hung and steamed, while a steam tunnel actually moves articles on hangers through a tunnel, steaming them and removing the wrinkles as they move through.

Steam cabinets—and tunnels to a lesser extent—can disrupt the flow of laundry through the OPL because they are time-consuming to operate. They also require a worker to load and unload the linens, which increases labor costs. As a result, only very large hotels with valet service or hotels that do frequent loads of curtains, bedspreads, and blankets find steam tunnels cost-effective. Most hotels that use no-iron linens do not require steam cabinets.

Flatwork Ironers and Pressing Machines

Flatwork ironers and pressing machines are similar, except that ironers roll over the material while presses flatten it. Also, items can be fed into ironers but must be placed on the presses manually. Either process is time-consuming and thus used only for items that require ironing. Some ironers also fold the flatwork automatically.

It is important for proper iron operation and maintenance that material arrives in the proper condition from the finishing process. For example, dirt left on linens because of improper rinsing can shorten ironer life. Too much sour left in the linens can cause them to roll during ironing, and too much alkali can cause linens to turn brown. Moisture extraction must be controlled, too. Linens should be moist before going into the ironer. Linens that are too dry will cause static electricity to build up on the ironer; on the other hand, linens that are too wet will be difficult to feed into the ironer.

It should be noted that older no-iron linens frequently have to be ironed. In reality, no-iron linens have two distinct lives. Initially, their performance is that of a true, no-iron fabric. However, this condition usually lasts less than half the article's total useful life. Over time, the crispness of no-iron linens is reduced, because repeated washings break down the fabric. Because linens are so expensive, many OPLs have discovered that buying an ironer is cheaper than buying new linens.

Folding Machines

Many folding machines do not actually fold the laundry, but hold one end of the item to be folded so that staff can fold it more easily. The most common folding machine acts as a passive partner, providing the worker with an extra set of "hands" to assist in folding linens.

Folding machines are now available, however, that virtually eliminate tumble drying and hand folding. These space-saving units dry, iron, fold, and often crossfold and stack flatwork. Some have microprocessor controls that determine fold points and trigger other related functions.

Rolling/Holding Equipment

Rolling and holding equipment is used for linen handling. Carts are used in most laundries to move and hold linens after they have been sorted for washing, drying, and finishing. Carts must be kept orderly so that staff can move freely through the OPL. They must also be carefully marked so that carts for clean linens are not mixed up with those used for soiled items.

Very large OPLs may have an overhead system of tracks to which laundry bags can be attached to hold linen ready to be sorted, washed, dried, or finished. Depending on the size of the OPL, overhead systems may be semi- or fully automated. Automated overhead systems have a number of advantages. First, they allow laundry to move in an orderly manner throughout the OPL. Second, one person can move all the carts simultaneously instead of many people having to move carts to and from washers, dryers, extractors, ironers, and other equipment on the OPL floor. This can represent considerable labor cost savings for large OPLs. Finally, overhead systems also provide extra storage space in case one step in the laundry process gets backed up, preventing a disorderly pileup of carts on the OPL floor.

There are a few basic guidelines for this equipment. First, transport devices should not have sharp corners or other parts that could tear linens. Second, they should be easy to use. They should not require workers to bend excessively or repeatedly to remove items from the bottom of a cart. Carrying should be avoided as a means of linen transportation. Third, make sure carts can fit comfortably through doorways. Fourth, holding space should be situated so that workers do not have to reach high or far back on shelves.

Preventive Maintenance

A detailed, strictly observed **preventive maintenance** program is essential to the efficient operation of an OPL. Lost productivity and expensive repairs easily justify the costs of these programs. The program should include a record of repairs or maintenance procedures and the total cost of each. When the total cost of the repairs and maintenance begins to approach the cost of the machine itself, the property should consider replacing it.

Typical examples of daily maintenance procedures include checking safety devices; turning on steam, water, and air valves; checking ironer roll pressure; and cleaning dryer lint screens.

Maintaining water and energy efficiency is an important aspect of preventive maintenance, as is reducing repair and downtime costs. Leaking valves, damaged insulation, and constricted gas, air, and water paths can be quite costly. Keep accurate records of utility use to identify such problems. Periodically check water levels in washers. Too much water results in decreased agitation and poor cleaning. Not enough water causes excessive mechanical action that can damage fabrics.

No matter how good maintenance precautions are, unexpected breakdowns or repair delays can occur. Many properties develop a contingency plan to help cope with unforeseen emergencies. A contingency plan should include an estimate of how long the stock of clean linen will last and at what point an outside laundry will need to be called.

Apply Your Learning 14.4

Please write all answers on a separate sheet of paper.

1. What is a tunnel washer and how does it work?

2. What is a microprocessor and what are its advantages?

3. What is the proper daily maintenance procedure for dryers?

4. Explain the differences between steam cabinets, steam tunnels, flatwork ironers, and pressing machines.

5. Why is a preventive maintenance program essential to the operation of an OPL?

6. Why should a property develop a laundry contingency plan and what should it include?

7. Since linens can be severely damaged by dumping chemicals onto them, manual dispensing machines usually have _____.

   a. ports or hoppers
   b. ports or dispensers
   c. tunnel washers
   d. microprocessors

8. A _____ washer can save energy, sewage, water, and chemical costs.

   a. 1200-pound capacity
   b. tunnel
   c. reuse
   d. conventional

Quick Hits

Chapter 14

SECTION 14.1—GENERAL FABRIC CARE

- Synthetic fabrics, introduced in the 1960s, led to the development of no-iron sheets. This eliminated or reduced the need for ironing, allowing many properties to switch from outside laundry services to the on-premises laundry (OPL).

- The main types of fabrics in today's marketplace include cotton, wool, acrylic, polyester, nylon, and blends.

- For most properties, the fabric of choice is a polyester/cotton blend (sometimes called **polycotton**) because it requires less care than all-natural fabric yet offers most of its comfort.

SECTION 14.2—LAUNDRY CYCLE

- The steps involved in the laundry cycle are: collecting soiled linens, transporting soiled linens to the laundry, sorting, loading, washing, extracting, finishing, drying, folding, storing, and transferring linens to use areas.

- Care should be taken to avoid further soiling or damage when collecting and transporting soiled linens.

- Soiled linens should be sorted by degree of soiling and type of fabric. These conditions will determine the necessary wash formula.

- Washing machines are rated for poundage; the weight refers to the clean, dry weight (CDW) of the fabric. Washers are most efficient and cost-effective when optimally loaded.

- The type of soil and fabric will dictate wash time, temperature, degree of agitation, which chemicals to use, and what procedures to follow. Each of these elements affects the others.

- The typical wash process consists of as many as nine steps: flush, break, suds, carryover suds/intermediate rinse, bleach, rinse, intermediate extract, sour/softener or starch/sizing, and extract.

- Finishing, which gives linens a crisp, wrinkle-free appearance, includes drying and ironing.

- After drying, linens should be removed from the dryer immediately for folding.

SECTION 14.3—CHEMICAL USE

- Although not always recognized as such, water is the major chemical used in the laundry process.

- Detergent is a catchall word for a number of cleaning agents that include **surfactants, builders** or **alkalies,** and **soaps.**

- **Surfactants** are chemicals added to synthetic detergents that aid in soil removal and act as antibacterial agents and fabric softeners. These include **antichlors, mildewcides, sours,** fabric softeners, and starches.

- **Chlorine** and **oxygen bleaches** help remove stains, kill bacteria, and whiten fabrics. If not carefully controlled, bleach can damage fabrics.

SECTION 14.4—EQUIPMENT USE AND MAINTENANCE

- Most washers are made of stainless steel and vary in size from 25- to 1,200-pound capacities. While newer washers are electronically programmed for automatic detergent and solution dispensing in correct proportions, machines that require manual dispensing usually have **ports** or **hoppers.** Microprocessors, one of the newest innovations, allow greater control over the washer's functions by allowing more flexibility and ease in programming.

- Dryers remove moisture from articles by tumbling them in a rotating cylinder through which heated air passes. Like washers, dryers must be maintained properly. Dirt or lint clogging the air supply to the dryer is the most frequent problem.

- **Steam cabinets** or **tunnels** effectively eliminate wrinkles from heavy linens. A steam cabinet is simply a box in which articles are hung and steamed, while a steam tunnel actually moves articles on hangers through a tunnel. Both are time-consuming to operate.

- Flatwork ironers and pressing machines are used to remove wrinkles. Ironers roll over the material while pressing machines flatten it. Either process is time-consuming.

- Some folding machines do not actually fold the laundry, but rather hold one end of the item so that staff can fold it more easily. Other units are now available that virtually eliminate tumble drying and hand folding.

- Rolling and holding equipment is used for linen handling. The equipment consists of carts and laundry bags which are used in overhead systems.

- A detailed, strictly observed **preventive maintenance** program is essential to the efficient operation of an OPL. Typical examples include checking safety devices; turning on steam, water, and air valves; checking ironer roll pressure; and cleaning dryer lint screens.

Careers

CHAPTER 15   CAREERS

Profile

Jeff Yamaguchi
Vice President of Residences,
MGM Grand Las Vegas

If Jeff Yamaguchi could have planned his career 20 years ago, he would probably be a doctor or scientist. He even earned a degree in biology and attended medical school.

"But then I thought, 'Do I want to go to medical school or go to work?'"

The answer wasn't that difficult for Yamaguchi.

Yamaguchi jumped into the hotel business at 17 when he took a bellman job at the Hacienda Hotel. He worked his way through college as a night auditor. Even though he loved the hospitality business, he was raised in a traditional Japanese family, and his father wanted him to further his career in the sciences. Yamaguchi knew he had a knack for math and analyzing difficult problems, but, he also loved the arts and had a creative side more aligned with the hotel business.

"As I got out of college, life got to mean more to me than book stuff," he says. "Now I'm more of an idea guy. I love coming up with concepts, and putting together programs to meet customer expectations. Yet, my analytical background benefits me when I have to solve a problem quickly."

Once he made the decision to stick with a hotel career, Yamaguchi went to work at the Beverly Hillcrest Hotel (now the Prescott Hotel) as a front office manager and controller. He then bounced around a bit, working in managerial positions for several hotels in Texas.

Yamaguchi's big break came in 1990 when he went to work for Marriott's vacation ownership division. Yamaguchi became a hot commodity in the fragmented timeshare business and joined Four Seasons in 1997. At 36, he not only runs the Carlsbad vacation club, but he is helping to mold an entirely new product for the luxury hotel chain.

"It's all about creating a product and making it speak for itself," he says.

"What I like about Four Seasons is that we are going to do it right. We're looking forward to making a name for ourselves in the vacation ownership industry and watching everyone else try to catch us."

In 2004, Yamaguchi became the Vice President of Residences for MGM Grand and is in charge of the six condo hotel towers replacing the MGM amusement park.

Reprinted with permission from Lodging, *May 1998, the management magazine of the American Hotel & Motel Association.*

Careers

Sections

15.1   Positions in Hospitality

AFTER STUDYING SECTION 15.1, YOU SHOULD KNOW HOW TO:

♦ List entry-level jobs in the lodging industry

♦ List skilled-level positions in the lodging industry

♦ List managerial positions in the lodging industry

♦ List the reasons that people enjoy hospitality careers

What *is* the **hospitality industry?** Some view the hospitality industry as comprising four sectors: lodging, food, entertainment, and travel. However, usually the hospitality industry is defined as mainly lodging and food service businesses. This definition can include school dormitories, nursing homes, and other institutions (see Exhibit 1).

The World Tourism Organization estimates that there are 14 million hotel rooms in the world. More than 4 million of those are in the United States. The number of rooms is increasing as new hotels, resorts, and other lodging facilities open every year. In the U.S., there are 200,000 hotel managers and assistant managers.

The food service industry is also growing. According to the National Restaurant Association (NRA), food service industry sales are more than four percent of the U.S. Gross Domestic Product. For every dollar spent on food, 45.3 cents are spent in a food service operation. More than 11 million people are employed in the industry.

Entry-Level Positions

Individuals with a high school education or less and no hotel or related experience are most likely to start their hotel careers with an entry-level job. Every department has at least one entry-level job classification. Starting here does not hinder one's ability to advance in the organization; *a*

Hotel Hershey

A postcard of an Egyptian hotel inspired the design of Hotel Hershey. Chocolate entrepreneur Milton Hershey built it during the Great Depression. He called it his yacht, his indulgence, but it became the livelihood of the townspeople, eliminating unemployment in the city.

During one of his visits to the construction site, he admired the bulldozers. The construction foreman told him that the bulldozers could do the work of 40 men. Hershey replied, "Well then, fire the bulldozers."

Exhibit 1
The Hospitality Industry

Lodging Operations	Food Service Operations	Other Operations
All-suite hotels	Commercial cafeterias	Airlines
Casino hotels	Education food service	Campgrounds
Conference centers	Employee food service	City clubs
Full-service hotels	Full-service restaurants	Country clubs
Limited-service hotels	Health-care	Cruise ships
Resorts	Lodging food service	National parks
Retirement communities	Quick-service restaurants	
Military housing	Recreational food service	
	Social caterers	

Exhibit 2
Representative Entry-Level Positions

Front Office

Bellperson
Apprentice telephone
  operator
Porter

Housekeeping

Housekeeper (room
  attendant, maid)
Supply clerk
Laundry attendant

Food Preparation

Vegetable preparer
Kitchen helper
Pantry helper
Storeroom helper
Warewasher
Steward

Engineering

Plumber's helper
Electrician's helper
Oiler's helper

Marketing

Clerk
Secretarial/Clerical
  (needed for several
  departments)
Clerk
Typist
File Clerk

Food and Beverage Service

Busperson
Barback
Counter server
Runner

Food Service Office

Checker
File clerk

Accounting

Checker
File Clerk

large number of today's hotel managers and executives began at this level. The experience and skills gained can help employees advance to the skilled level of hotel work.

Exhibit 2 lists some representative entry-level jobs.

Skilled-Level Positions

Employees at the second level, the skilled jobs, come from a variety of sources. Some are employees who moved up from entry-level jobs. Others are people who have learned a skilled trade in another industry and sought similar employment in a hotel. Some are graduates of the growing number of technical schools and junior colleges that offer hotel training, and others come from business schools or specialized high school training courses, such as *Lodging Management Program*.

A person who desires to work in food preparation might consider a school that trains cooks, bakers, and other food service personnel; graduates of these programs are in great demand by hotels and other food

Exhibit 3
Representative Skilled-Level Positions

Front Office
Front desk agent
Reservations agent
Telephone operator
Bell captain
Concierge

Housekeeping
Assistant housekeeper
Floor housekeeper (supervisor)
Laundry supervisor

Food Preparation
Baker
Roast cook
Garde-manger
Vegetable cook
Fry cook
Saucier

Engineering
Plumber
Electrician
Oiler
Upholsterer
Carpenter
Painter

Marketing
Sales representative

Secretarial/Clerical (needed for several departments)
Secretary
Administrative assistant
Accounting clerk
Bookkeeper
Receptionist
Accountant

Food and Beverage Service
Wine steward
Food server
Beverage server
Host/hostess
Captain
Headwaiter/headwaitress
Bartender

Food Service Office
Secretary
Accounting clerk
Bookkeeper
Receptionist
Accountant

Accounting
Accounting clerk
Bookkeeper
Accountant
Food and beverage controller
Night auditor
Cashier

service operations. People with military training in food service can usually find employment in hotel kitchens.

For those interested in a career as a bookkeeper, accounting clerk, secretary, or accountant, training at a reputable business school is a good start. The skilled-level jobs in the dining and banquet departments depend almost entirely on experience. The usual way to advance is to begin at an entry-level job and move up through the ranks. Mixology, or bartending, is taught at some vocational schools, although many bartenders are former food servers. Likewise, front desk agents and reservation agents might come from the ranks as bellpersons or from technical schools.

Exhibit 3 lists some representative skilled-level jobs encompassing different levels of responsibility, prestige, and salary.

Managerial-Level Positions

Training, experience, and individual initiative are the keys to attaining managerial-level (executive, managerial, and supervisory) positions. Many of these positions are offered to college-trained people, but opportunities will always be available for qualified employees who have worked their way up through the organization. Many division-head jobs are filled by those who excel in skilled-level position.

Many colleges and universities offer a four-year course in hotel management. Hotel school graduates learn a large amount of technical knowledge and typically receive some practical experience during their college program; however, few are ready for a manager's job upon graduation. A hotel school graduate must go through a **management internship**, or supervised training at a job site, before engaging in actual practice.

Many college graduates, armed with four years of theoretical and technical knowledge, become impatient when told they need experience before assuming high-level positions of responsibility. They do not realize that, though intellectually capable, they generally need more hands-on experience before assuming managerial positions. The crucial management skills of understanding, motivating, and directing people can best be developed through experience. It is vital that graduates understand and accept this situation, or their assets of enthusiasm, ambition, and confidence may gradually be replaced by disillusionment, lethargy, and dissatisfaction.

Some representative managerial-level positions are listed in Exhibit 4. Multi-unit companies may have area, district, regional, or corporate-level management.

Exhibit 4
Representative Managerial-Level Positions

Front office manager	Executive assistant manager
Controller	Convention manager
Executive housekeeper	Sales manager
Catering manager	General manager
Executive steward	Auditor
Food and beverage manager	Resident manager
Banquet manager	Chief engineer
Chef	
Executive chef	**Typical Multi-Unit Positions**
Food production manager	Director of training
Catering director	Vice president, finance
Restaurant manager	Vice president, real estate
Beverage manager	Director of franchising
Purchasing director	Area supervisor
Human resources manager	Regional director
Credit manager	

Why Hospitality?

Why do people go into the hospitality industry? If you were to ask people who have spent their careers in this business what they like most about it, you would get a wide variety of answers. Some of the most popular are:

- The industry offers more career options than most.

- The work is varied.

- There are many opportunities to be creative.

- This is a "people" business.

- Hospitality jobs are not nine-to-five jobs.

- There are opportunities for long-term career growth.

- There are perks associated with many hospitality jobs.

Despite these advantages, there are some aspects of the business that many people don't like:

- Long hours
- Nontraditional schedules
- Pressure
- Low beginning salaries

It is difficult to imagine another industry in which there are as many different kinds of work.

Management positions abound in the industry. Although hotels and restaurants may represent the largest sectors, they are by no means the only ones. Hospitality managers are needed in clubs, hospitals, nursing homes, universities and schools, cafeterias, prisons, corporate dining rooms, snack bars, management companies, airlines, cruise ships, and many other organizations. Even the royal palace of the Sultan of Brunei is run by the Hyatt organization!

Within these organizations you can go into marketing and sales, rooms management, housekeeping, cooking, engineering, dining-room management, menu planning, security, accounting, food technology, forecasting and planning, recreation, entertainment, guest relations, and so on. Moreover, there is a wide choice of places to live—warm climates and cold; cities, suburbs, and even rural areas; any region of the country or the world. There simply is no other industry that offers more diverse career opportunities.

Apply Your Learning 15.1

Please write all answers on a separate sheet of paper.

1. Why are there an increasing number of job opportunities available in the lodging industry?

2. What are the benefits of working in the hospitality industry?

3. What are the drawbacks of working in the hospitality industry?

For questions 4–9, identify whether the position is entry level, skilled level, or managerial level.

4. Chef

5. Receptionist

6. Carpenter

7. Steward

8. Controller

9. Auditor

15.2 *Choosing a Career*

AFTER STUDYING SECTION 15.2, YOU SHOULD KNOW HOW TO:

♦ Describe the career options available in lodging

♦ List the career opportunities available in food service

♦ Explain the career opportunities available in clubs

♦ Describe the career opportunities available with cruise lines

The type of business you choose for your first hospitality job puts you into a definite career slot. Skills and experience are highly transferable within a particular segment (such as resort hotels), but it can be more challenging to move between industry segments. Owners and operators of motels and fast-food restaurants often have incomes that are as high as, or higher than, those of managers at some deluxe hotels.

Lodging

There are many types of lodging properties to choose from. There are luxury hotels, full-service hotels, convention hotels, resorts, and casino hotels.

People who choose the lodging industry as a career often do so because they enjoy traveling and living in different places.

Hotel management personnel are in great demand, and since most larger hotels belong to chains, managers are often offered opportunities to move into new positions in different geographic locations.

Would you rather be part of a large chain or work for an independent operation? There are many opportunities in both areas. The arguments for working for a large chain include:

• Better training

• More opportunities for advancement

• Better benefits

A career with an independent operation also offers some advantages, however:

• More chances to be creative

• More control

• Better learning environments

Management Positions within Lodging Operations

Whether the lodging property is part of a chain or an independent operation, there are a wide variety of management positions open to you. Many people enjoy aiming for the top administrative job of general manager, but others prefer to specialize in such areas as:

• Catering

- Engineering
- Food and beverage
- Finance and accounting
- Human resources
- Marketing and sales
- Rooms management
- Management information systems (MIS)

The **general manager** is the chief operating officer of a hotel. The general manager supervises hotel staff and administers policies established by the owners or chain operators. Most general managers hold frequent meetings with their department heads. The general manager's main responsibility is the financial performance of the business. The compensation a general manager receives is often tied to the profitability of the business he or she manages. Hiring and firing when necessary is also part of a general manager's job.

Good general managers are skilled at getting along with people. They are able to forge positive relationships with employees, guests, and the community at large. They believe in teamwork and know how to get things done. Effective general managers are also technically proficient.

Catering managers promote and sell the hotel's banquet facilities. They plan, organize, and manage the hotel's banquets, which can range from formal dinners to picnic buffets. Knowledge of food costs, preparation techniques, and pricing is essential. Good catering managers are also aware of protocol, social customs, and etiquette. Creativity and imagination are useful qualities.

Chief engineers are responsible for the hotel's physical operation and maintenance. This includes the electrical, heating, ventilating, air conditioning, refrigeration, and plumbing systems. Chief engineers must have extensive backgrounds in mechanical and electrical equipment and may need numerous licenses.

Food and beverage managers direct the production and service of food and beverages. They are responsible for training the dining room and kitchen staffs and ensuring quality control. Food and beverage managers at large properties work with their head chefs to plan menus and with their beverage managers to select wines and liquor. At small properties the food and beverage manager has sole responsibility for these tasks. Menu pricing and cost control are also the province of the food and beverage manager.

Food and beverage managers must have a keen interest in food and wines and an up-to-date knowledge of food trends and guests' tastes. Because food and beverage service is offered from 15 to 24 hours a day, managers must be prepared to work long shifts and endure periods of pressure.

The **controller** is in charge of the accounting department and all of its functions, such as the management of credit, payroll, guest accounts, and all cashiering activities. The controller also prepares budgets and daily, weekly, and monthly reports showing revenues, expenses, and other statistics that managers require. Controllers are detail-oriented people and favor an analytical approach to business problems.

Human resources managers are responsible for recruiting and training the majority of the hotel's employees. They are also in charge of employee relations within a hotel. This includes counseling employees, developing and administering programs to maintain and improve employee morale, monitoring the work environment, and so on. An important part of the human resources manager's job is to oversee compliance with equal employment opportunity and affirmative action laws and policies. People who choose human resources as a career usually have a good deal of empathy and are excellent negotiators.

The marketing and sales function at a hotel consists of several different activities. Sometimes a large hotel will have two managers overseeing marketing and sales. In that case, the **marketing manager** develops and implements a marketing plan and budget. The marketing and sales manager is also in charge of corporate accounts and may work with an advertising and public relations agency. The **sales manager** conducts sales programs and makes sales calls on prospects for group and individual business. He or she usually reports to the marketing and sales manager. Marketing and sales people tend to be service-oriented and possess good communication skills.

Resident managers are often the executives in charge of a hotel's rooms division. Their areas of responsibility include the front office, reservations, and housekeeping, as well as sources of revenue other than the food and beverage department, such as gift shops and recreational facilities. In small hotels, resident managers are also in charge of security. Resident managers are good leaders and have many of the same qualities that general managers have.

Management information systems (MIS) managers are the computer experts in a hotel. They are in charge of the computers used for reservations, room assignments, telephones, guestroom status reports, accounting functions, and labor and productivity reports. They often know how to write simple computer programs and easy-to-follow

instructions for using computers. They have good problem-solving aptitudes and verbal and written communication skills.

The salaries for the hotel management positions just described vary according to the area of the country, the size of the property, and the work experience of the individual. However, Exhibit 1 gives a good indication of average management salaries in various positions.

Food Service

There are also a wide variety of job opportunities and geographic locations to choose from within the food service industry.

Independent Restaurants. At the top of the restaurant spectrum are luxury restaurants, which are for the most part owned and operated by independent entrepreneurs.

Guests at luxury restaurants usually receive superior service. Some luxury restaurants, for example, feature French service, in which meals are served from a cart or *guéridon* by formally dressed personnel. Tables are waited on by servers, a *chef du rang,* and an apprentice called a *commis du rang.* In the back of the house there is a classic kitchen, with an executive chef and a brigade of cooks organized into departments, each headed by a *chef de partie.*

Many hospitality students aspire to run and eventually own a luxury restaurant. The best way to the top is to work in a luxury restaurant and learn the ropes. Many of these restaurants are owned by an individual. They are usually sold to an employee or other entrepreneurs who can get financing when the owner retires.

Chain Restaurants. Chain restaurants recruit the majority of their managers from hospitality schools. Entry-level jobs for

Exhibit 1
Compensation: Lodging Properties

Position—Median Salaries	Nationwide	<150 rooms	150–350 rooms	350–550 rooms	550–800 rooms	>800 rooms
Dir. of Human Resources	$58,677	N/A*	N/A	$ 62,733	$ 73,632	$ 83,426
Dir. of Mgmt. Info. Systems	$55,227	N/A	N/A	$ 50,149	$ 59,481	$ 59,558
Dir. of Revenue Management	$67,116	N/A	N/A	N/A	N/A	N/A
Dir. of Sales	$67,662	N/A	N/A	$ 75,619	$ 86,745	$ 87,323
Dir. of Sales & Marketing	$69,763	$47,487	$47,487	$ 84,319	$ 97,058	$119,452
Director of Catering	$57,428	N/A	N/A	$ 58,989	$ 66,745	$ 93,907
Director of Food & Beverage	$67,364	N/A	N/A	$ 73,126	$ 85,672	$ 94,275
Director of Rooms	$60,850	N/A	N/A	$ 62,054	$ 67,652	$ 69,910
Executive Housekeeper	$38,810	$28,471	$28,471	$ 47,731	$ 57,338	$ 66,825
Front Office Manager	$39,496	$27,899	$27,899	$ 43,818	$ 46,899	$ 53,863
General Manager	$88,060	$50,053	$50,053	$132,022	$145,852	$172,872
Resident Manager	$74,181	N/A	N/A	$ 84,340	$ 93,727	$104,386
Restaurant Manager	$37,073	N/A	N/A	$ 39,021	$ 41,418	$ 42,648
Sales Manger	$38,938	$34,044	$34,044	$ 41,855	$ 44,902	$ 45,942

*N/A = Not available

Source: www.hospitalitycareernet.com. Visit this Internet site and click on to "career resources," then "HCE Hospitality Compensation Exchange" for the most up-to-date numbers.

graduates with hospitality degrees are often on the assistant-manager level, with progression to manager, then district manager for a group of restaurants, and then regional manager.

Restaurant chains are the fastest growing part of the restaurant business today. Many of these chains are made up of fast-food restaurants or, as they prefer to be called, quick-service restaurants.

Hospitality students often bypass fast-food management opportunities. This is often a mistake. These jobs may pay well and offer excellent benefit packages. Many McDonald's managers of single stores earn between $30,000 and $50,000 a year, plus benefits such as stock options and profit sharing. In addition, if you dream of owning your own franchise, the franchise company may help you if you've worked hard and well in one of their units.

Dinner houses, also known as casual restaurants, are another type of chain restaurant. Such well-known companies as Chili's Grill & Bar, T.G.I. Friday's, and Bennigan's lead the pack. These companies are popular career choices for hospitality graduates because they offer many opportunities for advancement.

Social Caterers. Social catering is another part of the food service industry that many hospitality graduates become interested in. Catering is another business that is most often started by independent entrepreneurs, as it requires very little start-up capital—facilities can be rented as needed, and equipment can usually be leased on a short-term basis from restaurant supply houses. Food servers can be hired as needed. In some cases, caterers provide only food; in others, they are responsible for tables, chairs, utensils, tents, servers, and decorations.

Contract Food Companies. Contract food companies are generally hired by organizations who provide food as a secondary business. The biggest users of contract food services are large manufacturing and industrial concerns in which workers have a short lunch period. Schools and colleges, hospitals, sports arenas, airlines, cruise ships, and even prisons use contract food companies. In the case of airlines, meals are cooked and prepackaged in central commissaries and then delivered to the airplanes for preparation and service as needed.

Because of the large volume of meals involved, contract food managers must be highly skilled in professional management techniques and cost control. Ccontract food companies usually hire people with experience within their industry and recruit from hospitality schools.

Institutional Food Service. Although contract food companies can supply food for schools and hospitals, some of these institutions handle their own food service programs. High school food managers work hard to come up with more creative and innovative menu plans to keep students in school cafeterias.

Colleges and universities have also experienced changes in their food service programs. Because more students live off-campus now, there is a trend toward flexible meal plans in which students have a choice of how many meals they wish to purchase.

Hospital programs are usually administered by a trained dietitian or a professional food service manager. Menus are generally simple and nourishing.

Management Positions within Food Service

A restaurant is usually a small business, with average sales of $535,000 annually. That means that most of the management opportunities in this field, even with large chains, lie in operations or "hands-on" management, as opposed to corporate staff jobs behind a desk.

The Chili's Grill & Bar restaurant chain staffs its units with a general manager and three restaurant managers. The general manager is responsible for overall operations, while each restaurant manager has specific functional duties—managing the dining room, handling beverage service, or supervising the kitchen staff. This simple management structure and division of duties is similar for many other commercial food service operations. Other typical food service management positions include chef, maître d', and banquet manager.

Clubs

Private clubs are another career option. Clubs are very different from other types of hospitality businesses because the "guests"—the club members—are also the owners in many cases. There are country clubs, city clubs, yacht and sailing clubs, military clubs, tennis clubs, even polo clubs—all with clubhouses and other facilities that must be managed. Some, like the Yale Club in New York City, offer complete hotel services. Large clubs have many of the same positions found in hotels and restaurants: a general manager, a food and beverage director, a catering director (weddings and parties are an important part of club operations), and a controller.

Today there are more than 14,000 recreational and social clubs in the United States. Most clubs are nonprofit, owned by and run for the benefit of the members. Some clubs are built by developers as part of housing developments and are proprietary, for-profit enterprises.

Many hospitality managers enjoy working in clubs. First of all, unlike chain food service and hotel operations, there is a chance to exercise one's own imagination and creativity in such matters as menu selection, party planning, and sporting events. Secondly, you interact with the owners (members) in a more direct way. Moreover, clubs with sports facilities often host celebrity tournaments.

Cruise Lines

There are opportunities both on shore and at sea within the cruise industry. Shoreside positions include marketing, accounting, provisioning, itinerary planning, and hotel operations. At sea, there are the same kinds of jobs any fine resort has. Salaries are competitive. Persons who are attracted by travel may enjoy operations jobs at sea but should be prepared to spend a minimum of nine out of every 12 months away from home. Living conditions don't allow for much privacy either, but many like the feeling of having an extended family that occurs on a ship.

Spas

The spa industry is a rapidly growing segmetn of hospitality. Modern spas offer services to help people relax and feel healthier. They include club spas, cruise ship spas, day spas, destination spas, medical spas, mineral springs spas, and resort/hotel spas.

The spa director is typically the employee in charge of the spa. Other important positions in a spa are estheticians, massage therapists, stylists, and front desk receptionists.

Apply Your Learning 15.2

Please write all answers on a separate sheet of paper.

1. What are the benefits of working for a chain hotel?

2. What are the benefits of working for an independent hotel?

3. List the management positions available in a lodging operation.

4. List the management positions available in the food service industry.

5. List the career opportunities available in private clubs.

6. List the career opportunities available in cruise lines.

15.3   Planning Your Career

AFTER STUDYING SECTION 15.3, YOU SHOULD KNOW HOW TO:

♦ Create a career ladder

♦ Assess your strengths and weaknesses

♦ Write a résumé

♦ Prepare for an interview

♦ Explain the elements of a good interview

♦ Compile a career portfolio

Many hospitality students have an idea of the job they want. Their parents, someone they admire, or a family friend may have advised them to take a particular position. Or they may have had an enjoyable part-time or summer job in a restaurant or hotel. Keep an open mind. Explore other career possibilities, so that you don't overlook opportunities that could be more appealing in the long run.

Career Ladder

Every job you take should move you closer to your final goal. If you look at jobs as step-ping-stones on a **career path** or **career ladder** (see Exhibit 1), there are several questions you should answer before you decide whether a job is right for you:

• What can I learn from this job that will contribute to my career goals?

• What are the long-term opportunities for growth in this company?

• What is this company's reputation among the people I know? Is it a good place to work? Does it deliver on its promises to employees?

• How good is the training program? Will the company really make an effort to educate me?

• What is the starting salary? What about other benefits? Do they add up to a competitive package?

• How do I feel about the location? Will I be living in a place where I can be happy? What about proximity to friends and relatives?

Your Résumé

A basic tool you will need when applying for a job is a well-prepared and attractive printed (not handwritten) résumé.

Exhibit 1
Sample Career Ladders—Lodging

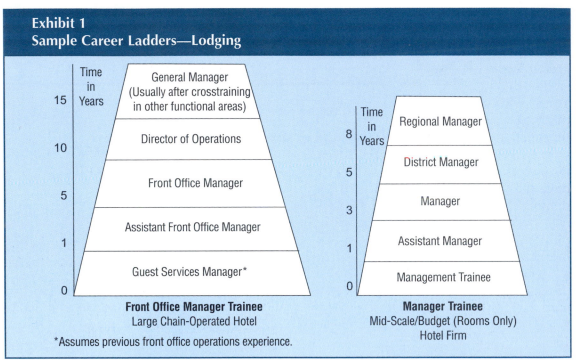

Front Office Manager Trainee
Large Chain-Operated Hotel

General Manager (Usually after crosstraining in other functional areas)
Director of Operations
Front Office Manager
Assistant Front Office Manager
Guest Services Manager*

Time in Years: 0, 1, 5, 10, 15

Manager Trainee
Mid-Scale/Budget (Rooms Only) Hotel Firm

Regional Manager
District Manager
Manager
Assistant Manager
Management Trainee

Time in Years: 0, 1, 3, 5, 8

*Assumes previous front office operations experience.

Source: The Council on Hotel, Restaurant and Institutional Education, *Guide to College Programs in Hospitality, Tourism, & Culinary Arts,* Seventh Edition (Richmond, VA: International CHRIE, 2002), p. 19. Reprinted by permission of John Wiley & Sons, Inc.

Purpose of a Résumé. Résumés and the cover letters that usually accompany them serve as screening guides. They are tools that the interviewer uses to decide whom to see. The purpose of your résumé, therefore, is to make certain that you will be one of the handful of people who will actually be interviewed.

A résumé is an advertisement for yourself. Its purpose is to convince the person doing the hiring that he or she should not fill the job without talking to you first. Résumés have other purposes as well. They introduce you to your prospective employer and provide a brief summary of your educational and employment background.

Contents of a Résumé. Once you understand the purpose of a résumé, the information that goes into one and in what order becomes clearer. Start with the length. Your résumé should not run more than one page. Interviewers don't have time to read more than that, and they don't need to read more in order to decide whether they want to interview you. What should be at the top of the page, after your name, address, and phone number? Whatever you can say that is most likely to make the interviewer want to read more about you.

Many of the best résumés start with a section called "Summary of Qualifications." Suppose you are applying for the front desk position and you have worked at another hotel before as a front desk agent. What you would want to put in this section is, "One year of experience as a front desk agent at a major hotel." In most cases you will not have had previous experience. That does not mean you are not qualified for the job.

Maybe you worked at a fast-food restaurant while you were in high school, in which case you could say, "Experienced at greeting and serving customers." It may well be that you've never held a job before. Your qualifications then might be something like the following: "personable, enthusiastic worker; quick learner; good team worker." This is the section that you use to market or sell yourself, to show that you have the skills, experience, and basic credentials for the job. If you have received any awards or recognition ("Named 'Employee of the Month'"), this is the place to mention it, to separate you from the crowd.

The next section of a résumé is often a direct presentation of your skills and experience. Here you will be more specific: "One year's experience as a front desk agent at the 100-room Hampton Inn. Duties included taking reservations, checking in and checking out guests, and handling complaints."

What if you've never held a front desk position before? You want to show that the jobs you have held or the work you've done has contributed to your ability to do the job in question. If you said that you were a "personable, enthusiastic worker," you might note that you were a shift leader at McDonald's last summer, or even "Head of the prom committee at Northside High."

List your education at the bottom of your résumé. Why not put your education at the top? Simply because most interviewers are not looking for a graduate of Northside High when they start going through résumés. They are looking for someone who can do the job. If they think you can do it, then they'll read your entire résumé carefully and call you in. If they don't, they don't care about your schooling.

Should you list your hobbies? Only if they relate to the job you're trying for.

Other personal information also has no place in a résumé. Your height, weight, age, race, or marital status should not be part of your résumé unless it bears directly on the job qualifications.

Finally, avoid gimmicks or being "creative" with your résumé. You want to present yourself as a professional, responsible, and reliable individual. Unusual résumés do not promote that image.

The Interview

Preparing for the Interview. You should know as much as possible about your prospective employer before you walk in the door. You want to be informed, because that will make it easier for you to converse and you will sound more enthusiastic.

Dressing for the Interview. The way you are dressed makes a big difference in the way you are perceived. If you are applying for a management position, you should consider how you would dress if you were working at the firm, and then dress slightly better. Research shows that reactions to clothing styles, colors, and combinations are fairly predictable. Remember, you want to project a professional, responsible image. The interview is not the time to make a bold or unusual fashion statement.

How to Be Interviewed. An interview is your opportunity to sell yourself, or rather to sell your prospective employer on offering you a job. Once you get the offer you can decide whether to take it, but first you must convince the interviewer to want to hire you.

Going into an interview with this attitude has several implications. First, it gives

Exhibit 3
Sample Information Interviewing Questions

- Describe what you do.
- How did you become interested in _____? (Fill in the blank: hospitality, hotels, restaurants, clubs, contract service, etc.)
- Which part of your job is most interesting, challenging, fun, difficult, etc.?
- What personal attributes are most important for success as a _____? (Fill in the blank: hospitality manager, hotel manager, restaurant manager, etc.)
- How did you get your job?
- What experiences have been most valuable to you in your career?
- What specific skills are required of you on a day-to-day basis?
- How often do you work late? weekends? holidays?
- Does your job require travel? How much?
- How does your job affect the rest of your life?
- What's the best educational preparation to become (whatever you are interested in)?
- Which professional journals, books, and organizations do you recommend?
- Who offers the best training in this field?
- What qualities and qualifications do you look for when hiring new employees?
- What reasons do you see for people leaving the industry?
- What do the next five years look like for your organization? the industry?
- If you were me, what would you do to get started in this industry?
- Whom else could I speak with to learn more?

you a sense of confidence. You are not going to sit back and wait to see what the interviewer asks, because he or she might not ask about the things that make you a superior candidate. You are going to control, to the extent you can, what is talked about. This is not as hard as it sounds. One good way to start off and gain control of the interview is to ask questions. If you have done your homework about the company, some questions will naturally occur to you. Asking questions shows that you are a person who is very interested in working for the company. The answers to your questions may give you clues that will help you sell the interviewer on hiring you.

Generally, industry recruiters look for people who possess specific skills and understand the dynamics of the changing business. They want good communicators

and leaders who can motivate others, show what needs to be done, and teach them how to do it. Recruiters look for well-rounded individuals who understand financial issues, legislative issues, ethical issues, and, above all, human resources issues.

Often, interviewers have a checklist of topics they want to cover in the interview. Don't be put off; you can still ask your questions in between their questions. Always answer their questions directly and honestly. If you don't know the answer to something, say so. The best thing you can do is sound positive. You want to be remembered after you leave the room as someone who is enthusiastic, confident, energetic, and dependable. Shape every answer to reinforce those images.

Under no circumstances should you say anything bad about a former employer.

To do so suggests that you might be disloyal or dishonest.

Finally, encourage the interviewer to make you an offer. Like any good sales person, ask for the order!

After you leave, always write a follow-up thank-you letter. Thank the interviewer for the time he or she spent with you and for considering you for the position. If you were impressed with the company, say so! Tell the interviewer that you're certain you can make a contribution and you hope you'll be hearing from him or her soon.

If you are offered a job, respond within the time requested. You might have additional questions, so contact the person making the offer to clarify details. If you need more time to make your decision, ask for it. When you have decided, be prompt in letting your prospective employer know. If you call to turn down the offer, follow up with a letter in which you thank the person for his or her interest in you.

Career Portfolio

It is important to periodically add to, sort, and reorganize all the information you gathered during the career planning process. One way to do this is to create a **career portfolio.** Some categories and materials that you might include in the career portfolio are self-assessment documentation, "what you've done" documentation (grade reports, test results, transcripts, diplomas, certificates, internships, licenses, professional certifications, complimentary letters from guests or clients, performance evaluations, etc.), and a networking list or references.

Apply Your Learning 15.3

Please write all answers on a separate sheet of paper.

1. What questions should you answer when deciding whether a job is right for you?

2. What is the purpose of a résumé?

3. What categories should a résumé have?

For questions 4 through 7, write whether the statement or question is appropriate or inappropriate for an interview.

4. I spent four years as the treasurer of the Model United Nations club.

5. I resigned from my previous position because my employer was unethical.

6. My salary minimum is $24,000.

7. Are most new positions due to turnover or internal promotions?

Quick Hits

SECTION 15.1—CHOOSING A CAREER

- The **hospitality industry** is made up of lodging, food, entertainment, and travel.

- Entry-level positions are the starting point for a hotel career for people with a high school education or with no hotel-related experience. These positions include such positions as bellperson, room attendant, warewasher, clerk, busperson, and file clerk.

- Skilled-level positions are often those employees who have moved up through the ranks or know a skilled trade. Some positions include front desk agent, housekeeping supervisor, baker, plumber, sales representative, receptionist, wine steward, and night auditor.

- Managerial-level positions include executive, managerial, and supervisory positions. They typically involve managing the work of other people. They require training, education, experience, and individual initiative. Some managerial positions are general manager, sales manager, catering director, auditor, chef, chief engineer, executive housekeeper, regional director, director of training.

- Careers in hospitality offer varied work, opportunities to be creative, a chance to work with people, and flexible work hours. However, they also require long hours, nontraditional schedules, pressure, and low beginning salaries.

SECTION 15.2—POSITIONS IN HOSPITALITY

- The lodging sector of hospitality includes luxury hotels, full-service hotels, convention hotels, resorts, extended-stay hotels, limited-service hotels, and casino hotels. There are independent properties and chain hotels.

- Some of the key managerial positions in lodging include general manager, catering manager, chief engineer, food and beverage manager, human resources manager, sales manager, marketing manager, resident manager, and systems manager.

- Managerial positions in food service include those found in independent restaurants, chain restaurants, social catering, contract food companies, and institutional food service.

- Management positions in food service typically include a general manager and managers with functional duties. They also include chef, maître d', and banquet manager.

- Clubs have many of the same positions found in hotels and restaurants. Clubs include country clubs, city clubs, yacht and sailing clubs, military clubs, tennis clubs, and polo clubs.

- The cruise industry offers positions both on shore and at sea. In addition to traditional hospitality jobs, there are also accounting, marketing, provisioning, and itinerary planning positions.

- The spa industry is a growing segment that promotes relaxation and health. Positions in a spa include the spa director, estheticians, stylists, massage therapists, and receptionists.

SECTION 15.3—PLANNING YOUR CAREER

- A career in hospitality should start before your first job. You should understand your goals and lifestyles and research companies that might be interested in you. This will help you plan your career.

- Every hospitality job you take should help you reach your final goal. Jobs are a **career ladder** that help you climb to your goal.

- A résumé advertises your skills and abilities. Its purpose is to land you an interview.

- Résumés generally should contain a summary of qualifications, a presentation of skills and experiences, and education.

- Interviews are most successful when you are prepared, properly dressed, and confident. It is important to ask questions during an interview so that you can learn more about the position and show that you are interested in working for the company.

- Always send a thank-you letter after an interview.

- Career planning information should be gathered in a career portfolio. This is an important tool that can help you throughout your career.

Glossary

abrasives—gritty substances used to remove heavy soils and polishes.

acids—weak citric acids and vinegar that can be used to clean glass, bronze, and stainless steel.

accounting posting formula—the formula used in posting transactions to front office accounts: Previous Balance + Debits – Credits = Net Outstanding Balance.

acute hazard—something that could cause immediate harm. For example, a chemical that could cause burns on contact with the skin is an acute hazard.

advance deposit guaranteed reservation—a type of reservation guarantee that requires the guest to pay a specified amount of money to the hotel in advance of arrival.

affiliate reservation network—a hotel chain's reservation system in which all participating properties are contractually related.

alkalies—chemicals that help detergents lather better and keep stains suspended in the wash water after they have been loosened and lifted from the fabric. Alkalies also help neutralize acidic stains (most stains are acidic), making the detergent more effective. They also have disinfecting powers.

amenity—a service or item offered to guests or placed in guestrooms for convenience and comfort and at no extra cost.

American Plan—a billing arrangement under which room charges include the guestroom and three meals; also called full pension.

antichlors—laundry chemicals that are sometimes used at the rinse point in the wash cycle to ensure that all the chlorine in the bleach has been removed.

authorization code—a code generated by an online credit card verification service, indicating that the requested transaction has been approved.

average daily rate—an occupancy ratio derived by dividing net rooms revenue by the number of rooms sold.

average rate per guest—an occupancy ratio derived by dividing net rooms revenue by the number of guests.

back of the house—the functional areas of the hotel in which employees have little or no guest contact, such as engineering and maintenance.

bar code—a group of printed and variously patterned bars, spaces, and numerals that are designed to be scanned and read into a computer system as label identification for an object.

break—a high-alkaline, soil-loosening product which is added in the second step of the typical wash cycle. The break cycle is usually at medium temperature and low water level.

builders—builders or alkalies are laundry chemicals that are often added to synthetic detergents to soften water and remove oils and grease.

call accounting system (CAS)—a device linked to the hotel telephone system that accurately accounts for guest telephone calls by identifying each phone number dialed from guestroom telephones and tracking charges.

capacity-constrained businesses—businesses that produce "products" or services that cannot be inventoried or stored for future use. Success depends on their ability to efficiently match productive capacity to consumer demand at any given moment.

career path/career ladder—a series of positions an individual may take on the way to his or her ultimate career goal.

cash bank—an amount of money given to a cashier at the start of each workshift so that he or she can handle the various transactions that occur; the cashier is responsible for this cash bank and for all cash, checks, and other negotiable items received during the workshift.

catering manager—the person in charge of the department within the food and beverage division of a hotel. Responsible for arranging and planning food and beverage functions for conventions and smaller hotel groups, and local banquets booked by the sales department.

central reservation systems—a network for communicating reservations in which each participating property is represented in a computer system database and is required to provide room availability data to the central reservations center on a timely basis.

chain hotel—properties that are affiliated with others. A chain property may be owned by a parent company, a franchise operation, or operated by a management contract company. A franchise and a chain operation are *not* the same; while a franchise property is part of a chain, a chain property is not necessarily a franchise.

chased-demand strategy—a management strategy in which capacity can, to a limited extent, be varied to suit the level of demand.

chief engineer—responsible for a hotel's physical operation and maintenance.

chlorine bleach—helps remove stains, kill bacteria, and whiten fabrics; it can be used with any washable, natural, colorfast fiber.

chronic hazard—something that could cause harm over a long period; for example, a chemical that could cause cancer or organ damage with repeated use over a long period.

city ledger—the collection of all non-guest accounts, including house accounts and unsettled departed guest accounts.

control folio—constructed for each revenue center and used to track all transactions posted to other folios (individual, master, non-guest, or employee). Control folios provide a basis for double entry accounting and for cross-checking the balances of all electronic folios.

controller—manages the accounting department and all of its functions, including management of credit, payroll, guest accounts, and cashiering activities.

corporate guaranteed reservation—a type of reservation guarantee in which the corporation signs a contractual agreement with the hotel to accept financial responsibility for any no-show business travelers it sponsors.

credit or debit card guaranteed reservation—a type of guarantee supported by credit and debit card companies; these companies guarantee participating properties payment for reserved rooms that remain unoccupied.

credit monitoring routine—compares a guest's current folio balance with a credit limit (also called a house limit) that is predetermined by management officials.

daily operations report—a report, typically prepared by the night auditor, that summarizes the hotel's financial activities during a 24-hour period and provides insight into revenues, receivables, operating statistics, and cash transactions related to the front office; also known as the manager's report.

deep cleaning—intensive or specialized cleaning undertaken in guestrooms or public areas. Often conducted according to a special schedule or on a special-project basis.

degreaser—products that act on a variety of greases and soils. They are also called emulsifiers or stabilizers.

delimer—substance that removes mineral deposits that can dull, scale, or discolor surfaces.

denial code—a code generated by an online credit card verification service, indicating that the requested transaction has not been approved.

deodorizer—chemical or powder that conceals the smell of cleaners in the room.

direct billing—a credit arrangement, normally established through correspondence between a guest or a company and the hotel, in which the hotel agrees to bill the guest or the company for charges incurred.

disinfectant—substance that kills bacteria, molds, and mildew.

due-outs—guests expected to check out on a given day who have not yet done so.

economy/limited service hotels—hotels that provide clean, comfortable, inexpensive

rooms and meet the basic needs of guests. They appeal to budget-minded travelers.

electronic locking system—replaces traditional mechanical locks with computer-based guestroom access devices. These systems eliminate the need for emergency and master keys.

emergency key—a key that opens all guestroom doors, even when they are double-locked.

employee folio—used to track employee purchases, compute discounts, monitor expense account activity, and separate authorized business charges from personal expenditures.

European Plan—a billing arrangement under which meals are priced separately from rooms.

express check-out—a pre-departure activity that involves the production and early morning distribution of guest folios for guests expected to check out that morning.

face—the pile of the carpet.

face fibers—yarns that form the pile of the carpet.

face weight—the measure of a carpet's pile. Equal to the weight of the face fibers in one square yard of carpet.

fiberglass cleaner—special cleaner designed to avoid scratching the surface of fiberglass materials.

fixed staff positions—positions that must be filled regardless of the volume of business.

flex time—schedules that allow employees to work hours other than the standard ones.

floor par—the quantity of each type of linen that is required to outfit all rooms serviced from a particular floor linen closet.

folio—a statement of all transactions affecting the balance of a single account.

food and beverage manager—directs the production and service of food and beverages.

forecasting—short-term planning that approximates the number of rooms available for sale on any future date.

franchising—permits another party (the franchisee) to sell products or services in the name of a specific company (the franchisor).

frequency schedule—a schedule that indicates how often each item on an area inventory list needs to be cleaned or maintained.

front of the house—the functional areas of the hotel in which employees have extensive guest contact, such as food and beverage facilities and the front office.

front office audit—a daily comparison of guest accounts (and non-guest accounts having activity) with revenue center transaction information.

front office auditor—an employee who checks the accuracy of front office accounting records and compiles a daily summary of hotel financial data as part of the front office audit; in many hotels, the front office auditor is actually an employee of the accounting division.

general manager—the chief operating officer of a hotel or restaurant.

global distribution systems (GDS)—a distribution channel for reservations that provides worldwide distribution of hotel reservation information and allows selling of hotel reservations around the world; usually accomplished by connecting the hotel company reservation system with an airline reservation system.

group résumé—a summary of all a group's activities, billing instructions, key attendees, rec-

reational arrangements, arrival and departure patterns, and other important information; usually stored in a binder at the front desk.

guaranteed reservation—a reservation that assures the guest that a room will be held until check-out time of the day following the day of arrival; the guest guarantees payment for the room, even if it is not used, unless the reservation is properly canceled.

guest cycle—a division of the flow of business through a hotel that identifies the physical contacts and financial exchanges between guests and hotel employees.

guest folio—a form (paper or electronic) used to chart transactions on an account assigned to an individual person or guestroom.

guest history file—a collection of guest history records created through sophisticated computer-based systems that automatically direct information about departing guests into a guest history database.

guest history record—a record of personal and financial information about hotel guests relevant to marketing and sales that can help the hotel serve the guest on return visits.

guestroom inspection—a detailed process in which guestrooms are systematically checked for cleanliness and maintenance needs.

hand caddy—a portable container for storing and transporting cleaning supplies. Typically located on the top shelf of the room attendant's cart.

hand-held technology—hand-held devices which store and transmit data. Often used for room inspections.

Hazard Communication (HazComm) Standard—OSHA's regulation requiring employers to inform employees about possible hazards related to chemicals they use on the job.

hoppers—openings in washing machines through which detergents can be poured. Also called ports.

hospitality industry—lodging and food service businesses that provide short-term or transitional lodging and/or food.

hot- or cold-water extraction—a deep-cleaning carpet method in which a machine sprays a detergent-and-water solution onto the carpet under low pressure and, in the same pass, vacuums out the solution and soil.

house count—a forecast specially prepared for food and beverage, banquet, and catering operations which generally includes the expected number of guests.

house limit—the amount which guests can charge to their accounts without partial settlement; this high balance amount is set by the hotel.

housekeeping status report—a report the housekeeping department prepares that indicates the current housekeeping status of each room, based on a physical check.

human resources manager—in charge of employee relations within an organization.

identification code—generally, the first few letters of a guest's last name. An identification code enables the guest accounting module to process a charge to the correct folio when two separate accounts exist under the same room number.

independent hotel—a property that is not affiliated with any other property, chain, or corporation.

individual folio—assigned to an in-house guest for the purpose of charting the guest's financial transactions with the hotel.

information directory—a collection of information kept at the front desk for front desk agents to use in responding to guest requests, including simplified maps of the area; taxi and airline company telephone numbers; bank, theater, church, and store locations; and special event schedules.

intangible products—the primary products of hospitality-oriented organizations. Intangible products such as comfort, enjoyment, and pleasant experiences relate to guests' emotional well-being and expectations. They present very different management and marketing problems than tangible products such as automobiles or boxes of cereal.

intersell agency—a central reservation system that contracts to handle reservations for more than one product line. They typically handle reservation services for airlines, car rental companies, and hotel properties.

inventory list—a list of all items within a particular area that need cleaning by or attention of housekeeping personnel.

job safety analysis—a detailed report that lists every job task performed by all housekeeping employees. Each job task is further broken down into a list of steps. These steps are accompanied by tips and instructions on how to perform each step safely.

late charges—charged purchases made by guests that are posted to folios after guests have settled their accounts.

late check-out—a room status term indicating that the guest is being allowed to check out later than the hotel's standard check-out time.

late check-out fee—a charge imposed by some hotels on guests who do not check out by the established check-out time.

lead-time quantity—the number of purchase units consumed between the time that a supply order is placed and the time that the order is actually received.

level-capacity strategy—a management strategy in which the same amount of capacity is offered, no matter how high the consumer demand.

management contract—a process in which a company operates a property for a fee.

management internship—supervised training that hotel school graduates must have before engaging in actual management; takes place at a job site.

market segmentation—a process whereby managers divide a varied market into distinctive and relatively homogenous subgroups or segments.

marketing manager—develops and implements a marketing plan and budget.

master folio—a folio used to chart transactions on an account assigned to more than one person or guestroom, usually reserved for group accounts; a master folio collects charges not appropriately posted elsewhere.

master key—a key that opens all guestroom doors which are not double-locked.

material safety data sheet (MSDS)—a form that is supplied by the chemical's manufacturer containing information about a chemical.

maximum quantity—the greatest number of purchase units that should be in stock at any given time.

metal cleaner—a chemical used to clean metal. May be either oil-based or water-based.

mid-range service—a modest but sufficient level of service which appeals to the largest segment of the traveling public. A mid-market property may offer uniformed service, airport limousine service, and food-and-beverage room service; a specialty restaurant, coffee shop, and lounge; and special rates for certain guests.

mildewcides—laundry chemicals added to the wash cycle to prevent the growth of bacteria and fungus on linens for up to 30 days.

minimum quantity—the fewest number of purchase units that should be in stock at any given time.

mitering—a method for contouring a sheet or blanket to fit the corner of a mattress in a smooth and neat manner. The results are sometimes referred to as "square corners" or "hospital corners."

Modified American Plan—a billing arrangement under which the daily rate includes charges for the guestroom and two meals—typically breakfast and dinner.

moments of truth—critical moments when guests and staff interact, offering opportunities for staff to make a favorable impression, correct mistakes, and win repeat customers.

multiple occupancy percentage—the number of rooms occupied by more than one guest divided by the number of rooms occupied by guests.

multiple occupancy ratio—a measurement used to forecast food and beverage revenue, to indicate clean linen requirements, and to analyze daily revenue rate; derived from multiple occupancy percentage or by determining the average number of guests per rooms sold; also called double occupancy ratio.

net cash receipts—the amount of cash and checks in the cashier's drawer, minus the amount of the initial cash bank.

non-affiliate reservation network—a central reservation system that connects independent (non-chain) properties.

non-guaranteed reservation—a reservation agreement in which the hotel agrees to hold a room for the guest until a stated reservation cancellation hour on the day of arrival; the property is not guaranteed payment in the case of a no-show.

non-guest folio—a folio used to chart transactions on an account assigned to (1) a local business or agency with charge privileges at the hotel, (2) a group sponsoring a meeting at the hotel, or (3) a former guest with an outstanding account balance.

non-recycled inventories—those items in stock that are consumed or used up during the course of routine housekeeping operations. Non-recycled inventories include cleaning supplies, small equipment items, guest supplies, and amenities.

no-show—a guest who made a room reservation but did not register or cancel.

occupancy percentage—an occupancy ratio that indicates the proportion of rooms sold to rooms available for sale during a specific period of time.

occupancy ratios—a measurement of the success of the hotel in selling rooms; typical occupancy ratios include average daily rate, revenue per available room, average rate per guest, multiple occupancy statistics, and occupancy percentage.

occupancy report—a report prepared each night by a front desk agent which lists rooms occupied that night and indicates guests who are expected to check out the following day.

Occupational Safety and Health Act (OSHA)—a broad set of rules that protects workers in all trades and professions from a variety of unsafe working conditions.

operating ratios—a group of ratios that assist in the analysis of hospitality operations.

organization chart—a schematic representation of the relationships between positions within an organization, showing where each position fits into the overall organization and illustrating the divisions of responsibility and lines of authority.

overage—an imbalance that occurs when the total of cash and checks in a cash register drawer is greater than the initial bank plus net cash receipts.

overflow facilities—a property selected to receive central system reservation requests after room availabilities in the system's participating properties within a geographic region have been exhausted.

oxygen bleach—helps remove stains, kill bacteria, and whiten fabrics; is milder than chlorine bleach and is generally safe for most washable fabrics.

paid-in-advance (PIA) guest—a guest who pays his or her room charges in cash during registration; PIA guests are often denied in-house credit.

par—the standard quantity of a particular inventory item that must be on hand to support daily, routine housekeeping operations.

par number—a multiple of the standard quantity of a particular inventory item that represents the quantity of the item that must be on hand to support daily, routine housekeeping operations.

performance standard—a required level of performance that establishes the quality of work that must be done.

permanent folio—used to track guest folio balances that are settled to a credit card company.

perpetual inventory—a system in which receipts and issues are recorded as they occur; this system provides readily available information on inventory levels and cost of sales.

physical inventories—taking a physical count of all the linen and recording the amounts on an inventory count sheet. This inventory should be conducted at least quarterly (if not monthly).

PIA (paid-in-advance) guest—a guest who pays his or her room charges in cash during registration; PIA guests are often denied in-house credit.

pile—the surface of a carpet; consists of fibers or yarns that form raised loops that can be cut or sheared.

pile distortion—face fiber conditions such as twisting, pilling, flaring, or matting caused by heavy traffic or improper cleaning methods.

polycotton—a polyester/cotton blend.

ports—openings into washing machines through which detergents can be poured. Also called hoppers.

POS (point-of-sale) system—a computer network that allows electronic cash registers at the hotel's points of sale to communicate directly with a front office guest accounting module.

posting—the process of recording transactions on a guest folio.

prepayment guaranteed reservation—a type of reservation guarantee that requires a payment in full before the day of arrival.

preventive maintenance—a systematic approach to maintenance in which situations are identified and corrected on a regular basis to control costs and keep larger problems from occurring.

primary backing—the part of the carpet to which face fibers are attached and which holds these fibers in place.

productivity standard—an acceptable amount of work that must be done within a specific time frame according to an established performance standard.

property management system (PMS)—a computer software package that supports a variety of applications related to front office and back office activities.

rack rate—the standard rate established by a hotel for a particular category of rooms.

reader board—a posting or closed-circuit broadcast of daily events at a hotel.

real time capability—refers to simultaneous processing.

recycled inventories—those items in stock that have relatively limited useful lives but are used over and over in housekeeping operations. Recycled inventories include linens, uniforms, major machines and equipment, and guest loan items.

reference code—generally, the serial number of a departmental source document.

referral group—independent hotels which have banded together for some common purpose.

registration record—a collection of important guest information created by the front desk agent following the guest's arrival; includes the guest's name, address, telephone number, and company affiliation; method of payment; and date of departure.

reservation record—a manual record created by the reservationist as a result of the initial inquiry procedures. Typical data are: date of arrival, type and number of rooms requested, and number of persons in the party.

resident manager—in charge of the rooms division.

revenue center—an operating division or department which sells goods or services to guests and thereby generates revenue for the hotel. The front office, food and beverage outlets, room service, and retail stores are typical revenue centers.

revenue forecast report—projects future revenue by multiplying predicted occupancies by current house rates.

revenue per available room (RevPAR)—a revenue management statistic that measures the revenue-generating capability of a hotel.

room attendant's cart—a lightweight, wheeled vehicle used by room attendants for transporting cleaning supplies, linen, and equipment needed to fulfill a block of cleaning assignments.

room rate—the price a hotel charges for overnight accommodations.

room rate variance report—a report listing rooms that have not been sold at rack rates.

room status discrepancy—a situation in which the housekeeping department's description of a room's status differs from the room status information that guides front desk employees in assigning rooms to guests. Discrepancies can seriously affect a property's ability to satisfy guests and maximize rooms revenue.

room status report—a report that allows hotel employees to identify the occupancy, status, and condition of the property's rooms, typically prepared as part of the night audit. Generated daily through a two-way communication between housekeeping and the front desk. Indicates the current status of rooms according to housekeeping designations, such as on-change, out-of-order, and clean and ready for inspection.

rooms availability report—lists, by room type, the number of rooms available each day (the net remaining rooms in each category).

rooms division budget report—compares actual revenue and expense figures with budgeted amounts.

rotary floor machine—floor care equipment that accommodates both brushes and pads to perform such carpet-cleaning tasks as dry-foam cleaning, mist pad cleaning, rotary spin

pad cleaning, or bonnet and brush shampoos. On hard floors, these machines can be used to buff, burnish, scrub, strip, and refinish.

routine maintenance—activities related to the general upkeep of the property that occur on a regular (daily or weekly) basis and require relatively minimal training or skills to perform.

safety stock level—the number of purchase units that must always be on hand for smooth operation in the event of emergencies, spoilage, unexpected delays in delivery, or other situations.

sales manager—conducts sales programs and makes sales calls on prospects for group and individual business. Reports to the marketing manager.

secondary backing—the part of a carpet that is laminated to the primary backing to provide additional stability and more secure installation.

self check-out terminal—a computerized system, usually located in the hotel lobby, that allows the guest to review his or her folio and settle the account to the credit card used at check-in.

semipermanent folio—used to track "bill to" accounts receivable.

service—meeting customer needs in the way that they want and expect them to be met.

shading—a carpet condition that occurs when the pile is brushed in two different directions so that dark and light areas appear.

shortage—an imbalance that occurs when the total of cash and checks in a cash register drawer is less than the initial bank plus net cash receipts.

sizing—laundry chemicals added to the wash cycle to stiffen polyester blends.

skipper—a guest who leaves with no intention of paying for the room.

soap—a kind of detergent. Neutral or pure soaps contain no alkalies; built soaps do. Built soaps are generally used on heavily soiled fabrics; pure soaps are reserved for more lightly soiled items. Soaps are destroyed by sours.

source document—a printed voucher, usually serially numbered for internal-control purposes, from a revenue-producing department showing an amount that is charged to a folio.

sours—mild acids used to neutralize residual alkalinity in fabrics after washing and rinsing.

split folio—a folio in which a guest's charges are separated into two or more folios.

staffing guide—a system used to establish the number of labor hours needed.

steam cabinet—a box in which articles are hung and steamed to remove wrinkles. Steam cabinets are typically used to remove wrinkles from heavy linens such as blankets, bedspreads, and curtains.

steam tunnel—a piece of laundry equipment that moves articles on hangers through a tunnel, steaming them and removing the wrinkles as they move through.

support center—an operating division or department which does not generate direct revenue but plays a supporting role to the hotel's revenue centers. Support centers include the housekeeping, accounting, engineering and maintenance, and personnel functions.

surfactants—laundry chemicals that aid soil removal and act as antibacterial agents and fabric softeners.

SWOT—an acronym for *strengths, weaknesses, opportunities,* and *threats.*

SWOT analysis—an important step in the strategic planning process; it helps companies assess how well they are serving their current markets.

synthetic detergents—synthetic detergents are especially effective on oil and grease. Builders or alkalies are often added to synthetic detergents to soften water and remove oils and grease.

system update—a fully automated audit routine that accomplishes many of the same functions as a non-computerized night audit; daily system updates enable file reorganization, system maintenance, and report production, and provide an end-of-day time frame.

systems manager—manages a hotel's computerized management information systems. May write simple computer programs and instruction manuals for employees.

target markets—the market segments for which a property is best suited.

transaction file—a record in which important front office events and decisions are recorded for reference during subsequent shifts. Also called a log book.

travel agent guaranteed reservation—a type of reservation guarantee under which the hotel generally bills the travel agency after a guaranteed reservation has been classified as a no-show.

trial balance—in the night audit, the process of balancing front office accounts with transaction information by department.

tunnel washer—a long, sequential laundry machine that operates continuously, processing each stage of the wash/rinse cycle and extracting in another section of the machine.

Underwriters Laboratories (UL)—an independent, nonprofit organization that tests electrical equipment and devices to ensure that the equipment is free of defects that could cause fire or shock.

upselling—a sales technique whereby a guest is offered a more expensive room than what he or she reserved or originally requested, and then persuaded to rent the room based on the room's features, benefits, and his or her needs.

variable staff positions—positions that are filled in relation to changes in hotel occupancy.

voucher—a document detailing a transaction to be posted to a front office account; used to communicate information from a point of sale to the front office.

walk-in—a guest who arrives at a hotel without a reservation.

walking—turning away a guest who has a reservation because of a lack of rooms.

wet vacuum—floor care equipment used to pick up spills or to pick up rinse water that is used during carpet or floor cleaning.

wetting agents—a chemical that breaks down the surface tension of the water and allows water to get behind the dirt to lift it off the surface.

wicking—a carpet condition that occurs when the backing of the carpet becomes wet and the face yarns draw the moisture and color of the backing to the carpet's surface.

world-class service—a level of service which stresses the personal attention given to guests. Hotels offering world-class service provide upscale restaurants and lounges, exquisite decor, concierge service, opulent rooms, and abundant amenities.

yield statistic—the ratio of actual rooms revenue to potential rooms revenue.

zero out—to settle in full the balance of a folio account as the guest checks out.

Index